CONFLICT AND COMMUNITY IN SOUTHERN ENGLAND

Essays in the Social History
of Rural and Urban Labour
from Medieval to Modern Times

Edited by
BARRY STAPLETON

ALAN SUTTON · Stroud

ST. MARTIN'S PRESS · New York

First published in the United States of America in 1992

All rights reserved. For information, write:
Scholarly and Reference Division,
St. Martin's Press Inc. · 175 Fifth Avenue
New York · NY 10010

ISBN 0-312-08611-3

Library of Congress Cataloging in Publication Data

Conflict and community in southern England: Essays in the social
history of rural and urban labour from medieval to modern times/
edited by Barry Stapleton.
    p.   cm.
    ISBN 0–312–08611–3
    1. Social conflict–England–History. 2. Working class–England–
History. I. Stapleton, Barry.
HN398.E5C66   1992
305.5′0942–dc20
                                                            92–18693
                                                            CIP

First published in the United Kingdom in 1992 by
Alan Sutton Publishing Limited
Phoenix Mill · Far Thrupp · Stroud · Gloucestershire

British Library Cataloguing in Publication Data

Conflict and Community in Southern England
    I. Stapleton, Barry
    942

ISBN 0–7509–0161–6

Typeset in 10/11 Goudy.
Typesetting and origination by
Alan Sutton Publishing Limited.
Printed in Great Britain by
The Bath Press, Bath, Avon.

The editor and publishers acknowledge
with thanks the financial contribution
towards the publication of this volume
received from the Marc Fitch Fund.

Contents

List of Maps

List of Tables

Contributors

Bob Bushaway
Associate Member, Department of Modern History, University of Birmingham

Publications include   *By Rite: Custom, Ceremony and Community in England, 1700–1880* (1982), and a number of articles on popular culture and social crime in the eighteenth and nineteenth centuries.

Graham Davis
Principal Lecturer in History, Bath College of Higher Education

Publications include   *The Irish in Britain 1815–1914* (1991), *Bath beyond the Guidebook* (1988), and a number of articles on late eighteenth- and nineteenth-century economic and social history.

Christopher Durston
Senior Lecturer in History, St Mary's College, Strawberry Hill

Publications include   a number of articles on the English Revolution, and two books *The Family in the English Revolution* (1989) and *Princes, Pastors and People: the Church and Religion in England, 1529–1689* (1991).

John Hare
Peter Symonds' College, Winchester

Publications include   *Battle Abbey* (1985), and numerous articles on aspects of medieval social and economic history and on medieval archaeology.

Celia Miller

Formerly Part-time Tutor, Department of Extra-Mural Studies, University of Bristol

Publications include   *Rain and Ruin, The Diary of an Oxfordshire Farmer: John Simpson Calvertt 1875–1900* (1983), editor and *The Account Books of Thomas Smith, Irely Farm, Hailes, Gloucestershire, 1865–71* (1985).

Jeff Porter

Senior Lecturer in Economic History, University of Exeter

Published work includes   articles on Victorian Labour history and a chapter on 'Rural Social Structure and Society' in G.E. Mingay (ed.), *The Agrarian History of England and Wales*, Vol. VI.

Mick Reed

Lecturer in Information Technology

Publications include   articles on nineteenth-century peasant and farm service, social change and social conflict and religion and cooperation.

John Rule

Professor of History, University of Southampton and former editor of *Southern History*

Publications include   *The Experience of Labour in Eighteenth Century England* (1981), *Albion's Fatal Tree* (with E.P. Thompson, D. Hay *et al*), *Outside the Law* (ed.) (1983), *The Vital Century 1714–1815* (1992), *Albion's People 1714–1815* (1992) and a wide range of articles on the history of crime, protest and trade unionism, popular religion and fishing and mining communities.

Barry Stapleton

Principal Lecturer in Economic History, University of Portsmouth

Published work covers   eight centuries from *Odiham Castle 1200–1500, Castle and Community* (1983) and (with J.H. Thomas) *The Portsmouth Region* (1989), to articles on the demography of, and sources for, local communities from the sixteenth to the nineteenth centuries and on Malthus and migration.

George Watts
Formerly Senior Counsellor, Open University

Published work includes *The Learning of History* (1971), and a wide range of articles on the medieval economy and medieval peasant movements especially in Southern England, and the history of disease.

Roger Wells
Senior Lecturer in Modern History, Brighton Polytechnic

Publications include *Insurrection; the British Experience 1795–1803* (1983), *Wretched Faces; Famine in Wartime England 1793–1801* (1988), *Class, Conflict and Protest in the English Countryside 1700–1880* (1990) co-edited with Mick Reed, and numerous articles on eighteenth- and nineteenth-century English social history.

Foreword

It is a most agreeable task to be asked to provide a foreword for this volume of essays which has sprung, in a form of long jump, from the *Southern History* conference which was held in Portsmouth in 1984, a stimulating and enjoyable occasion at which I chanced to be in the chair. That was indeed a matter of chance, for I am not generally known to be either a conflict historian or a practitioner of history from below, and I had as much to learn from the conference papers as readers will have from this volume. It is salutary to be reminded that people are frequently, even generally, disputatious and prone to have conflicting customs, interests, or beliefs that are liable to be expressed in open, often violent, protests and disputes – and rewarding to find a group of scholars whose own friendliness expresses, at least in part, their agreement on the interest and importance of historical disagreements. The historians contributing to this volume demonstrate, collectively, the continuity of conflict and unrest: but not the continuity, from the thirteenth century to the late nineteenth century, of the causes or forms of unrest. The essential interest of the volume lies, rather, in the particular forms taken by social tensions and protests in different places and different times. The other side of the coin of social protest, distinguishing it from personal or individual violence, is that the protesters all felt some common bond, whether of local community, occupation status, or religion. Hence the volume is also about the beliefs and customs, as well as material conditions, which bind people together in groups, communities, or social classes.

All these studies are, by definition, set in one part or another of southern England, be it Wiltshire, Hampshire, Gloucestershire, or Devon, Newbury, Exeter, or Bath. The geographical coherence which this may imply is, however, rather misleading. None of the authors would claim that there is some special 'southern' ingredient in their analysis, except that in the modern chapters they are dealing with places relatively far removed from the great centres of nineteenth-century smokestack industries. Rather, the authors are united by their use of the approaches, materials, and techniques of local history for their proper purposes: to examine interesting and important questions – in this case, social relations, social behaviour, and social developments – in depth, in particular places. When the area of study is sufficiently compact and localized it is possible to exploit the full array of available sources and bring down to earth airy generalizations that rest more on abstractions than on the actions or thoughts of identifiable people. This is what has been done in these essays, and they are a signal achievement of the Southern History Society.

February 1992

F.M.L. Thompson
Institute of Historical Research
University of London

Acknowledgements

Collections of essays usually take much longer to appear in print than the work of a single individual, and this book is no exception. It originated from the *Southern History* conference of 1984 in which the theme was 'Peasants and Proletarians in Southern England'. That conference was successfully held, thanks not only to the contributors but also to the financial generosity of the Nuffield Foundation. Since much of the content of the papers at this small conference was developing new and important themes, it was felt that it should be made available to a wider public, and the decision to publish was taken. Thus this volume largely represents the conference papers with one exception, that by John Hare, to whom I am personally most grateful for producing his chapter at short notice to fill the space of a long awaited, but never produced, original contribution. My apologies, as well as thanks, must go to my other fellow contributors who have had to wait an unconscionably long time to see their efforts finally reach the printed page and who are in no way responsible for the delay.

Two contributions have been previously published: Christopher Durston's in *Southern History*, vol. 6 (1984), and Mick Reed's in *History Workshop Journal*, no. 18 (autumn 1984). The former is published here by permission of the editor and Alan Sutton Publishing, and the latter is included by permission of Oxford University Press and the editorial board. I am most grateful for their cooperation.

The 1984 conference was notable also for its good-humoured and able chairman, Professor Michael Thompson, for whose guidance and erudition all those who attended were most grateful. Since then, Michael Thompson has kept an interest in, and encouraged the publication of, this volume and for that and the foreword he has produced, I am happy to indicate my deep gratitude.

In my own institution a number of people have given valuable assistance. Bill Johnson of the Geography Department produced a number of maps and diagrams, and in my own Department of Economics Gill Batchelor, Carol Lacey and Val McDermott have all, at different times, assisted with typing and administration. My grateful thanks to all and also to everyone at Alan Sutton Publishing, especially Clare Bishop, for much friendly assistance. Finally, I am pleased to acknowledge the financial support of the Marc Fitch Fund, without which this volume would still be awaiting publication.

Introduction

The image of the poor as peasants tied to the soil of their native communities in England is an enduring one despite much evidence to the contrary. From at least the later Middle Ages onwards there were local popular customs which undoubtedly encouraged those born into a community to remain knitted into the fabric of their locality. This framework of custom encompassed most forms of relationship in the local community and provided a dynamic ideology to which the labouring poor could relate. However, it was an ideology to which their social superiors devoted much time and energy in attempts to reduce, or eliminate, the poor's participation (Bushaway). Nevertheless, custom rarely could provide much needed employment, find a likely spouse or feed a growing family and for these reasons, if no others, many had inevitably to leave their birthplaces to seek opportunities elsewhere. Thus the population of communities was fluid and changing. Those despairingly leaving one place would be replaced by others arriving in hope, looking for better prospects in order to sustain often large families without having to resort to parish poor relief (Stapleton) provided by their local superiors.

Thus, both mobility and custom were possible areas of discord between the poor peasantry and wage labourers and the better off in communities in southern England and unrest occurred in rural and urban areas alike not simply in more modern times with the growth of industrialization, but discontent and disorder were demonstrably part of the fabric of society from the Middle Ages onwards.

Both urban and rural disaffection were prevalent in the medieval period. For example, the city of Winchester, an important administrative centre, frequently visited by medieval monarchs, was shown to have a regular pattern of disorder related to prostitution, animosity towards minorities and foreigners and the perennial problem of the consumption of too much alcohol. In addition, national instability in the mid-thirteenth century and in 1381, releasing underlying economic and social tensions, caused higher levels of violence in the city, as they did again in 1450. Similarly, the medieval countryside was far from peaceful, constant friction between landlords and tenants being evident especially on the estate of Titchfield abbey in southern Hampshire. In particular years, especially 1381 and 1450 when peasant rising were more normally associated with the eastern part of England, more widespread rural unrest could be seen right across the south from Somerset to Sussex (Watts).

One cause of these signs of discontent may have been the exploitative feudal system which undoubtedly created strains especially in medieval rural society. Much of this may well have been the result, in the fifteenth century, of the tensions caused between lord and tenant as serfdom declined at varying rates and lords sought, generally unsuccessfully, to control remaining serf families (Hare). But such strains did not disappear when the system did, as can be clearly seen in early modern Berkshire where, after involvement in Lollardy in the later Middle Ages, the town of Newbury demonstrated an ability for some of its residents to participate in a number of radical developments – for example early Protestantism in the sixteenth century, the English revolution and the Restoration in the seventeenth century and food riots in the eighteenth century – disturbances which again suggest socio-economic tensions in the community (Durston).

Conflict continued into the modern period with a major causal factor being the emergence earlier in southern England than in the north of a proletariat dependent on the sale of its labour – the landless and wage-dependent agricultural labourers as well as the 'putting-out' workers in the textile industries of the south-west. Such labourers were vulnerable not only to changes in the employment market but also as consumers to changes in the food market, thus helping to explain the widespread food rioting in eighteenth-century southern England (Rule) and the increased expenditure on poor relief. The transition from the patriarchal 'living-in' system of agricultural employment prevalent before the nineteenth century to that of a purely contractual relationship between farmer and worker highlighted the inferior and insecure position of ordinary farm labourers and thus provided further tensions in rural society (Miller).

Associated with these tensions and the disturbances in the countryside is the growth of rural crime, of which the Captain Swing episodes of 1830 are perhaps the best known example.

However, crime in the countryside as well as in the towns, was endemic and a good deal of it appears to have been a form of social protest and a defence against hunger (Wells). The problem of hunger, as well as employment, underlay the conflict between authority and the net fishermen of Devon in the nineteenth century. Landowners and magistrates wished to conserve the salmon stock and protect landed privileges and such action resulted in conflict between the net fishermen and police and bailiffs especially on the north Devon rivers Taw and Torridge (Porter).

Attempts to control the activities of social inferiors in the nineteenth century are also examined in rural south-east England, where gentry and capitalist farmers' efforts at social control were frequently frustrated by parish officials who themselves were often small family producers who might otherwise have been considered beneficial to a developing capitalist economy (Reed). Similarly, in nineteenth-century urban Bath the ruling elite were themselves experiencing their own internal conflicts, exacerbated by attitudes to the control of the urban poor whose existence in the slum quarter of the town distinctly marred the image of genteel Bath propagated diligently by the city fathers, and consequently affected municipal policy (Davis).

Local attitudes to the poor may well have been an important if not decisive element in the conflict which so frequently is found in English historical communities. For many who sank into poverty, however, it was to be a lifetime experience, frequently inherited and often inescapable. It remains to be seen whether, in those places where the poor were humanely treated within a caring community, the level of social and economic tension was reduced and hence peasants or proletarians could live out their lives with a measure of dignity and social harmony.

1
Popular Disorder in Southern England, 1250–1450

D.G. Watts

This essay examines critically certain conventional interpretations of the 1381 rising and of the occurrence of popular disorder in southern England during the later middle ages.

It has for many years been an accepted proposition that the Peasants' Revolt was essentially a south-eastern phenomenon, in which the most prominent areas were the counties of Kent, Essex, Suffolk and Norfolk. Writing in 1906, for example, Charles Oman argued that in 1381, "in Surrey, Sussex or Hertfordshire, and still more in the remote counties, the riots and outrages were sporadic and short-lived".[1] In 1962 Steel wrote, "the only serious trouble occurred in the south and east of England, apart from certain isolated exceptions".[2] R.H. Hilton, writing in 1973, elaborated the argument:

> The risings in the west and north were . . . secondary to the great rebellion in the south-east. In so far as the explanation for the movement is to be found in the nature of local and political relations it is this area which we must examine . . . This was the most industrialized and commercialized part of the country and this therefore was the area where lord–peasant relationships . . . were pushed to the limit . . . the English peasants' revolt could only begin in market-oriented south-east England.[3]

Inevitably these arguments have been embodied in the standard and widely read accounts of the period: Fryde, in his Historical Association booklet of 1981, for instance, described the revolt as taking place in the "areas of most rapid economic change".[4] In the process, explanations of events around London – which it might be argued were the outcome of the particular, local and temporary circumstances of that year – have been magnified into some very general propositions about social and economic developments in England over a long, if unspecified, period.

These propositions embody a number of assumptions. First, that in the later middle ages certain groups of English counties had distinctive

provincial characteristics; secondly that some counties were more indus-
trialized and commercialized than others; thirdly that social relationships
were different in these various localities; and of course, lastly that as a
result these localities exhibited more or less evidence of disorder. These
assumptions require critical examination.

Northern England, the counties north of the rivers Mersey, Trent and
Humber, will not be considered in this paper. Those northern counties had
long traditions of violence and disorder, though the disorder was often
differently motivated and took different forms from that in the rest of the
kingdom. Words like "remote" and "isolated" have different connotations
in Cumberland and Northumberland than in Hertfordshire or
Buckinghamshire, and northern historians can no doubt explain why their
"peasants" were less involved in the events of 1381 than those elsewhere.[5]
Indeed, the particular northern happenings in the towns of York, Beverley
and Scarborough, and near Chester, have been discussed by R. B. Dobson.[6]

The area considered in this essay will include some of the counties, like
Sussex, mentioned by Oman; a middle band of counties such as Hampshire and Berkshire; and so-called "remote" counties such as Wiltshire,
Somerset and Devon. From an economic point of view, these counties can
only with difficulty be described as less commercialized than those further
east. Sussex and Hampshire faced Normandy across the Channel: Devon
looked to Brittany and the coastline of the Bay of Biscay and all were
accessible to Genoese, Florentine and Venetian merchants. Within
Hampshire were the cloth manufacturing centre of Winchester, and
Southampton, a major port for imports of wine and materials for the
textile industry, and for exports of cloth and wool: the county, which
contained the great international fairs of Weyhill and St. Giles, both
visited by Covetousness in *Piers Plowman*, can hardly be said not to have
been market-orientated. To the north-west, Bristol was growing rapidly as
a port and a commercial centre for the rich agricultural and woollen
manufacturing district of the Cotswolds, north Somerset and Wiltshire. In
the many small towns of the area were communities of merchants, weavers
and what Eleanor Carus-Wilson called an "industrial proletariat", who
were turning their profits to, amongst other things, rebuilding their
magnificent parish churches.[7] Elsewhere, Reading and Newbury in
Berkshire, Salisbury in Wiltshire and Exeter in Devon were important
provincial market centres in the fourteenth century. Just across the Severn
were the iron miners of the Forest of Dean; and still further west, the
Cornish tin-miners constituted a working community with as much
independence of authority as any in England, as the events of 1497 were to
demonstrate.

If then, we hesitate to describe the south-western counties as more
"backward" than those of the east, perhaps an explanation of events can

be framed around Dobson's notion of "seignorially oppressive" regions with a population more quiescent, more servile, less prone to violence and disorder.[8] A cursory inspection of any set of court or coroner's records makes it clear that it cannot. We can agree with V.H. Galbraith that "from start to finish (the inferior classes) were full of ferment and violence and their criminal records, preserved in the plea rolls, are far in excess, having regard to population, of those of later times".[9]

Our short tour of the south-western counties begins on the Isle of Wight in 1282, with a dramatic tithe dispute:

> When armed men arrived for defence reasons, the monks (of Quarr Abbey) and their servants raised a hue. As soon as news of the hue reached the castle (Carisbrooke), the bailiff sent Roger, his clerk, for information. But when Roger tried to parley with the armed men, he was greeted with a shower of arrows. On hearing this, the bailiff set off and, passing through Newport, gathered together a band of men. However it was still impossible to approach. The arrows fell, killing a horse, wounding one man under the breast and another in the middle of his hip. Finally the bailiff managed to arrest the men . . .[10]

Another activity on the Isle of Wight was wrecking. At Brightstone in 1321, for instance, 42 named wreckers had taken £5,000 worth of goods from the Portuguese ship *Jesus Christ*, and in 1325 at "Havenmouth" 104 wreckers, among them men from the Hampshire mainland, despoiled the Spanish vessel *Ship of St. Mary*.[11]

Across in Hampshire itself, the New Forest was the scene of constant mayhem. To take just one example, in 1278-9 "Brother Hugh (of Beaulieu Abbey) and others came armed with bows and arrows, axes, swords, hauberks and other weapons and assaulted [two fishermen] and wounded [their] servants".[12] The two fishermen were in fact *agents provocateurs* acting for the citizens of Southampton, quite literally testing the water. Along the coast at the growing port of Portsmouth, we do not know who the persons were who in 1325 killed John Doye when he came there on the king's business: perhaps they were the same persons who broke into the prison at Portsmouth and released the prisoners several times in the same year.[13] At the county town of Hampshire in 1314, 69 men, described as leading citizens, attacked the Hyde Abbey manor of Barton just outside the city, assaulted the occupants, broke the doors, carried away goods and timber, destroyed the sluices and flooded 100 acres of meadow.[14] Hampshire also provides a good example of armed resistance by agricultural tenants, from Hayling, the island east of Portsmouth, in 1338:

The king lately took into his hands the priory of Hayling with other alien priories . . . and committed the custody of it to the prior . . . the prior says that, although he and his predecessors time out of mind have had divers villeins in the manor of Hayling . . . yet these have now by confederacy among themselves and others refused (to do services and have) rescued distraints . . . with armed force[15]

South-east Hampshire also gives us an example of forcible resistance to royal taxation, at Portsdown in 1354.[16] Both Hayling and Portsdown were within a few miles of the Abbot of Titchfield's manors of Portchester and Wallsworth, which are discussed below.

Further north, in Oxfordshire but not far from Reading, in 1375 "very many evildoers, gathered together with others armed, came to Huntercombe . . . entered the manor of the abbot of Dorchester there by armed force without any legal process, held the manor as a fortress, threatening to kill the abbot and all his men . . .".[17]

Wiltshire too was the scene of disorder and violence of all kinds. Prolonged resistance to the landlord, based on the claim that it was ancient demesne of the Crown, began on the Abbot of Bec's manor of Ogbourne in 1309, saw the wholesale refusal of services in 1327, and continued throughout the fourteenth century.[18] In the nearby market town of Marlborough in 1329 nine men assaulted the constable of the castle there and took away "divers sums of money which he had upon him".[19] And in the principal town, Salisbury, the major rising of 1380–1 can be seen in the context of a long history of often violent disputes between the citizens and the bishop. The citizens had refused to pay tallage in 1302; in 1343–5, 33 citizens attacked the bailiff who was presiding over the bishop's court; at the end of the century, in 1391, citizens "in no small number" rose in insurrection and formed unlawful assemblies; there seems to have been further trouble in 1395; in 1450 it was a Salisbury man who led the mob that killed Bishop Ayscough at the village of Edington; and what have been described as "even deeper antagonisms" were stirred up in 1465.[20]

In Somerset, too, the events of 1381 were rooted in a seed-bed of popular violence. In 1331 for instance, 13 men broke into John de Say's house at Martock and carried away "deeds, writings and other muniments"; and in 1335 eight Somerset men attacked Margaret de Beaupre, imprisoned her, mowed her crops and assaulted her men and servants.[21] In far away Devon, the tenants of Tavistock had pursued their claim to ancient demesne status throughout the thirteenth century:[22] and it was in Devon that in 1346 it was reported that John Lersedeken had "assembled a large number of armed members of his confederacy and is running about that county and elsewhere to kill John Cole, resisting attachment by armed force and wholly refusing to satisfy the king".[23]

In Dorset, as in the Isle of Wight, wreckers were regularly at work, in 1362 for instance despoiling the goods of the king's clerk John de Stretle, chancellor of the Black Prince, on a vessel which had been driven ashore near Weymouth: while the pirates operating out of Weymouth and Dartmouth in the 1350s were only the forerunners of a tradition of seagoing disorder that was to last more than 400 years.[24]

In the south-west, then, as elsewhere in medieval England, people of all ranks of society were accustomed to defend or assert their interests violently, with arms, and when necessarily murderously. The maintenance of public order was as problematic in Somerset or Dorset as it was in Essex or Kent: and the fine line between the hoodlum and the aggrieved tenant everywhere was difficult to draw. But the counties of the south and west provide us with as many examples of determined, concerted and persistent opposition to a landlord's demands as they do of wanton violence. One such example is from the estates of Titchfield Abbey in southern Hampshire.

The Premonstratensian Abbey of Titchfield had been founded in 1232, in the process becoming endowed with estates in Titchfield itself and in half-a-dozen neighbouring villages.[25] The Titchfield canons set out from the first to maximize their income by more clearly defining and enforcing what they saw as their tenants' obligations. They were resisted. There are signs that even before the foundation the tenants in Titchfield had been developing arguments for privileged status based on the proposition that the manor was ancient royal demesne. By the 1240s there was a "querela" between the new abbot and the tenants of the neighbouring manor of Swanwick. In 1246 and 1256 the tenants of Titchfield too were objecting to some of their services. By 1271 there was a full-scale dispute, pursued by a writ of *monstraverunt* and hearings before the King's Bench.[26] A settlement reached in 1275 was a compromise heavily weighted in the landlord's interest; but arguments continued until 1319 in both Swanwick and Titchfield.

Across Southampton Water, in the abbey's manor of Cadland, resistance to the landlord followed the same pattern and lasted even longer. It began with a dispute about tallage in 1247, continued with opposition to carrying services, and persisted as an argument about electing a reeve which was still dragging on in 1365. In another of the abbey's manors at Portchester, in the shadow of the royal castle there, yet another series of disputes centring on ancient demesne status lasted from 1267 to 1309. And in the more rural manor of Wallsworth, on the mainland opposite Portsmouth, and unprotected by any supposed ancient demesne status, the tenants put up a particularly spirited opposition between 1262 and 1342 to the imposition of a variety of agricultural services. These arguments between the Abbot of Titchfield and his tenants died down for some years before the Black Death, and although there was renewed activity, in part associated with the Statute of Labourers, in the 1350s and '60s, the indications are that in this instance a century of disputes from 1240 to 1340 had resulted in compromises, at least on agrarian issues, acceptable to both sides. Only at the coastal village of Hook did opposition, sometimes violent, continue until 1405, but now on a different issue, the maintenance of a chapel-of-ease.[27]

An interesting feature of these Titchfield disputes is that they were closely paralleled by very similar incidents on the great Worcestershire manor of the Premonstratensian Abbey of Halesowen which was the mother abbey of Titchfield. There are strong indications that the Premonstratensian abbots discussed common problems and policies of this kind during their regular meetings. The disputes at Halesowen, as at Titchfield, began in the 1240s, continued with proceedings in the King's Bench court in 1278, and were for the time being ended with a settlement largely in the landlord's interest in the 1290s.[28] But a notable difference between our evidence for Titchfield and that at Halesowen is that we know that in the latter resistance to manorial demands continued up to and beyond 1381: "in the period between 1312 and 1348 each of the males identified in the court rolls performed on average 0.32 trespasses against the lord per year: while in the period from 1350 to 1386 the mean was 0.73". There were major disputes at Halesowen in 1380 and 1386, and the settlement of 1387, apparently final, was largely to the advantage of the tenants.[29]

That the Premonstratensians were not the only landlords in south and west England who provoked concerted and effective resistance to their policies is shown by the examples of Crondall, in north-eastern Hampshire, and the nearby manors of Whitchurch and Hurstbourne Priors in central Hampshire which were among the estates of the Priory of St Swithun's (that is, the cathedral) in Winchester. The disputes here, again based on the notion of ancient demesne, had begun in 1280, and were resumed in 1364–5 with writs of *monstraverunt* followed by a settlement in Crondall largely in the tenants' interest.[30] What gives additional interest to the Crondall instance is that Crondall was one of the first manors, in March 1377, to ask for an exemplification of Domesday Book during the series of events in south central England associated with the "Great Rumour" that preceded the revolt of 1381.[31]

Hampshire tenants then seem to have been pioneers of the use of ancient demesne arguments in resisting landlords' demands. As well as Titchfield, Swanwick, Cadland and Portchester on the Titchfield Abbey estates, and Crondall, Whitchurch and Hurstbourne Priors on the St Swithun's estates, there are other early Hampshire instances from Andover, Basingstoke, Ramsdean, Tisted, Barton Stacey and Priors Dean.[32] Some of these disputes were sustained over three or four generations. Similar prolonged disputes elsewhere in the south and west have already been noted at Tavistock, Ogbourne and Halesowen.

That articulate opposition to landlords, as well as being sustained through time, could also be co-ordinated across estate and shire boundaries is demonstrated by the events of the "Great Rumour" of 1376–8. This remarkable movement, well described by Rosamund Faith, took place through at least 40 communities.[33] Though we do not know in detail what happened in all of these, the events seem to have taken the form of riotous protests against landlords' demands followed by requests for exemplifications of Domesday Book to support the tenants' assertions. Seeking such exemplifications was a development of the older procedures such as the writ *monstraverunt* used in ancient demesne cases. The whole movement seems to have been coordinated by itinerant "counsellors", men literate and with some legal training who knew their way around the procedures of the London courts.

What is notable is that this was a movement of the south and west. Of the forty communities listed by Faith, one, Ottery St Mary, was in Devon, not far from the stubborn manor of Tavistock. Two villages in Hampshire, Crondall and Whitchurch, had been amongst the pioneers of the use of ancient demesne procedures. There were also five more villages in Hampshire, one of them, Ashmansworth, being as geographically "remote" as is possible in southern England.[34] There were eight communities in Surrey; one in Oxfordshire; three in Berkshire; two in Sussex; and 18 in Wiltshire. Several places, among them Farnham, Melksham and Bradford-on-Avon, were market towns rather than villages. Some – Whitchurch to Winchester, Wylye to Salisbury – were within a few miles of the scenes of disturbances in 1381. At the same time Wroughton in Wiltshire was close to the Ogbourne villages which had resisted the Abbey of Bec for so long. We may conclude that "isolated" "sporadic" and "short-lived" are not very helpful words with which to describe the popular movements of the south and west, at least for the greater part of the fourteenth century.

In attempting to give an account of the events of 1380–1 in the south and west we come to appreciate Dobson's verdict that "remarkably little research upon the problems of the Peasants' Revolt has been attempted during the last 60 years".[35] The chroniclers knew little of the south-west, and what they say about it is frustratingly vague. There are large and inexplicable gaps in the evidence from the public records (or at least in our present knowledge of those records). Andre Réville's extracts, published

Medieval England

Scale

0   50   100
                   miles

in 1898, though invaluable, are tendentious and in places inaccurately transcribed.[36] In 1906 Oman took these sources and repainted them with a very broad brush.[37] Since then, too many historians have drawn uncritically on Oman, and have woven explanatory theories around his weaknesses.

In attempting to piece together what might have happened in Hamp-shire, we are fortunate in being able to draw on Derek Keene's detailed knowledge of Winchester in this period.[38] Oman had more or less invented a colourful story in which a "wealthy draper" (William Wigge) had led a group of "the lower class of craftsmen" against the "burgess oligarchy of mayor and aldermen" in Winchester; "no doubt" says Oman "he had gone against his own class owing to some old municipal grudge".[39] What is really known about this incident?

Our only detailed evidence of events in Hampshire comes from the royal escheator's account of the goods of 25 men who had been involved.[40] The account describes the 25 as having been insurgents against the king, of taking part in an insurrection in the aforesaid county (Hampshire) and as inducing others to take part. Keene believes that 14 of the insurgents can be shown to have come from Winchester, nine of them being known property holders or guild members: one (William Wigge) was later to be mayor of Winchester, and another (Henry Clerk) would be a member of Parliament. Four men (not including Wigge) were specifically said to have committed crimes in Winchester, one, Geoffrey Talbot, on a particular day – 25 June 1381. Five of the Winchester men (including Wigge) were active in the fulling and dyeing trades, one was a hosier, another a blacksmith. On the other hand, one man, Thomas Fauconer, was also described as "alias Thomas Palmer of the county of Surrey"; and another (William Tiptoft) who had two acres of winter corn, two acres of spring corn and two bullocks at "Purton" was evidently a genuine peasant. Eight other named men cannot be identified by location or chattels, and Keene suggests that they are from "Hampshire generally".[41]

There was then an urban rising in Winchester in 1381 in which some cloth workers were involved. But we do not know that the cloth workers led the rising or that the rising was against the "urban authorities"; the fact that John Fisshe's chattels were in the hands of the Prior of St Swithun's suggests that the rising may have been against those unpopular landlords, Hyde Abbey and St Swithun's Priory. In fact, we do not know what the motives of any of the participants were, whether there were any rural risings as well, whether something similar also happened at Southampton, what actually occurred, or for how long. Réville had begun the process of distorting this ambiguous evidence by including in his transcript details only of chattels related to the textile industry: in the event, even Keene's conclusion that "the Winchester outbreak appears to have arisen from tensions within the community of citizens" is no more than a well-informed guess.[42]

There are a few hints that the Hampshire rising went beyond Winchester. On 16 July the king appointed John Montagu and others to put down the insurrection in Hampshire and Wiltshire.[43] We know that the authorities believed that Kentish insurgents had tried to stir up the population in Hampshire and Sussex.[44] According to Froissart, the fleet which had assembled at Plymouth, apparently in mid-June, put to sea "or else they feared lest the commons about Hampton, Winchester and Arundel would have come upon them".[45] But the scale of the Hampshire rising must for the present remain an open question.

As to Sussex, it seems unlikely that the people there needed inspiration from Kent. Oman thought that the riots there were sporadic and short-lived: the escheator's accounts which had listed 25 men in Hampshire listed only ten for Sussex.[46] However, there were major risings in the south of the county, including an attack on Lewes Castle, so that by July the authorities had filled Arundel and Lewes Castles with their prisoners.[47] But the most striking feature of events in Sussex is that less than two years after the often brutal suppression of the summer of 1381, the Earl of Arundel's castle at Lewes was attacked again in February 1383:[48]

> William Grete of Lewes, William Wodeland of Clyve by Lewes and other insurgents in the county of Sussex, came armed to Lewes, broke his closes and gates . . . threw down his buildings, consumed and destroyed ten casks of wine . . . and burned his rolls, rentals and other muniments.

The combative spirit of Sussex was to be again evident in 1450.

The most interesting of the events of the 1380s in the south and west is the rising in Wiltshire, which began in September 1380, before the proclamation of the third Poll Tax and nine months before the risings in the east. On September 3rd one John Haukewode of Salisbury and the common people of Salisbury came to Salisbury, the suburban village of Fisherton Anger and other unnamed places in Wiltshire with swords, shields, bows and arrows. A second attack on Salisbury seems to have taken place in March 1381, still before the eastern risings, when a band of people who were described as having no land or tenements in the city or anywhere else entered Salisbury by night, destroying the new fortifications there, attacked and wounded townspeople, prevented the election of bailiffs and for several days committed all kinds of misdemeanours.[49] These disorders certainly spread as far as Mere, 25 miles to the west, where the already semi-derelict royal castle was looted,[50] and were presumably still going on in July when John Montagu was given his commission to put down the rising in Hampshire and Wiltshire. Haukewode was pardoned in 1384.[51] Oman dismissed the significance of this remarkable Wiltshire rising on the grounds that the escheator had been unable to find any rebels or their chattels.[52] Dobson mentioned it briefly in his chronological table but not in the body of his text. McKisack, Fryde, Hilton and others do not mention it at all.[53]

Even though the events of June 1381 in Somerset have been more fully documented than those of Wiltshire they still raise difficulties of interpretation.[54] Events began in Bridgwater, with the revival of a bitter dispute, which had already been going on in 1380, between the Augustinian Hospital of St John and the vicar of the parish church supported by a large number of townspeople. This dispute then provided a pretext for a group of men described by Dobson as "gentry" to further what seem to have been local feuds by marching across Somerset as far as Ilchester, 20 miles to the east, burning, looting and committing at least two murders. This was not therefore a wholly urban rising; and at the same time, on the basis of the account in the Patent Roll Dobson concluded that it was "certainly not a peasant revolt": yet a draft letter of manumission of July, identified by Barbara Harvey, was intended not for gentry but for villein tenants in Somerset, and prepared on their behalf.[55] Somerset, then, seems to be another county in which more happened than our existing sources reveal.

That the identification of a single piece of evidence can transform our understanding of events is well illustrated by the case of Cornwall. Oman had concluded: "nor are there any special misdoings reported from Dorset, Devon and Cornwall".[56] But the publication in the *Calendars of Inquisitions Miscellaneous* of a commission of inquiry into unlawful assemblies in Cornwall enabled Dobson to include this "unexpected example" in the preface to his second edition.[57] It revealed several weeks of chaos in central Cornwall in the summer of 1381, the misdemeanours including Sir William Botreaux and 80 armed men plundering his neighbour's estate, while his tenants Richard and William Eyre with 300 men were attacking the property of Bodmin Priory.

We can anticipate that stories of this kind will also come to light for Dorset and Devon. As to Berkshire, we have only one minor example of disorder, from Blewbury, but Reading was one of the towns from which, according to Froissart, the London rebels expected to get reinforcements.[58]

The 1381 rising and its repression did not of course bring popular discontent in the south and west of England to an end. We have already noticed the attack on Lewes Castle in 1383, the continued bitterness in Salisbury, and the struggle over the chapel at Hook. An interesting illustration of the changing motives for discontent comes from mid-Wiltshire in 1428 when six villagers of Edington met at the cross on Tinhead Hill and took an oath not to pay more than a penny for church dues. They were taken before the bishop at Ramsbury 20 miles away to be forced to abjure.[59] That in the fifteenth century a mixture of anti-clericalism and political grievance was replacing manorial resentments in the motives of popular movements is evident from the dramatic events of 1450 in the south. The year began with the brutal murder of Adam Moleyns, Bishop of Chichester, by unpaid soldiers and sailors at Portsmouth (so that Portsmouth ends our period under an interdict).[60] In June hundreds of Sussex men joined Jack Cade at Blackheath.[61] In rural Wiltshire Bishop Ayscough's carriage was looted at Edington and the next morning the bishop himself was dragged from the church and hacked to pieces.[62] His murder precipitated widespread attacks on church property. The bishops' palaces at both Winchester and Salisbury were stormed, and episcopal property was looted throughout Wiltshire. The authorities' estimate of the gravity of these offences was conveyed in the distribution of the quartered limbs of Cade and his principal supporters. Salisbury received one of the quarters of Cade himself: Chichester, Portsmouth and Winchester only limbs of lieutenants.[63] But this review of popular movements over two centuries is most suitably ended at a scene in the market place of the little Dorset town of Sherborne, with the entire adult population gathered to receive each a sixpennyworth share of the bishop's looted property.[64]

In summary, in 1381 the south and west of England was not "remote": its ports and markets were in direct and regular contact with the great cities of Renaissance Europe. Nor was it uncommercialized: those same ports and markets handled a large proportion of the wine trade and the products of the woollen industry.[65] The risings in the south and west were not "sporadic": they were further expressions of a long, often violent, history of resistance to landlords and to the authorities in general in both town and country which stretched from the early thirteenth to the late fifteenth century and beyond. Nor were the risings "isolated". Winchester and Salisbury were surrounded by villages in which "ancient demesne" disputes had dragged on for generations and through which the Great Rumour had spread. Indeed, it might be argued that during the thirteenth and fourteenth centuries, in their concerted and ingenious use of ancient demesne procedures and in their employment of "counsellors" the western villagers were more sophisticated than those of other parts of the country. Fryde attributes the high proportion of evasions of the 1377 Poll Tax (43% in the south-west and 48% in the north) to impoverishment; just as likely an explanation is more effective resistance.[66] Though the events of 1381 itself remain obscure, we have quite enough evidence to rebut any suggestion of a cowed or acquiescent population. Some of the incidents of 1381 and 1450 are better seen as outbursts of bitter resentment against a regime which might change at the top, but which always looked inefficient, corrupt and oppressive to the citizen. As Conscience said:

> (Lucre) makes bishops of men who can scarcely read. She provides livings for parsons and for lawless priests to spend their lives with mistresses . . . Heaven help that land where she wins the king's favour![67]

It has not been the purpose of this paper to minimize the significance of the remarkable events in London and the south-east in 1381: of course, nothing quite like them occurred elsewhere. What has been questioned is the attempt to explain the background of those events by the use of a negative stereotype of the south and west. If south-west England was just as market-orientated and commercially minded, its inhabitants as resentful of corrupt authority and landlord control as anyone else, and as capable of cutting throats, then we cannot interpret the south-eastern rising as the product of a peculiarly "advanced" society. We need to look for other explanations.

Notes

1   C. Oman, *The Great Revolt of 1381* (Oxford, 1906), p. 90.
2   A. Steel, *Richard II* (Cambridge, 1962), p. 58.
3   R.H. Hilton, *Bond Men Made Free* (Temple Smith, 1973), pp. 166, 175.
4   E.B. Fryde, *The Great Revolt of 1381* (The Historical Association, 1981), p. 9; *see also* M. McKisack, *The Fourteenth Century* (Oxford, 1959), pp. 407–19.
5   For events in the north, see, for example, "The Turbulent Border", chapter V in W. Rollinson, *A History of Cumberland and Westmorland* (Phillimore, 1978).
6   R.B. Dobson (ed.), *The Peasants' Revolt of 1381* (2nd edn., Macmillan, 1983), p. 284 sq.
7   E.M. Carus-Wilson, "Evidences of Industrial Growth on some Fifteenth Century Manors", *Essays in Economic History* II, (ed.) Carus-Wilson (Arnold, 1962), p. 165; M.K. James, "The Fluctuations in the Anglo-Gascon Wine Trade during the Fourteenth Century", *Essays in Economic History* II, op.cit., pp. 136–41.
8   Dobson, op.cit., p. 18.
9   V.H. Galbraith, "Thoughts about the Peasants' Revolt", *The Reign of Richard II*, (eds.) F. du Boulay and C.M. Barron (Univ. of London, 1971), p. 55.
10 S.F. Hockey, *Quarr Abbey and its Lands* (Leicester U.P., 1970), p. 108.
11 *Cal(endar of) Pat(ent Rolls)* 1371–21, p. 604; *Cal.Pat.* 1324–7, pp. 139–40.
12 D.J. Stagg (ed.), *New Forest Documents 1244–1334* (Hampshire County Council, 1979), p. 129.

13 *Cal. Pat.* 1324–7, p. 139.

14 D. Keene, *Survey of Medieval Winchester I* (Winchester Studies 2, Oxford, 1985), p. 395; *Cal. Pat.* 1313–17, pp. 145–6.

15 *Cal. Pat.* 1338–40, p. 65.

16 R.H. Hilton, "Resistance to Taxation and to other State Impositions in Medieval England", *Genèse de l'État Moderne* (Paris, 1987), p. 172: Portsdown was a Hundred not a village, and included Wallsworth.

17 *Cal. Pat.* 1374–7. p. 220.

18 M. Morgan, *English Lands of the Abbey of Bec* (Oxford, 1946), p. 106.

19 *Cal. Pat.* 1327–30, p. 435.

20 F. Street, "The Relations of the Bishops and Citizens of Salisbury between 1225 and 1612", *Wiltshire Archaeological Magazine* 39 (1915–17), p. 185 sq.; *Victoria County History of Wiltshire* VI (Oxford, 1962), pp. 102–3.

21 *Cal. Pat.* 1330–4, p. 239; *Cal. Pat.* 1334– 8, p. 215.

22 P. Vinogradoff, *Villainage in England* (Oxford, 1892), p. 119.

23 *Cal. Pat.* 1345–8, p. 113.

24 *Cal. Pat.* 1361–4, p. 290; *Cal. Pat.* 1358–61, pp. 276, 585.

25 D.G. Watts, "Peasant Discontent on the Manors of Titchfield Abbey", *Proceedings of the Hampshire Field Club* 39 (1983), pp. 121–35: the first reference to ancient demesne (*tamquam dominici homines nostri*) is in *Calendar of Close Rolls* 1227–31, pp. 132–3.

26 *Monstraverunt* was the conventional name for a writ by which the tenants of former royal demesne land claiming to be overburdened with dues and services could initiate proceedings against their present landlords.

27 Watts op.cit., pp. 131–2; more material on the dispute at Hook appears in *John Lydford's Book*, (ed.) D.M. Owen (Devon and Cornwall Record Society, new ser. 20, 1975), pp. 112–16.

28 R.H. Hilton, "Peasant Movements in England before 1381", *Essays in Economic History* II op.cit., p. 83; Z. Razi, "The Abbots of Halesowen and their tenants", *Social Relations and Ideas*, (ed.) T.H. Aston (Cambridge, 1983), pp. 151–67.

29 Razi op.cit., p. 165.

30 F.J. Baigent (ed.), *The Crondal Records I* (Hampshire Record Society, 1890), pp. 43–7.

31 R. Faith, "The Great Rumour of 1377 and Peasant Ideology", *The English Rising of 1381*, (eds.) R.H. Hilton and T.H. Aston (Cambridge, 1984), pp. 43–74.

32 R.S. Hoyt, *The Royal Demesne in English Constitutional History 1066–1272* (Cornell U.P., 1950), pp. 137, 138, 215, 221; K.A. Hanna, *The Cartularies of Southwick Priory* (Hampshire County Council, 1988), pp. 304–5.

33 Faith op.cit., pp. 71–3.

34 Ashmansworth is in the heart of south central England, close to its highest point on Inkpen Beacon, half-way beween London and Bristol and between Southampton and Oxford, and on minor roads.

35 Dobson op.cit., p. 11.

36 A. Réville, *Le Soulevement des Travailleurs d'Angleterre en 1381* (Paris, 1898), pp. 278–85.

37 Oman op.cit., passim.

38 Keene op.cit., pp. 396–7.

39 Oman op.cit., p. 98.

40 Public Record Office E136/195/1; and Réville op.cit., pp. 278–9.

41 Keene op.cit.

42 Keene op.cit.

43 Réville op.cit., p. 282.

44 *Cal. Pat.* 1381–5, p. 80.

45 Dobson op.cit., p. 143.

46 Oman op.cit., p. 98.

47 *Victoria County History of Sussex VII* (Oxford, 1940), p. 16; and *VCH Sussex I* (London, 1905), pp. 511–12; *Cal. Pat.* 1381–5, p. 73.

48 *Cal. Pat.* 1381–5, p. 259.

49 Réville op.cit., p. 281; *Cal. Pat.* 1377–81, p. 631.

50 Réville op.cit., p. 281.

51 Réville op.cit., p. 280; *Cal. Pat.* 1381–5, p. 399.

52 Oman op.cit., p. 138.

53 Dobson op.cit., p. 43; Fryde op.cit.; Hilton 1973 op.cit.; McKisack op.cit.

54 Dobson op.cit., pp. 279–84.

55 B. Harvey, "Draft Letters of Manumission and Pardon for the Men of Somerset", *English Historical Review* 80 (1965), pp. 89–91.

56 Oman op.cit., p. 140.

57 Dobson op.cit., p. xxv; *Calendar of Inquisitions Miscellaneous IV* 1377–80, pp. 101–2.

58 Réville op.cit., p. 280, and *Cal. Pat.* 1381–5, p. 75, which shows that Réville omitted the reference to Blewbury, where the disorder took place; Dobson op.cit., p. 194.

59 E.F. Jacob, *The Fifteenth Century* (Oxford, 1961), p. 496.

60 G. Kriehn, *The English Rising of 1450* (Strasbourg, 1892), p. 83.

61 W.D. Cooper, "Participation of Sussex in Cade's Rising", *Sussex Archaeological Collections* XVIII (1866), p. 17 sq.

62 Kriehn op.cit.

63 H.M. Lyle, *The Rebellion of Jack Cade 1450* (The Historical Association, 1950), pp. 14–15.

64 Kriehn op.cit., p. 84.

65 See, for example, O. Coleman, "Trade and Prosperity in the Fifteeth Century", *Economic History Review*, 2nd ser. XVI (1963), pp. 9–22: Coleman refers to London, Southampton and Bristol as "the big three" and as "the three busiest ports in England", pp. 18–19.

66 Fryde op.cit., pp. 11–12.

67 J.E. Goodridge (trans.), *Piers the Plowman* (Penguin, 1959), p. 87.

2

The Lords and their Tenants: Conflict and Stability in Fifteenth-Century Wiltshire

J.N. Hare

Peter Symonds' College, Winchester

I

Later Medieval Wiltshire witnessed a growing prosperity that was reflected in the taxation returns,[1] in countless manorial records, and in the active building work in many country churches.[2] This prosperity left intact many of the traditional features of its rural economy: the regional divisions, particularly those between the chalkland and elsewhere; the pattern of manors and great estates; the manorial demesnes and the customary virgates or peasant holdings. But there was also to be much change and by the end of the fifteenth century lords had generally leased out their demesne arable and flocks, and the peasantry now showed much greater variation in the scale of their holdings, a group of large-scale peasant aristocrats or gentleman farmers having emerged. Some of the changes were to be the product of the demographic decline of the later Middle Ages, and others were influenced by the county's development as one of the main cloth production centres during the great expansion of this industry in England from the late fourteenth century onwards: already by 1377, Salisbury had become the sixth most populous provincial town in England, and the west Wiltshire industry rapidly grew thereafter. The expansion of this industry would increase the demand for labour, for raw materials, for food and for services. As such its impact would extend far beyond the cloth workers or clothiers, and into agriculture and the lives of the peasantry. Many of the rural changes were already underway by the end of the fourteenth century, and this study seeks to examine some aspects of the relationship between lord and tenant as they developed in the fifteenth century in one part of southern England. It is not an attempt to examine conditions on a single estate, rather to view the problems on a wide range of manors belonging to different lords, whether lay or ecclesiastical, great or small.[3]

Amidst this prosperity, the risings of 1450 provide the most striking example of conflict. Throughout the summer, from the end of June to the beginning of September, there were a series of riots and attacks on property and persons, events that included the killing of the bishop of Salisbury, William Ayscough, just outside Edington priory church. Ayscough, an influential figure in the discredited government of Henry VI, was to provide the focus for most, but not all, the disturbances: he was murdered, his baggage train and some other property had already been attacked, and his manor houses or palaces at Salisbury, Potterne, Ramsbury and Woodford were all sacked. In part, therefore, the Wiltshire risings need to be seen as part of the wider political protest against the failures of government policy that is so evident in the risings of Jack Cade and the rebels' programme in Kent. But in Wiltshire, as elsewhere, there was a further element, that of social and economic discontent which reflected the economic recession that had struck those areas increasingly dependent on the manufacture and export of cloth. In Wiltshire, it was the cloth-producing areas in general and the men associated with the industry in particular who were heavily involved in the risings: of those indicted and whose occupations are described, at least 30 per cent belonged to this industry. Peasants or husbandmen were also active, with about 25 per cent of the indictments suggesting that the person accused was engaged in agricultural production. But again their distribution seems significant, and the areas outside the cloth producing districts do not seem to have been involved.

It would seem difficult to view these events as part of a rural conflict between lord and tenant. Conflicts with Bishop Ayscough as a landlord seem to have been greater in the towns of Salisbury and Sherborne than on the rural manors, and although the attacks on his properties in Ramsbury, Potterne and Salisbury included the destruction of records, none of his rural tenants seems to have been indicted for their part in the risings. These risings were not merely a political protest against misrule, but nor can they be seen as a peasants' revolt. Tensions between lord and tenant certainly existed, and the political crisis combined with the economic recession provided a situation in which a variety of individual and group grievances could surface. Despite this, no specific evidence of peasant or tenant complaints has been found.[4] In order to study the relationship between lord and tenant in this period, attention must be turned to the less dramatic episodes and to the evidence of innumerable manorial account and court rolls. This will be done by examining two aspects of peasant conditions: the continuation of serfdom or villeinage, and developments in the lord's capacity to exact rent and income from his tenantry. The first of these concerned a small and diminishing part of the rural tenantry, but the latter concerned them all.

Wiltshire

II

In Wiltshire, as elsewhere, the fifteenth century was to see a major decline in the presence of serfdom. Previously, the burdens of personal servility had rested on the customary tenants. Now, in the changed economic conditions of a declining population and with the lords unable to enforce the conditions of personal unfreedom on new tenants, fewer families remained subject to these restrictions. As families died out in the male line, as serfs left for the vacant land that was now available elsewhere, as other families bought their freedom, or as sons escaped for education or for the church, so did the number subject to the effective burdens of villeinage decline. By the sixteenth century, few such families remained, although this did not diminish the irksome character of the restraints or of the extra financial impositions upon them. Holding bond land no longer implied the burden of personal servility: most customary or bond land was now held by men who were legally free.[5]

Already by the fifteenth century, the burdens of serfdom rested on a small minority of the village families. This situation was the result of death, a failure to produce male heirs and of the readiness of villeins to flee the manor, together with a changed economic and social environment which made it difficult for lords to impose harsh conditions on men who were not previously unfree. Like their social superiors, peasant families might fail to produce male heirs,[6] and a villein family would disappear. Thus at Durrington 71 per cent of the old tenant families who had combined holding bond land and the personal burdens of servile status, disappeared from the manor between 1334 and 1359. In the latter year a note was made on the rental as to which of the tenant families were free and which were of villein blood: only five of the nine virgators fell into the latter category, and three of these had gone by 1411/12.[7] Similarly at Combe Bisset by about 1380 only four of the fourteen customary virgators were described as bondmen by blood.[8] Villein families continued to disappear in the fourteenth century, helped by the failure to keep serfs on the lord's land. The steady trickle of villeins repeatedly fined for being outside the lordship is reflected in the five examples from the small manor of Hilmarton, or on manors like Hannington, Stockton and Wroughton.[9] While villeinage was to continue to decline, the evidence suggests that in Wiltshire it had ceased to affect more than a small minority of the tenant population by the end of the fourteenth century.

Serfs were not just a declining minority, but they were a group distinguished by legal rather than economic factors. Freemen now held bond or customary land, and we can even find serfs holding specifically free tenures. Looking at the survival of villeinage in the fifteenth century, it needs to be borne in mind that this was no longer a status that affected a large part of the village population. Serfs were no different from the rest except that they had potentially severe extra financial burdens: the requirement to pay a fine if they wished to stay outside the lordship, for the marriage of their daughters or at death. The scale of such payments may be seen at Stockton, where in 1390 the lord received 6s. 8d. for one merchet, or marriage, payment, and 23s. 4d. for the merchet of four daughters of Thomas Self, while in 1397 William Palmer paid 8s. for his two daughters.[10] Serfdom seems to have survived rather more fully on the chalklands, a reflection of the greater traditionalism of this area in its agricultural organization.[11] Elsewhere, at places like Bromham, Abyndscourt, Eastrop, Purton and over the Berkshire border at Coleshill, personal servility appeared virtually or absolutely non-existent.[12] By contrast chalkland manors such as Enford, Stockton, Wroughton, Urchfont and Durrington had a small but significant group of villeins. Thus the records of the Wiltshire estates of St Swithun's cathedral priory, Winchester, provide minimum figures for the fifteenth century at Enford of four distinct villein family groupings, together with some subdivisions, and at Wroughton there were five or six such families.[13] A similar pattern is reflected on the eight Wiltshire manors of Glastonbury abbey in 1518, on the rental of which the scribe took care to record the description *nativus de sanguine* (bondman by blood) in a different coloured ink.[14] Outside the chalklands, only a single manor had a villein family (Nettleton with one) while in the chalklands themselves, although some manors also produced no serfs, the manors of Idmiston and Damerham provided eighteen bondmen from seven families.

It is difficult to distinguish any other factor significantly affecting the survival of serfdom: whether the distinction between lay and ecclesiastical estates, the influence of markets or towns, or any relationship to trends in economic prosperity or decline. Some of the factors affecting the survival of serfdom were – like family fertility – beyond the control of estate owners, and moreover, as in other aspects of estate policies the same administrators were involved in running both lay and ecclesiastical estates, as with John Whittocksmede, who served Hyde abbey, Battle abbey, the Hungerfords and Bishop Ayscough.[15] There was an accidental element to the survival of serfdom. If some families died out in the male line, others increased the number of serfs. Thus when a survey of bondmen was made at Durrington in 1453, and again in 1454, the number of villein families had risen to six, but these represented the descendants of only three such families. Some families purchased their freedom from their lord, and on one large estate, that of St Swithun's priory, Winchester, a chronology for this can be established.[16] The priory manors were found in

Wiltshire and Hampshire. Of the forty-six known manumissions, the vast majority (thirty-seven) occurred within the period from 1390 to 1450, with by far and away the highest concentration in the decade 1410–19, when fifteen grants were made. Here they seem to have preceded the main manumissions on the estates of the bishopric of Worcester, and probably those on the estates of Ramsey abbey.[17] The smaller Wiltshire figures need to be used with caution, since there were only eight recorded manumissions in the priory register, but they seem to parallel the pattern of the estate as a whole. The paucity of manumissions after 1450, probably reflects the fact that by then there were few villein families left to buy their freedom.

But although serfdom thus affected only a small part of the tenant population, landlords were keen to maintain the financial benefits. Hence lords as diverse as Sir John Fastolf, Winchester College and Glastonbury abbey are seen taking care to record which of the customary tenants were legally unfree, or seeking to keep a note of the movements of their villeins. Thus in 1423, the court at Wroughton recorded that Robert Jumpere had fled the lordship. As a comparatively recent newcomer to Wroughton, this would not have been of great significance to the lord, except that Jumpere was a villein belonging to another of the cathedral priory's manors, at Houghton in Hampshire.[18] It was thus important to establish his movements so that he could be prevented from acquiring his freedom by default.

Serfdom was thus a legal and not an economic state and could apply to rich and poor alike. Landlords can be found attacking men of wealth: if the latter were the lord's bondmen, then their property could also be. One notable example was John Halle, one of the great merchants of Salisbury in the mid-fifteenth century and a dominant figure in the political life of one of the greatest cities of the kingdom. Thrice Member of Parliament for the city and four times mayor, he led it in its struggle with the bishop, at a time when this long-standing conflict reached a peak.[19] Yet he was accused by the Prioress of Amesbury of being her bondman and her officials went as far as seizing some of his property. In the end the case was resolved in 1468 by the arbitration of no less a personage than the king's brother, George, Duke of Clarence.[20] The accusation of serfdom may have been a longstanding one. This possibility is suggested by the decision of the city council in 1456, that its members should not engage in personal invective, singling out John Halle and his rival William Swayne as causing such disturbances. Amongst the specific words banned from future use were 'ceorl' and 'knave', both of which could imply villeinage and unfree status as well as being more general terms of abuse.[21]

Another, but better known example of villeinage striking at the rich may be seen at Castle Combe, a village that grew enormously in the early fifteenth century as a centre of the cloth industry.[22] While many of the men who benefited from this prosperity were outsiders and freemen, William Haynes was not, the family already being referred to as villein by blood in 1392. William was a wealthy clothier as well as a man of standing in the local community and a former warden of the goods of the parish church.[23] As a bondman his property was his lord's. At his death, the council of Sir John Fastolf his lord, valued his goods and chattels at 3,000 marks (£2,000). Even the more lenient local jury still assessed his moveables, debts, household goods, merchandise, stock and all else at 300 marks, after allowing for the payment of certain outstanding commitments, such as the £20 bequest for making the new bell tower of the parish church. In view of later developments, the jury seems to have underestimated his wealth, for in the following years his widow was able to pay Fastolf £140 for gaining possession of his lands and for permission to hold them and marry, while the new husband also had to pay a fine of £40 for admission to his wife's property.[24]

Haynes and Halle may have gained most of their wealth from industry or trade, but there were also rich villeins who had acquired their wealth from agriculture and from the increasing opportunities in Wiltshire for self advancement, either through the accumulation of agricultural holdings, or through the leasing of the demesnes.[25] The Goddards were a family who leased several demesnes in north-east Wiltshire in the fifteenth century including the large manors of Aldbourne and Ogbourne St George, and later at Overton. By 1510, Thomas Goddard of Ogbourne was being formally referred to as a gentleman, while the scale of their wealth was reflected in the 1525 lay subsidy returns, when John Goddard was assessed with goods to the value of £440 and Thomas Goddard at Ogbourne was assessed at £640. But in 1478 they were involved in a case in the royal court resulting from the accusation of villeinage. John Yorke, late of Ramsbury had taken £50 of the family's goods and chattels on the grounds that the Goddards were his villeins of the manor of Upham. The Goddards sued Yorke and eventually the jury declared in their favour.[26] On a smaller scale is the later case provided by the abbot of Malmesbury's seizure of Robert Carter's stock on the grounds of the latter's bondage. A sizeable block of livestock had been seized whether it was the 109 sheep, five bullocks, ten cows and nine calves claimed by Carter or the fifty-three sheep and eight lambs claimed by the abbot.[27] Some families remained unfree well into the sixteenth century, such as the Alweys of Colerne. They tried to secure their manumission from New College, Oxford, and when they sought this under Henry VIII they secured the support of men of influence such as Sir Henry Long, the bishop of Winchester, the archbishop of Canterbury and later of Thomas Cromwell himself. The warden, however, refused and claimed that the statutes of his college prevented him from making such a grant.[28]

Such cases also serve to remind us of the limited and essentially financial aspect of fifteenth-century villeinage for a small but significant number of people, some of whom were fully accepted as villeins while others had left the manor, although with their legal status still in doubt. But for the lord these all offered the potential for financial reward. The abbess of Amesbury would not have been interested in John Halle as an extra tenant or ploughman. Nor should Fastolf's financial success in the case of William Haynes allow us to forget that serfdom was dying out at Castle Combe. Haynes had died in 1434, but already many of the other villein families had disappeared. A few years later, in 1443/4 a list of the surviving villeins was compiled.[29] There were then only three remaining in Castle Combe of whom two belonged to one family (the Newmans). The third member of this family now lived at nearby Slaughterford. Another villein lived at Hawkesbury (Glos.) and a further one lived with his family at Tetbury (Glos.). As for William Haynes, he had left three children, of whom only the son remained at Castle Combe. A fine was paid for the marriage of his two daughters in 1434 and both had left Castle Combe for towns elsewhere in the county, migrating to Trowbridge and Malmesbury. The survival of the family as a bond one thus depended on William's son Thomas, who remained at Castle Combe and who in 1455 paid a fine to inherit his father's land.[30] He had, perhaps, too much to lose by leaving the manor. Fastolf's council might try to squeeze the maximum financial returns from villeinage and from the Haynes family, but they could not stop its decline. Only the Newmans and Thomas Haynes now remained, and they not for long: Thomas Haynes purchased his freedom in 1463, and a William Newman and his son in 1482.[31]

Such families remind us that a silent struggle was going on, and that the lords were losing it, or accepting the inevitable by taking the short-term benefit of manumission in return for the long-term loss. The Weylot family of Durrington provides a good example of this losing battle. The family was not one which went back on the manor before the Black Death and it does not appear on the rentals until 1388.[32] They were evidently and specifically regarded as unfree during the fifteenth century, so that it seems likely that they had come from one of the other Winchester College manors. They constituted one of the active and influential families of the village in the fifteenth century, and by 1453 there were three branches of the family resident there.[33] Gradually they sought and achieved their freedom. A Thomas Weylot probably achieved manumission since he is seen heading the free jurors in 1484 and 1485.[34] Another Thomas Weilot was staying outside the lordship at the neighbouring village of Fittleton by 1502, and his death and the fact that he had three sons who were also bondmen, was carefully recorded in the Durrington manorial court of 1509: two remained with their mother at Fittleton and another had moved on to the nearby village of Alton.[35] Thomas was evidently a man of substance leaving bequests to five of the local churches and making specific bequests of 274 sheep together with one sheep for each of his god children. Despite his unfree status he was able to have his will proved at the Prerogative Court of Canterbury, like any other freeman.[36] A third Thomas Weilot (alias Barbour), moved from Durrington to another Winchester College manor at Combe Bisset. There he undertook the leasing of the demesne from 1491 until 1523 and established his family, but it is not clear whether he may have already moved before this undertaking. Although his place of origin is never noted on the Combe Bisset records, comparison of the documents here and at Durrington show that he had come from the latter manor, where the same surname and alias was to be found. Though he was a newcomer to Combe Bisset and does not appear on any of the earlier rentals, the college took particular pains to record his servile status, even on the account rolls where he is generally described as nativus de sanguine. Despite, the change of manor, which might otherwise have led to his villeinage being forgotten, his lord was evidently keen that his tenant should not so easily escape his servile status. But all this was to be in vain and at his death, he too was treated like a freeman and had his will proved at the Prerogative Court of Canterbury.[37] Since there were four or five sons and a daughter, Winchester College was the loser.

Serfdom has been treated on an individual level and this reflects both the scale of its survival in fifteenth-century Wiltshire and the evidence. Although the manorial evidence may conceal revolt and conflict within the village,[38] no example of any such action has been found in Wiltshire at this period. The nearest known contemporary example was at Faccombe over the border in north-west Hampshire, and where villeinage would certainly seem to have been an issue of conflict. In 1425 three of the lord's bondmen by blood assaulted the lord. Two of these then removed sheep and corn seized on behalf of the lord. One of them, Richard Gosyn, had already refused to accept his villein status, having refused to do his labour services and having married his daughter outside the lordship without permission, an action concealed by the homage. Subsequently, Richard and other armed men prevented the steward holding the manorial court, and four villeins left the manor. In 1426, members of the Gosyn family and others dragged the lord outside the manor house and killed him. But the list of tenants drawn up, in 1427, in the aftermath of these disturbances, suggests a much larger scale of serfdom than has been found on our Wiltshire manors. Of the tenants, other than cottagers, three held by charter, seven were customary tenants and as many as thirteen were villeins by blood. The court of that year also recorded four vacancies, produced by villeins who had suffered from the punishments of hanging or forfeiture, and eight villeins who had fled, although some of these were later to reappear. Was it the exceptional scale of serfdom that led to trouble? The battle seemed to end in victory for the new lord, and in 1427, three of the vacant holdings were filled and two of the villeins returned, formally accepting their position as 'the lord's villein by blood, together with their offspring born or to be born thereafter'. It may, however, have been a pyrrhic victory, for villeinage declined: in 1433 there were five grants of manumission, and after 1435 the villein incidents became less prominent.[39]

Serfdom was thus a matter of concern for landlords for whom it could mean extra payments or even money for manumission, and it would have been of great concern to those families who might have to suffer its financial or social costs. But it had ceased to be typical. Examination of the richer peasant farmers of the Wiltshire villages reveals families like the Goddards who were accused of villeinage, families like the Martyns of Durrington who bought their freedom[40] and the vast majority for whom there is no hint of villeinage. It was to be the same among the rest of the tenantry. For the mass of the population serfdom had become irrelevant: it had withered away.

III

Serfdom applied to a small, and diminishing, band of individuals within the village, but the burden of rent was something which affected all members of the rural community. As at other periods, examination of the level and changes of rent can reveal something of the often silent conflict between lord and tenant. How far were lords able to maximize and tenants able to minimize the level of rent payments? Such a study can help us to see changes in the demand for land and in economic prosperity, as well as shifts in the balance between lord and tenant. A few general comments need, however, to be made about the use of this evidence, much of which is based upon the examination of manorial account rolls which have been heavily criticized as being potentially misleading guides to the rural economy. Nevertheless, with care, such material can tell us much about the economic developments of the time; they are sources that we cannot afford to neglect.[41] It would not be enough to examine the annual rent payments in isolation, it is also necessary to consider the level of entry fines (the payments made when a new tenant entered his tenement) and what proportion of his expected manorial income was actually being received by the lord. Each of these items in turn poses its own problems. In comparing rent totals, it is important to ensure that the same items are being compared. As lords leased the manorial demesne or the manorial sheep flocks, extra items might be added to the manorial rent total, so that the higher rent might reflect these organizational changes, rather than increased exactions by the lord. Such changes would thus render invalid any comparison between the figures from different years. Moreover, there are very few manors where enough material has survived, or been studied, to allow useful conclusions to be made as to any movements in the level of fines. Such evidence has therefore been supplemented by reference to the annual income of the manorial court, in which entry fines were a major, but not the only source. The resultant figures are particularly difficult to use in the early fifteenth century, since at this time and in the previous decades a long decline in the use of manorial courts was taking place, resulting in a fall in profits that might have nothing to do with the entry fines.[42] Subsequently, such figures become more useful. Finally, it is not enough to look at the arrears entry to establish how much of the lord's income he had failed to collect. Arrears included short term debts that would soon be paid off and old debts that would never be, debts that arose from a single account, and those that represented many years accumulation of a single rent item. They represented both debts that were collectable and those that were not, a distinction familiar to contemporaries.[43] They may provide a better indication of the lord's conservatism than of his indebtedness, as can be seen in the arrears at Urchfont in 1481. Here the total arrears of £99 9s. 1d. compare with a cash livery to St Mary's abbey, Winchester of £62 12s. 7d. in the previous year, and suggest a case of seigneurial crisis. But over a third of these arrears came from the accumulated debts from two rents and a payment by a freeman, the annual value of all three merely amounting to 16s. 3d. A second group of debts (£11 6s.) went back to the days of seigneurial sheep farming, some to 1462. The debts of the current officials of the manor came to over £43, but most or all of these were ultimately paid off. Of the £99, less than £6 came from the debts of past lessees or rent collectors, a much more encouraging situation for the lord than might have at first sight appeared. Any comments made on indebtedness must be based on a study of the debts and not just on the arrears totals.[44]

In an earlier attempt to sketch changes in rent, Dr Scott treated the fifteenth century as a whole,[45] conveying a picture of general rent falls and decayed rents. Such a picture, however, fails to do justice to the regional and chronological variations and the changes that were taking place in the economy of the county. Although the later Middle Ages was to see a decline in the area of arable and settlement, as reflected in the landscape remains of deserted and shrunken villages and in the deserted lynchets that alone had allowed the cultivation of steep chalkland slopes,[46] such a process was neither uniform nor necessarily here characteristic of the fifteenth century. A more useful framework, based upon the study of a large number of manors, would be to divide the period into three: the first half of the century; the mid-century recession from 1450 to about 1470, and the late fifteenth-century recovery.

Much of the county shows little evidence of declining demand for land during the first half of the century. To the west of the county, in the area that was witnessing a considerable growth in the cloth industry,[47] rent totals rose slightly at both Trowbridge and Castle Combe. At the latter, the exceptional quantity of the surviving materials make it possible to see clearly the impact of the industry in what may have been one of its fastest growing centres: the large number of landless men who now worked in the village rose from 45 in 1417 to 54 in 1435 and 70 in 1443 and 1450, some 50 houses and 2 mills were rebuilt during Fastolf's lordship (1409–59), and the manorial courts show the presence both of rich clothiers and an urban proletariat.[48] The remarkable growth of the cloth industry meant that court receipts also remained buoyant reaching over £20 on eleven occasions, including annual figures for £106 and £89. The profits from villeinage have already been referred to, but all tenants paid entry fines and the level of these reflected this expanding prosperity.[49] At the urban centre of Trowbridge, the movement of court profits showed signs of growth in this period, and the rent total was rising in the 1440s as it was also to do at Warminster, another centre of the cloth industry. Around the latter town, rent totals on the Hungerford manors showed significant rises.[50] Beyond the immediate area of the cloth industry rents were generally stable or even showed slight rises. The thriving industrial areas in the west of the county and around Salisbury would have generated considerable demand for wool, meat, and grain as well as providing the opportunities for additional by-employment in the area around. Such stable or rising rents were to be found in the chalklands at Durrington, Collingbourne and Everleigh. Elsewhere, at Bromham rents fluctuated more from year to year than on most manors and reached a peak in the 1430s. There was no evidence of a rise or fall in entry fines here, although the high level of fines for three holdings between 1433 and 1436, in the last few surviving court rolls, may represent a sign of increased demand. This possibility is reinforced by the figures for the court profits which, as on other manors, had shrunk early in the century but now recovered to reach the levels of the later fourteenth century.[51]

There were, however, some manors that showed declining rent totals. These included a few small chalkland manors, as at Stockton, Combe Bisset and Kingston Deverill, probably all manors relatively short of arable land.[52] More interestingly all the manors studied in the north of the county show falling rents in this part of the century, for example at Stratton, Oaksey and Poole where the impact of the expansion of the Wiltshire cloth industry would have been felt much less. Here was an area which conformed more to the general national norm with peasants leaving and rents falling.[53] Finally the first part of the century did not show any serious general problem in collecting what was due. On the estates of the duchy of Lancaster debts were few, small and paid off, and mainly seemed to be short term debts resulting from wool and sheep production. At Bromham, arrears were not regular until after 1425 and even then they were short term. Wiltshire was not unaffected by the general changes in seigneurial economies familiar elsewhere in the later Middle Ages, but these changes had largely taken place in the fourteenth century. Most of Wiltshire in the early fifteenth century witnessed a stability in the demand for land, as the prosperity of the cloth industry brought expansion into the local economy and extra demand for food and raw materials.

By contrast, the 1450s and 1460s show a very different picture from such stability and prosperity. Those areas that hitherto escaped declining rents now showed falling rentals, and those areas where the rents had previously fallen now showed stability. The period had been ushered in by the risings of 1450, which themselves had reflected the reaction to the recession in the cloth industry.[54] Figures for cloth exports through Bristol, London and Southampton, the main outlets for Wiltshire cloth show that considerably less cloth was being exported in the 1450s and 1460s, a damaging blow to an area that had become increasingly dependent on cloth production.[55] Wool prices also fell in mid century, those for the chalk downlands reaching their lowest level.[56] Most of the manors studied showed growing difficulties in collecting income and consequently mounting arrears as at Bromham and All Cannings.[57] In the west of Wiltshire cloth area, Trowbridge showed falling rents, generally lower receipts from the manorial courts, and growing arrears from about 1456. In this area, the diminution of the rents was mainly in the cottage tenements, as at Warminster, Upton Scudamore, Sutton Veny, and Heytesbury,[58] reflecting difficulties among the wage earning classes during the recession. At Castle Combe, the declining demand for such men is reflected in the falling capitage payments, from seventy payers in 1450 to forty-four in 1481, and with a sharp fall in value in the 1450s.[59] In marked contrast was the situation at Durrington and Winterbourne Stoke among those who produced food for the industrial food market, where it was the holders of the standard virgate holdings who also benefited from the rent reductions. For several years, Winchester College, the lords of Durrington, had failed to extract the full rental and part of it had been pardoned.[60] Then in 1461, it reduced all the rents: a virgate from 20s. to 16s. a half virgate from 9s. to 7s., the lessee also had his rent reduced as were the rents of demesne acres and three cottages.[61] At Winterbourne Stoke, on the Hungerford estate, the decayed rent entry rose from £2 3s. 11d. in 1448 to £8 7s. 1d. in 1465. The tenements which thus gained rent reductions comprised twenty-one virgates, two half-virgates, a parcel of land but only three cottages.[62] Several manors show evidence of increased difficulty in raising the rent apart from Durrington, this being the case also at Bromham, Wroughton and All Cannings. But behind the general financial difficulties of the lord at this period there seems to have been two different types of manors and economies. Within the industrial area where the wage earners would have found particular difficulties with rent payments, rent reduction focused on the cottages. In the essentially agricultural communities, that produced food and raw materials for the market and were now suffering from a contraction in demand for the latter, reductions occurred in the agricultural farms. Such difficulties reflect the way in which much of Wiltshire had become dependent on the prosperity of the cloth industry. The wholesale character of such rent cuts at Durrington and Winterbourne Stoke may also raise the question as to whether some sort of communal action was taking place.

As in the first period, the manors in the north of the county again diverge. But their earlier falling rents now cushioned the northern manors against the impact of this mid-century depression and rents remained stable, or in the case of Poole, actually rose, while elsewhere lords ran into difficulty. Rents here had not been distorted from the general decline of the later Middle Ages by the prosperity of the cloth industry. It was a part of the county which no longer seemed so unattractive compared to the areas further south.

Subsequently, the situation began to change in the landlord's favour, and the worst of the depression was completed by the early 1460s. Rents thereafter remained stable or indicated some signs of growth. This slow recovery showed itself in different ways. On some manors the value of the demesne lease rose, as at Wroughton where it increased by £1 from £9 13s. 4d. between 1461 and 1488. Elsewhere the decayed rent entry might fall, as at Wexcombe where it declined from £3 10s. 3d. to £2 0s. 10d. between 1448 and 1485, while at Durrington in the 1460s some of the vacant tenements were now retaken and the decayed rent entry fell from £8 14s. 1d. in 1461 to £6 18s. 2d. in 1463 and £6 10s. 9d. in 1468. Finally, new rent items might be introduced as at Wexcombe and Wilsford which, if not great in monetary terms, do indicate a distinctive improvement in the position of the landlord.[63] Moreover, the lords were collecting the bulk of their supposed revenue and there seems no general problem of rent collection at such manors as Wexcombe, Wilsford, Stratton, on the manors of the Duchy of Lancaster, or at Kingston Deverill, Wroughton, or Bromham. Even apparently large debts were cleared as at Urchfont and All Cannings.[64] There were, however, occasional difficulties as with a group of debts at Enford in the 1480s, or at Durrington in the 1470s.[65] Unfortunately not enough entry fines have been examined to make any clear conclusion as to their trends, although there were some signs of recovery. But at Bromham the court profit rose substantially to a higher level from the 1490s, and this probably reflected increased entry fines.[66] In general, therefore, the recovery of the cloth industry and perhaps the start of a more general growth of population began to create improved conditions for the landlord such as were eventually to lead to the changed balance of the sixteenth century.

Such a study can tell something about the changes that were taking place and about the impact on the countryside of industrial expansion. These changes also suggest that the important distinctions in examining the balance of lord and tenant, as expressed in rents, fines and indebtedness, were regional rather than seigneurial or communal. There is little to support the view that the key factor in seigneurial finances was the efficiency of its administration rather than the effect of economic developments.[67] In a given area and time, manors belonging to different lords showed similar trends. By contrast, estates with different manors in different parts of the county showed differences as individual manors followed the regional or local trends. This was the case with the duchy of Lancaster manors in the early and mid-fifteenth century[68] or on the Winchester College manors of Durrington and Combe Bisset earlier in the century.

IV

The relationship between lord and tenant, thus showed mixed fortunes on each side. The lord had sought to control the remaining serf families and to make his financial gain, but had generally failed to halt the decline of serfdom. It disappeared as a significant part of most villagers' lives, and Wiltshire does not seem to have been slow in this respect. The study of rents has suggested something of the result of the bargaining that underlay the taking and granting of land. For most of the time lords benefited in most of the county from the good fortunes of the cloth industry. There is nothing here to compare with the comment of the keeper of the manors of Blockley and Wick Episcopi on the bishopric of Worcester estates who in 1435 explained that the arrears could not be collected at present, "for all the tenants of the said manors from which the said arrears ought to be levied would leave the aforesaid manors immediately after such a decision"[69] but something of that fear may have lain behind the wholesale cuts in arable rents during the mid-century recession. The decline in serfdom was final, that in rents was temporary, and the slow recovery in the later fifteenth century was to become the more familiar sixteenth century rent rise.[70] The nature of the village society with which the lord had to deal had also changed. The traditional pattern of a broad upper range of virgate holders had now gone, to be replaced by a much smaller new peasant aristocracy, each of whom might hold several virgates or a substantial part of the main demesne.[71] This essay has suggested ways in which the Wiltshire evidence both reinforces and modifies our understanding of the economic and social developments of the period. Regional variations existed on a local as well as on a national scale, and through local studies we may come to a fuller and more rounded understanding of the varied and changing character of the economy of later Medieval England. Nowhere does such work seem more necessary than in those areas most closely associated with the great expansion of the cloth industry.

Notes

1 R.S. Schofield, 'The Geographical Distribution of wealth in England 1334–1649', *Economic History Review* 2nd, 18 (1965), 503–9.

2 Some of the churches are examined in detail in Royal Commission on the Historic Monuments of England, *Churches of South-East Wiltshire* (1987), although the development is less obvious in this part of the county.

3 Further documentation for this is provided in Hare, *Lord and Tenant in Wiltshire, c.1380–c.1520 with particular reference to regional and seigneurial variations*, unpublished Ph.D. thesis University of London (1976). For the agricultural background see R. Scott, 'Medieval Agriculture' in (ed.) R.B. Pugh, *The Victoria County History of . . . Wiltshire*, V.C.H. Wilts. IV (1959); Hare, 'Change and Continuity in Wiltshire agriculture: the Later Middle Ages' in (ed.) W. Minchinton, *Agricultural Improvement: Medieval and Modern*, Exeter papers in economic history, 14 (1981), pp. 1–18; and id. 'The monks as landlords: the leasing of the demesnes in southern England', in (eds.) C.M. Barron and C. Harper-Bill, *The church in pre-reformation society* (Woodbridge, 1985) pp. 82–94. For a survey of the cloth industry see E.M. Carus-Wilson, 'The woollen industry before 1550', in *V.C.H. Wilts*, IV; and see also A.R. Bridbury, *Medieval English Clothmaking* (1982). The account rolls have been dated by the year of the close of the account.

4 This paragraph is based upon J.N. Hare, The Wiltshire risings of 1450: political and economic discontent in mid-fifteenth century England, *Southern History*, 4 (1982), pp. 13–32.

5 R.H. Hilton, *The decline of serfdom in Medieval England*, 1969; A. Savine, 'Bondmen under the Tudors', *Trans. Royal Hist. Soc.*, 17, 1903; D. MacCulloch, 'Bondmen under the Tudors', in (eds.) C. Cross, D. Loades and J.J. Scarisbrick, *Law and Government under the Tudors* (1988).

6 K.B. McFarlane, *The nobility of later Medieval England* (1973), pp. 146–9, 172–6.

7 W(inchester) C(ollege) M(uniments) 5601Ca.

8 WCM 4352.

9 Bad(minton) Mun(iments) 110/5/3; C.B. Fry, *Hannington: the records of a Wiltshire village* (1935), p. 101; B(ritish) L(ibrary) Add(itional) R(ol)l. 24345; W(inchester) C(athedral) L(ibrary) Box 52.

10 BL Add. Rl. 24349, 24355.
11 Hare, Change and Continuity, pp. 5–11.
12 L.C. Latham, *The decay of the manorial system*, unpublished MA thesis, University of London, 1928, 80–3; P(ublic) R(ecord) O(ffice), SC2/208/18, 19, 21–6.
13 Hare, *thesis*, p. 244.
14 BL Harl(eian) Mss. 3961.
15 J. Wedgwood, *A History of Parliament*, vol I. Biographies, p. 945; Hare, thesis, p. 319.
16 WCM 5655 d & c. Based on W(inchester) C(athedral) L(ibrary), Register [of the Dean and Chapter] vol I & II; & (ed.) J. Greatrex, *The Register of the Common Seal* (Hampshire Record Series, II, 1978).
17 C. Dyer, *Lords and peasants in a changing society* (Cambridge, 1980), p. 272. At Ramsey, the evidence begins in the 1430s from whence manumissions remained consistently higher than on the St Swithun estate, J.A. Raftis, *Tenure and Mobility* (Toronto, 1964), pp. 184–5.
18 WCL Box 52, 1423 i, ii, & 1424.
19 J. Wedgwood, *A History of Parliament*, vol I (1936), p. 407; F. Street, 'The relations of the bishop of Salisbury and the citizens of Salisbury between 1225 and 1612', *Wilts. Archaeol. Mag.* 39 (1916), pp. 234–43; R. Benson and H. Hatcher, *Old and New Sarum or Salisbury* (1843), chap. XIII. On his new town house see, Royal Commission on Historical Monuments, *City of Salisbury*, vol I (1980), pp. 103–4.
20 W(iltshire) R(ecord) O(ffice) 214/8; M.A. Hicks, 'Restraint, mediation and private justice: George, Duke of Clarence as "good lord"', *Journal of Legal History*, 4 (1983), pp. 56–72.
21 WRO G23/1/2 (Salisbury City Records Ledger Book B), f. 31 r. & v. On an attempt by a Wiltshire lord, Edington Priory, to secure the return of a villein 'worth 100 marks' from a town, Newbury, to its manor of Coleshill (Berks.), see R. Faith, 'Berkshire: fourteenth and fifteenth centuries' in P.D.A. Harvey, *The Peasant Land Market in Medieval England* (Oxford, 1984), pp. 174–5.
22 E.M. Carus-Wilson, 'Evidences of Industrial growth on some fifteenth century manors', in (ed.) E.M. Carus-Wilson, *Essays in Economic History*, II (1962), pp. 159–67; Latham, thesis, pp. 182–90.
23 G.P. Scrope, *History of the manor and ancient barony of Castle Combe*, private print, 1852, p. 165; Latham, thesis, p. 188; Carus-Wilson, *Essays*, II, pp. 162–3.
24 BL Add. Rl. 18478 m. 10; Scrope, *Castle Combe*, pp. 223–5; Carus-Wilson, *Essays*, II, pp. 162–3.
25 Hare, thesis, pp. 283–93; J.N. Hare, 'Durrington: a chalkland village in the later Middle Ages', *Wilts. Archaeol. Mag.* 75 (1980), pp. 143–7; J.N. Hare, 'The demesne lessees of fifteenth-century Wiltshire', *Agricultural History Review* 29 (1981), pp. 8–15.
26 Hare, *Ag. H. R.*, 29, pp. 11–12, Wilts. Arch. Soc. MSS vol 241, *The Goddard Family*, p. 61.
27 Hilton, *The decline of serfdom*, pp. 54–5.
28 A. Savine, *T.R.H.S.* 17 (1903), p. 277; *Letters and Papers of the reign of Henry VIII*, XIII, i, p. 108.
29 BL Add. Mss. 28208 f. 32v.; Scrope, *Castle Combe*, p. 217.
30 Scrope, *Castle Combe*, p. 225.
31 Scrope, *Castle Combe*, pp. 226, 289.
32 WCM 5596.

33 Hare, thesis, pp. 215–16.

34 WCM 5656g.

35 WCM 5656l, & m.

36 PRO Prob 11/16/14.

37 PRO Prob 11/21/12.

38 R.H. Hilton, *The English peasantry in the later Middle Ages* (Oxford, 1975), p. 63.

39 This paragraph is based upon Latham, thesis, pp. 176–81.

40 Hare, *Wilts. Archaeol. Mag.* 75, pp. 146–7.

41 Carus-Wilson *Essays*, II, 158–9; Hare thesis, pp. 142–3.

42 Hare, thesis, pp. 144–54.

43 R.R. Davies, 'Baronial accounts, incomes and arrears in the later Middle Ages' in *Economic History Review* (1968), 2nd, 21, p. 221.

44 Hare, thesis, pp. 155–64.

45 Scott, 'Medieval Agriculture' in *V.C.H. Wilts.*, IV, 41.

46 For a recent discussion of some of the deserted villages of the county, see M. Aston, 'A regional study of deserted settlements in the west of England', in (eds.) M. Aston, D. Austin and C. Dyer, *The rural settlements of Medieval England* (Oxford, 1989), pp. 105–28.

47 E.M. Carus-Wilson, 'The woollen industry before 1550', in *V.C.H. Wilts.*, IV, pp. 128–38.

48 Latham, thesis, p. 185; BL Add. Rl. 18478; BL Add. Mss. 28211 f. 2; BL Add. Rl. 18481; Scrope, *History of Castle Combe*, pp. 249–50; Carus-Wilson, *Essays*, II, 161–6.

49 Hare, thesis, table IV, p. 154; Carus-Wilson, *Essays*, II, 166.

50 Hare, thesis, table I, p. 151; WRO 845/Manorial Papers/14.

51 Hare, thesis, p. 147.

52 At both Stockton and Kingston Deverill the lack of sheltered land may have led to the seigneurial sheep flock being composed entirely of the more hardy wethers, with new stock being brought from outside.

53 Hare, op. cit., table IX & XIII, pp. 173, 177.

54 Hare, *Wiltshire risings*, pp. 15–19.

55 E.M. Carus-Wilson and O. Coleman, *England's Export Trade* (1963), pp. 140–3, 148–9.

56 T.H. Lloyd, *The movement of wool prices in Medieval England* (Econ. Hist. Rev. Supplement, 1973), table I, column 4.

57 Hare, thesis, tables V & VII, pp. 162, 164.

58 WRO 845 Manorial Papers/14; PRO SC6/1061/20, 1059/18, 1054/8.

59 BL Add. Rl. 18481; BL Add. Rl. 18250. 1450 70 payers; 1451 69; 1452 62; 1455 56; 1457 44; 1459 30 (BL Add. Rl. 18481, 18482, 18483, Latham, p. 185; Add. Rl. 18486 m.9).

60 1458 £6 18s. 6d.; 1459 £2 8s. 11d.; 1460 £2 6s. 8d.; 1461 £11 9s. 7d.

61 WCM 6016. In 1441 there were 10 cottages recorded.

62 PRO/SC6/1062/9, 13.

63 Hare, thesis, table XIII, p. 177.

64 Hare, thesis, table VII, p. 164.

65 WCM 6035.

66 Hare, thesis, table III, p. 153.

67 J.R. Lander, *Conflict and stability in fifteenth-century England* (1969), p. 30.

68   Hare, thesis, table VIII & IX, pp. 172–3.
69   C. Dyer, 'A redistribution of incomes in fifteenth-century England?' in (ed.) R.H. Hilton, *Peasants, knights and heretics* (Cambridge, 1976), p. 203.
70   E. Kerridge, 'The movement of rent 1540–1640', in Carus-Wilson, *Essays*, II, for rent rises in Wiltshire.
71   For a good example of this development at Durrington see Hare, *Wilts. Archaeol. Mag.* 75, 1980, pp. 145–7.

3

'Wild As Colts Untamed': Radicalism in the Newbury Area during the Early-Modern Period

C.G. Durston
St Mary's College, Strawberry Hill

I

In an article published in 1978, in which he investigated traditions of lower-class radicalism during the sixteenth and seventeenth centuries, Christopher Hill remarked:

> I suggest as a hypothesis for further investigation that there may have been a continuing underground tradition – not necessarily organization – in which we can identify certain heretical and seditious beliefs.[1]

While studying the Berkshire county community in the early seventeenth century,[2] the present writer discovered that the town of Newbury enjoyed a considerable reputation as a centre of radical opinions on both religious and political issues. Further investigation has revealed that such a reputation extended over a much longer period. This essay outlines the evidence which suggests that, during a period of two centuries or more, many of Newbury's inhabitants harboured radical opinions, and then offers some possible explanations for this fact.

Newbury lies on the River Kennet, in the 'champion' mixed farming district of south-west Berkshire. Its population rose from about 1,600 in the mid sixteenth century to over 4,000 by the early nineteenth century.[3] During the early-modern period it was an important market town, particularly for the corn trade, lying on two major trade routes, the main West Country road from London to Bath and Bristol, and the road from Southampton to Oxford and the north.[4] The manufacture of woollen cloth was an important element of the town's economic life from the early fifteenth century, and by Henry VIII's reign Newbury was a centre of cloth production of national significance. By 1600, cloth production had spread out to the surrounding villages; the inhabitants of Shaw, Speen, Thatcham and Greenham were employed in the cottage production of yarn, and Benham Valence, Thatcham, Colthrop and Brimpton possessed their own fulling mills. Broadcloth manufacture in Newbury entered a period of serious decline in the economic depression of the 1620s, and was further hit by the dislocation of the Civil War years. By the early eighteenth cetury it had been almost entirely replaced by the making of poor quality shalloons.[5]

From the early sixteenth century the town was dominated by a small oligarchy of aldermen, often master clothiers, whose extensive powers were confirmed in a new town charter granted by Elizabeth I in 1596.[6] The authority of these aldermen was largely unaffected by interference from the gentry of the surrounding rural area. However, despite being one of Berkshire's wealthiest boroughs, Newbury returned no M.P.s to Westminster during the period under discussion.

II

The earliest suggestions of Newbury's radical proclivities date from the fifteenth century. In the aftermath of Cade's rising in Kent in 1450, Henry VI's government felt it necessary to exhibit at Newbury part of the quartered body of one of the leading rebels. Newbury nevertheless retained its hostility towards the government, and support for Richard Duke of York, whose restoration to high office had been demanded by Cade. In 1460, when the struggle between York and the government reached a climax, commissioners were sent to Newbury, and several of the townspeople executed for treason. In 1483 the town was once more a focal point for resistance to the government, when the Berkshire rebels who supported the Duke of Buckingham's rising against Richard III rendezvoused there.[7]

Newbury was also during the late fifteenth century a conspicuous Lollard centre, which according to Thomas Man contained:

a glorious and sweet society of faithful followers who had continued the space of fifteen years together till at last by a certain lewd person whom they trusted and made of their counsel they were betrayed; and then many of them to the number of six or seven score were abjured, and three or four of them burnt.[8]

In January 1491 Thomas Taylor, a Newbury fuller, was charged with a number of heretical beliefs, including objecting to pilgrimages and claiming that 'it was better to give a penny to a poor man than to go to Santiago'. Later in the month a further six suspects were examined by an episcopal court. All were extremely hostile to priests whom they described as 'scribes and pharisees who deceived the people and did not profit them, leading them to temptation as the blind lead the blind'. The hearings continued in February when further suspects expressed disbelief in transubstantiation, objected to images in churches and looked for an imminent second coming of Christ.[9]

Despite pressure from the bishop, heretical opinions seem to have persisted. In the winter of 1502/3 a woman from Bisham in east Berkshire claimed during examination that 'those whom ye call heretics which were brand(ed) at Newbury were apostles and martyrs of Christ', and in 1504 a layman and a curate from Newbury were charged with possessing heretical books. In the autumn of 1521 several suspected Lollards being examined by the Bishop of Lincoln, revealed the names of a number of people in Newbury who still subscribed to Lollard beliefs.[10]

In view of this strong association with Lollardy, it is not surprising to find that Newbury was quick to embrace Protestantism in the mid sixteenth century. Writing in 1660, Thomas Fuller remarked that Newbury 'started the first . . . in the race of the Reformed Religion' and that 'the town appears the first fruits of the Gospel in England.'[11] In 1556, during the Marian reaction, several inhabitants of Newbury were burnt at the stake in the town.[12] During the period 1560 to 1640 many of Newbury's inhabitants clearly desired a more reformed Church than that established by the Elizabethan settlement. A recent study of puritanism in Elizabethan Berkshire found Newbury to be 'one of the most interesting and important areas of the county for the student of puritanism'.[13] For nearly thirty years from 1568 the minister at Newbury was the noted puritan preacher Hugh Shepley, and for much of this period the master of the grammar school was another puritan, Robert Wright. In 1619 the Newbury living came to another staunch puritan William Twisse. Twisse objected strongly to the publication of James I's *Book of Sports*, and during the 1640s was prolocutor of the Westminster Assembly of Divines. Twisse's friend Thomas Porter, who also favoured reform in the Church, was master of the grammar school in the early seventeenth century; he emigrated to New England in 1634, and helped found the town of Newbury in Massachusetts.[14]

These men were clearly popular within the town, and their opinions influential. There is much evidence of enthusiasm for preaching in the wills of townspeople, and in 1627 a weekly lectureship was established by the will of one Thomas Bennett. Thomas Fuller comments on Twisse's popularity, stating:

> though generally our Saviour's observation is verified 'A Prophet is not without honour save in his own country' – yet here he met with deserved respect.[15]

On several occasions during the 1630s Twisse's churchwardens were in dispute with the Bishop of Salisbury. In 1631 they were accused of selling the church organ and of neglecting to present in the church courts women who refused to wear veils while being churched, and five years later they were in trouble for ignoring instructions from the conservative Laudian hierarchy to remove the Communion table to the upper end of the chancel and surround it with rails.[16] By the 1630s an early separatist congregation was also meeting at Newbury.[17] Mrs Connolly's study of Berkshire puritanism concluded that in the period preceding the Civil War:

> Newbury had a national reputation for religious zeal, unshared with any other town in the county.[18]

The same period from 1560 to 1640 witnessed a number of incidents in the Newbury area involving the voicing of subversive opinions and threats to public order, which caused concern to both the local and national authorities. In 1593 one Stephen Bachiler was reported to the Privy Council for delivering in a sermon at Newbury 'very lewd speeches, tending seditiously to the derogation of Her Majesty's Government', and in 1615 Thomas Standen was arrested for making 'certain lewd speeches touching His Majesty' in an inn at Speenhamland just outside the town.[19] In 1604 Robert Brooke, vicar of the neighbouring parish of Enborne, was accused of tearing up a prayer book and a copy of Archbishop Bancroft's ecclesiastical canons, and of 'casting abroad a libel in contempt of the religion established in His Majesty's dominion'. He only avoided serious punishment through the intercession of a sympathetic local gentleman.[20]

A serious threat to order developed in the winter of 1630, when many of the townspeople were suffering great hardship as a result of a poor harvest and widespread unemployment. At the beginning of November 'a great company of poor people' assembled outside the town at Greenham 'then and there to watch for carts laden with corn coming that way towards Reading'. No violence occurred on this occasion, but the following week at Speen a crowd attacked some carts and assaulted their owners. The local justice subsequently examined a number of 'poor ragged women whereof many of them were very aged', committing seven to the house of correction and ordering another five to be whipped 'for further terror and example of others'.[21] Later in the 1630s Newbury was in trouble with Charles I's government for refusing to contribute towards ship money. The town was one of the earliest centres of resistance in Berkshire, and in January 1637 its mayor was summoned to the Privy Council to explain its backwardness.[22]

III

Newbury's reputation as a centre of disaffection is perhaps most clearly seen during the mid seventeenth century. In February 1643 the royalist Lord Grandison wrote to Prince Rupert:

> . . . there is two gentlemen now come from Newbury frightened from thence last night by intelligence they had of some of the enemy forces, [that they] were to come into Newbury, invited thither by the townsmen, who have only reported the plague to be there to keep the King's troops out. How slight soever this may be, sure I am that that disaffected town cannot be too much punished by your Highness for at my coming from Basingstoke, they stopped all our baggage and had detained it but they heard we were strong enough to revenge it.[23]

Several months later, when Newbury's mayor wrote secretly offering his help to the king, Charles I is reported to have remarked that he was glad there was 'one righteous man left in Sodom'.[24] The following autumn the townspeople prepared a great welcome for the Earl of Essex's army which was returning from raising the seige of Gloucester, only to be disappointed by the surprise arrival of the royalists.[25] At the end of 1643 the governor of the royalist garrison at Donnington castle, which overlooked the town, complained that he had:

> such ill neighbours as the factious town of Newbury which lately betrayed some of His Majesty's friends, not so much as giving me notice that I might in time have relieved them.[26]

In August 1644 a Royalist newsbook described Newbury as 'the very Colchester of Berkshire'.[27]

Following the ending of the first civil war, a number of radical religious sects appeared in the town. Edmund Calamy states that at this time it was 'overrun with strange opinions and divided into many parties',[28] and the activities of one anabaptist group were described in an anonymous pamphlet, *A Looking Glass for Sectaries or True Newes from Newbury*, published in December 1647.[29] Prominent in this group was a school-mistress, subject to fits and convulsions, who believed she was to be taken up bodily into heaven. A large crowd gathered on the appointed day to watch her fail in her attempt.

In view of Newbury's attachment to the parliamentary cause and some of the more radical forms of Protestantism, it is not surprising that serious trouble occurred in the town following the restoration in 1660. In June 1662 three aldermen were removed from office under the act for regulating corporations.[30] The following year Newbury's presbyterian minister, Benjamin Woodbridge, was ejected and replaced on the king's presentment by a more conservative incumbent, Joseph Sayer; and in February 1664 Thomas Voysey, the popular presbyterian minister of Thatcham, was charged at Reading Assizes with complicity in a plot to assassinate Charles II and imprisoned in Windsor.[31]

A violent reaction to these events broke out in April 1664, when a large crowd interrupted Sayer and the aldermen who were meeting in the church vestry to choose new churchwardens. Sir Thomas Dolman, the local justice called in to investigate the disturbance, commented on their 'insolent and tumultuous manner' and 'strange rudeness and reproaches'. The ringleaders demanded a say in the choice of churchwardens, but Dolman believed that this was merely a pretext 'to engage the multitude in a tumult and sedition and cast contempt upon the King's authority'.[32] He advised that the ringleaders should be charged at the Quarter Sessions the following week and discussed the possibility of packing the grand jury with outsiders who would declare the incident a riot. He concluded his report to the Lord Lieutenant:

> The plain trouble is, my Lord, this place is in very great disorder, the multitude upon all occasions flying as high as they dare against the King and the Church . . . My Lord this town is on those terms that they only want an opportunity to begin a rebellion, and I believe three parts of four would quickly take arms.[33]

Dolman later suggested that the real reason for the riot was that the presbyterians in the town were infuriated that Sayer had persuaded about 300 people to receive communion over the Easter weekend. Their leader was one William Milton who ran a coffee house in the town and held conventicles in his house. Milton, according to Dolman, was:

> a very rigid presbyter, has been a rebel in the armies from his cradle, comes not to church because Mr Sayer was presented by His Majesty, keeps a coffee house where all the malcontents of this place frequently meet with great confidence in his secrecy. This fellow is of high value amongst all the non-conformists and being seditious to the highest point and bold, having little to lose, they think him a fit instrument to belch out all their affronts against the book of common prayer and conformity.[34]

Further disorders occurred several days later when Dolman was examining Milton at the mayor's house. A large crowd assembled in an attempt to rescue Milton, and shots were fired. Dolman led his guards into the street and 'forced the seditious rabble into their houses'. He later discovered that during the night:

> Some odd fellows, whose names we cannot learn, have thrown so many handfuls of dirt upon the sign of the Crown [Inn] that it is but discernable what sign it is.[35]

His explanation was that the rioters were angry with the inn-keeper who had testified against Milton, but the act was also probably symbolic. Dolman's intervention appears to have forestalled further trouble; the ringleaders were indicted at the Abingdon Assizes in 1665 and heavily fined.[36] His first hand testimony, however, reveals the continuing popularity of nonconformity, and the close connexion between dissent and political disaffection in the town.

Despite the efforts of Sayer and Dolman, nonconformity remained popular in Newbury. In 1669 a survey carried out by the Bishop of Salisbury revealed that at least 600 people regularly attended presbyterian services on Sundays. They were described as mainly 'ordinary persons', though the wife of one local gentleman, Mrs Roger Knight, also attended, and some of those purged from the corporation in 1662 were named as 'abettors'. The survey commented:

> these meetings consist of such as have been engaged (as generally the whole town was) in the late war against the King.[37]

By the 1660s there were also Quakers in the town. The bishop's survey mentions meetings at the houses of Robert Wilson and Thomas Merrimans and there was a regular monthly meeting from 1674.[38]

IV

While the evidence for Newbury's radicalism is strongest for the seventeenth century, there are indications that a tendency towards unorthodoxy and unruliness persisted. Newbury remained a strong non-conformist centre throughout the eighteenth century. Following the 1689 Toleration Act, the presbyterians built themselves a meeting house in 1697. An Independent meeting house was erected in 1717, and the Baptists erected a place of worship in 1702. The Quakers continued to worship in a building near St Bartholomew's Street.[39] The early Methodists met near Cheap Street, and were preached to on several occasions by John Wesley. Wesley's entry in his journal for 1 March 1790 reads:

I left Brentford early in the morning and in the evening preached at Newbury. The congregation was large and most of them attentive but a few of them were wild as colts untamed. We had none such at Bath the following evening but all were serious as death.[40]

The eighteenth and early nineteenth centuries also witnessed periodic outbreaks of unrest and disorder in and around Newbury. A riot occurred in 1706 when a crowd attempted to rescue four impressed men; several soldiers were assaulted and one died of his injuries. One of the soldiers later testified that he had 'desired the people in Her Majesty's name to separate but some of [th]em answered they did not care for anybody'.[41] There was more trouble in 1766 when the series of food riots that hit Berkshire in that year originated at a market in the town.[42] In 1800 several hundred labourers gathered at Thatcham in an attempt to force up wages,[43] and in 1830 the 'Captain Swing' machine breaking riots began in Berkshire, and were concentrated in an area within a ten mile radius of Newbury. According to Hobsbawm and Rudé these riots at once stage 'threatened to engulf the whole Hungerford and Newbury area in a general labourers' insurrection'.[44]

V

For several centuries or more, therefore, Newbury contained many people who harboured unorthodox religious and political opinions and who could be provoked into active and violent opposition to the ecclesiastical and secular authorities. During the seventeenth century in particular the town enjoyed a widespread notoriety as a centre of radical anti-authoritarian attitudes. Attempts to account for this must involve discussion of the commercial and industrial make-up of the town, the pattern of local authority and the possibility of the existence of a local radical tradition.

As an important market town, lying on major east–west and north–south trade routes, Newbury was visited by a constant stream of travellers, traders and itinerant workers. These people brought with them a great variety of news and opinion, to which the townspeople were exposed in their market-place and inns. In their work on the 1830 riots, Hobsbawm and Rudé discovered that trouble was most likely to occur near 'more important centres of trade and communications, and therefore of news, discussion and action'.[45] If the trading communities were more exposed to radical ideas, they also contained the social elements which provided a receptive audience for them. Buchanan Sharp has recently stressed the involvement in popular disorder of artisans, 'skilled men in rural areas or small towns working in non-agricultural employments',[46] and R. Tudor-Jones in his study of congregationalists in England stated that:

> The Newbury Independent Church reflected the economics of the market town amongst its hearers with three gentlemen and forty tradesmen.[47]

Newbury traded principally in corn and cloth; both may have rendered it particularly susceptible to disturbance. Dissatisfaction and resentment develop quickly amongst the hungry and are likely to lead to rioting where basic foodstuffs are bought and sold. The 1630 riots in Newbury were provoked by the shipment of grain out of the area at a time of great scarcity and in 1766 the townspeople were again roused to direct action by the exceptionally high prices in the market. In his study of eighteenth-century food riots, Walter Shelton acknowledged the 'provocative nature of grain exports in a time of expected famine',[48] and John Stevenson similarly found that 'transhipment points, market towns and ports' were particularly prone to disturbance.[49]

Newbury was for several centuries the home of, and visited by, large numbers of clothworkers, a notoriously unruly group well known for their heretical beliefs. Some of the Newbury Lollards were clothworkers, and Lollard ideas may have originally reached the town along the trade routes from the clothing regions of Essex, the 'breeding grounds for Lollardy'.[50] Professor Dickens has stated that:

> certain periods at least saw a flow of information and ideas between the communities of Buckinghamshire, of East Anglia, of London and the Thames Valley. Tudor provincial society contained large mobile elements, and the part played by wandering clothworkers in the dissemination of heresy has already been observed.[51]

Christopher Hill also believes that 'Lollardy and later heresy are found especially in clothing counties'.[52]

The connection between clothing and non-conformity remained strong down to the late seventeenth century; in 1675 many of those presented by the churchwardens for non-attendance at church were clothworkers.[53] The town authorities were also clearly anxious to regulate their numbers in the town; the Quarter Session records for the late seventeenth century contain numerous cases of the ejection of weavers, and the authorities insisted that all lodgers should obtain a certificate allowing residence.[54] Nor were the radical ideas confined to the industry's wage labourers. During Elizabeth I's reign three of the prominent master clothiers, Philip George, Philip Kystell and John Holmes, were noted puritans.[55]

The cloth-producing communities of early-modern England were particularly vulnerable to periodic economic recessions, causing a drop in demand and inevitable unemployment amongst the clothworkers. With the makeshift relief systems unable to copy with such crises, the unemployed became desperate and direct action often ensued. The disturbances at Newbury in 1630 followed the lay-off of large numbers of clothworkers during the recession of the 1620s. The mayors of Newbury and Reading reported to the Privy Council in December 1630 that:

> the manufacture of mingled and coloured cloth was much decayed in respect of what it was formerly, whereby the petitioners were much prejudiced and many poor people left destitute of work and employment to their utter ruin.[56]

The extent of the problem was revealed in another report compiled several months later. At this time over 100 families were completely dependent upon work provided by the workhouse, and the poor rate was 'very great and exceedeth very much our neighbouring parishes proportionately'.[57] In such circumstances tension was heightened throughout the community, resentment developed, and the likelihood of violence increased.

If Newbury was exposed to a wide range of radical ideas and contained receptive socio-economic groups, such attitudes were perhaps able to gain a firm hold because of the outlook and authority of the town's governors. As mentioned above the aldermen controlled virtually all aspects of town life; their relative autonomy may help to explain the persistence of radical opinions in Newbury, as on occasions they clearly took a lenient attitude towards those who professed them. The puritanism of some of the master clothiers, who also sat as aldermen, has already been noted. In 1662 several members of the corporation were ejected by the government, and they were later reported to be involved in presbyterian conventicles.[58] In his report about the 1664 riot, Sir Thomas Dolman attached much of the blame for the incident to the attitude of the mayor, whom he claimed was 'more forward to excuse this riot than to take notice of it'. According to Dolman the mayor 'suffers himself to be governed in secret by those that do what they can to hinder obedience to the King and his laws and conformity to the Church'. Dolman feared that, unless the Privy Council intervened, the next mayor would be 'of the same temper'.[59]

Even if the borough authorities had wished to enlist outside help to quash heterodoxy, it is doubtful whether it would have been available. During Elizabeth I's reign Newbury was the most poorly served deanery in the archdeanery of Berkshire; deanery surveys in 1561 and 1586 reveal large numbers of non-resident clergy.[60] In addition, for much of the early seventeenth century there was only one resident justice in the Newbury division of the county, as opposed to four or five in the other divisions, a fact which clearly reduced the power of central government and was mentioned as a matter of concern by several justices in the 1630s.[61] While Sir Thomas Dolman of nearby Shaw may have been appalled by the condition of Newbury and have regretted his lack of jurisdiction over the borough, his feelings were not shared by most other gentry families in the surrounding district. The dominant local families of the Chokes, Fullers, Goddards and Knights were conspicuous in their support for puritanism or non-conformity.[62]

The *Victoria County History* for Berkshire states 'all through the history of Newbury, popular movements centred around ecclesiastical institutions',[63] and Newbury's religious radicalism was clearly fostered and preserved through the influence of secular and ecclesiastical teachers. From the mid sixteenth century the town was served by a succession of preachers, notably Shepley, Twisse and Woodbridge, whose influence over the inhabitants was remarked upon by contemporaries.[64] In 1664 Thomas Voysey, vicar of Thatcham, was reported to have had a 'strange influence' over the rioters.[65] In addition, the town was regularly visited by itinerant preachers; Man, the Lollard, preached at Newbury; in 1593 Stephen Bachiler, vicar of Wherwell, Hampshire, was accused of delivering a seditious sermon in the town; and in 1640 one Barnard preached in support of the presbyterian Scots covenanters.[66] After the restoration the presbyterian conventicles were addressed by visiting preachers.[67] Townspeople were also subjected to radical views at an early age in their schools. Amongst the masters of the grammar school were the puritans Robert Wright and Thomas Parker, and in the 1640s a school-mistress was prominent amongst the anabaptists.[68]

Thus far, the reasons put forward to explain Newbury's radicalism correspond closely to those discussed in recent studies by Buchanan Sharp and Peter Clark. From a study of riot in the west of England during the period 1586 to 1660 Dr Sharp concluded:

Food riots occurred most frequently in the rural broadclothmaking areas of Western England . . . in the new-drapery towns of Essex and Suffolk, and in the clothing areas of Berkshire and Hampshire. Although the social status of participants in these riots was not always recorded, such evidence as is available invariably characterizes the rioters as clothworkers – weavers, spinners, fullers, and the like . . . Capitalists had come to dominate the broadcloth industry and the new drapery – products, aimed at an export market, which demanded considerable investment in raw materials and in the distribution of the finished product . . . The locations of such industries were amongst the most disorderly places in the kingdom and the connection between landlessness, rural industrialism and direct action can hardly have been accidental.[69]

From his investigation into similar radical trends in Gloucester between 1540 and 1640, Dr Clark identified economic instability, industrial malaise (especially in the cloth industry), social polarization, and the existence of a powerful puritan oligarchy as contributing factors in the town's radicalism. He suggested that all communities evidencing such tendencies in the seventeenth century were both dominated by 'puritan potentiores' and suffered from 'acute economic and social instability'.[70] Newbury conforms to such a pattern, but the greater length of its radical complexion prompts consideration of one further explanation – whether radical views may have persisted because they were handed down in the form of an ongoing local tradition.

It is extremely difficult to establish conclusive proof of the existence of underground traditions of radicalism. Individuals were naturally reluctant to own up to proscribed opinions when confronted by those who might have left documentary evidence about them, i.e., the prosecuting authorities; they were less likely to have been willing, given the opportunity, to explain how they acquired such views. However, it remains true that significant numbers of people in Newbury over a period of at least two centuries did consistently voice opinions on religious and political matters which challenged the established authorities, a fact which may not be entirely explained by the town's socio-economic make-up.

That these people were consistent in their radicalism throughout their lifetimes is suggested by Dolman's comments in 1664 that William Milton had been 'a rebel in the armies since the cradle', and that 'most of the ordinary rabble in this riot were such as had been in arms against the King'.[71] The 1669 bishop's survey also commented that the town's conventicles were frequented by 'such as having been engaged . . . in the late war against the King'.[72] One should, therefore, perhaps not discount the possibility that these strongly held attitudes were passed down within families. Christopher Hill has pointed out how easy it is to underestimate the importance of the verbal transmission of ideas,[73] and Dr Sharp has acknowledged the existence of a 'tradition of artisan radicalism' in the West Country, stretching from the seventeenth to the nineteenth century.[74] In an attempt to explain why labour disputes erupted at Thatcham on several occasions in the early nineteenth century, Hobsbawm and Rudé speculated that 'it may be too that a local tradition of labour militancy played a part'.[75]

Those historians who suspect the existence of such underground radical traditions, can turn for support to some recent sociological research. In their book *Political Socialisation*, Richard and Karen Dawson and Kenneth Prewitt suggested:

. . . outlooks and identifications regarding ethnic, racial, religious, social class and regional groupings as well as certain basic political attachments are acquired at an early age. They too are transmitted by the family . . . The evidence is that these types of political orientations tend to be developed early, persisted in long, and that they are transmitted at least initially through the family . . .[76]

They also found that ideas acquired in this way were very difficult to displace, and concluded:

The persistence of partisan attachments or particular political perspectives within geographical regions, among members of specific sub-groups and persons who share a particular position in the socio-economic structure, result in part from the tendency of those group-related attitudes to be passed on within a family from one generation to the next.[77]

These conclusions, the result of a study of modern American communities, should apply even more strongly to a small community of early-modern England, less exposed to other sophisticated mechanisms for the dissemination of information and opinion. We should perhaps therefore suggest that heretical and seditious attitudes may have persisted for so long in Newbury during the early modern period not only because of the efforts of teachers, the particular economic and social structure of the community and the attitudes of those in authority locally, but also because the acquisition of such opinions was an important element in the cultural inheritance of successive generations of townspeople.

Notes

1　Christopher Hill, 'From Lollards to Levellers' in Maurice Cornforth (ed.), *Rebels and Their Causes: Essays in Honour of A.L. Morton* (1978), pp. 62–3.

2　C.G. Durston, 'Berkshire and Its County Gentry', Unpublished Reading University Ph.D. thesis (1977).

3　Walter Money, *A History of the Ancient Town and Borough of Newbury in the County of Berkshire* (1887), p. 571.

4　A. Everitt, 'The Marketing of Agricultural Produce' in J. Thirsk (ed.), *The Agrarian History of England and Wales*, Vol. 4 (1967), pp. 495–500.

5　W. Page and P.H. Ditchfield (eds.), *The Victoria County History of Berkshire*, Vol. 1, p. 393: Vol. 2, p. 198: Vol. 3, p. 138; R.F. Dell, 'The Decline of the Clothing Industry in Berkshire', *Transactions of the Newbury District Field Club* Vol. 10, No. 2, pp. 50–64; Daniel Defoe, *A Tour Through England and Wales, Divided into Circuits or Journeys* (Everyman Edn. 1959), Vol. 1, p. 288.

6 V.C.H. Berks, Vol. 3, pp. 139–40.
7 Money, Newbury, pp. 182–8.
8 Josiah Pratt (ed.), The Acts and Monuments of John Foxe, Vol. 4 (1877), p. 213.
9 J.A.F. Thomson, The Later Lollards 1414–1520 (Oxford, 1965), pp. 75–9.
10 Ibid., pp. 82–3, 92–3; Acts and Monuments, Vol. 4, pp. 235–40.
11 Thomas Fuller, The History of the Worthies of England (1660) (1811 edn.), Vol. 1, p. 87.
12 Acts and Monuments, Vol. 8, pp. 201–19; Money, Newbury, pp. 209–10.
13 M. Connolly, 'The Godly in Berkshire from the reign of Elizabeth to c. 1642', Unpublished Reading Univ. M. Phil. thesis (1977), p. 126.
14 Ibid., pp. 126–34; Dictionary of National Biography William Twisse (1578?–1646).
15 Fuller, Worthies, Vol. 1, p. 93.
16 Connolly thesis, p. 132.
17 Henry W. Clark, The History of English Non-Conformity, Vol. 1 (1911), p. 301; Edward Whitaker Grey, The History and Antiquities of Newbury and its Environs (Speenhamland, 1839), pp. 121, 127.
18 Connolly thesis, p. 133.
19 J.R. Dasent (ed.), Acts of the Privy Council 1592–3, p. 268 (1901) Council to Bishop of Salisbury 29 May 1593; Acts of Privy Council 1615–6, p. 254 (1925) Warrant to John Hawkins 11 July 1615.
20 H(istorical) M(anuscripts) C(ommission), Salisbury Mss. Vol. 17, pp. 73, 76–7, 98–9, 118.
21 P(ublic) R(ecord) O(ffice), State Papers Charles I, SP.16. 172.4. William Hunt to Council 15 Dec. 1630, SP.16. 176.35. Gabriel Dowse to Council 6 Dec. 1630.
22 P.R.O. SP.16. 344.12 Council to Mayor Newbury 15 January 1636/7, Privy Council Registers P C 2, 47 f. 164 Appearance of Mayor 25 January 1636/7.
23 W.A. Day (ed.), The Pythouse Papers (1879), p. 8, Grandison to Rupert 8 February 1642/3.
24 I.G. Philip (ed.), The Journal of Sir Samuel Luke, Oxford Records Society Publs., Vol. 29 (1947), pp. 73–4, 12 May 1643.
25 B(ritish) L(ibrary) Thomason Tracts E.67.38, True Informer 23 September 1643.
26 Bod(leian) Lib(rary) Rawlinson Mss. D. 395 f. 141. Casimirus Stuart to Lord Percy 12 November 1643.
27 BL E. 9.5. Mercurius Aulicus No. 34. 24 August 1644.
28 Edmund Calamy: The Non-Conformists Memorial (1802 edn.), Vol. 1, pp. 290–1.
29 BL E. 419.20. 12 December 1647.
30. C(alender) of S(tate) P(apers) D(omestic) 1661.2. p. 419 Certificate of Commissioners for Regulating Corporations 26 June 1662.
31 Money, Newbury, pp. 504–6, Calamy Memorial Vol. 1, pp. 295–6. Calamy claims the charges against Voysey were fabricated by a local landowner upset by his preaching. He remained in prison for over a year before being released and returning to his native Devon.
32 P.R.O. State Papers Charles II. SP. 29. 96. 110. Dolman to Lovelace 14 April 1664.
33 P.R.O. SP. 29. 96. 97. Dolman to Lovelace 12 April 1664.
34 P.R.O. SP. 29. 96. 129. Dolman to Lovelace 17 April 1664.
35 Ibid., and see P.R.O. SP. 29. 96. 114. Dolman to Lovelace 15 April 1664.
36 The Newbury churchwardens accounts for 1665 include payments to witnesses who testified at Abingdon, Money Newbury, p. 537; see also the wrongly dated entry in C.S.P.D. 1675–6, p. 479. Gohory and Gallwey to King.

37 G. Lyon Turner (ed.), *Original Records of Early NonConformity Under Persecution and Indulgence* (1911), Vol. 1, p. 110.

38 *Ibid.*, Berkshire Records Office, Newbury Corporation Mss. D/F2 B2/1. Newbury and Oare monthly meeting minutes 1674–1779. For the attempt of the town authorities to prevent these meetings see Berks. R.O. N3/20 Quarter Sessions Journal ff. 162–3, 174, 186, 213, and Joseph Besse, *A Collection of the Sufferings of the People Called Quakers* (1713), Vol. 1, pp. 29, 34, 36.

39 Grey, *History*, pp. 121–9.

40 John Wesley, *The Journal of the Reverend John Wesley* (1906 edn.), Vol. 4, p. 496.

41 BL Harley Papers, Ms. Loan 29, 193, f. 12. Deposition 12 January 1706, ff. 31–3. Examinations of William Littler and John Kay 21 January 1706, f. 59. Examination John Southby 2 February 1706, *HMC Portland Mss.*, Vol. 4, pp. 279, 281, 284, Vol. 8, pp. 211–2.

42 Walter J. Shelton, *English Hunger and Industrial Disorders* (1973), pp. 24, 32, 39, 42; *Oxford Gazette and Reading Mercury* No. 238 August 1766. I am grateful to Mr Richard Williams for this reference.

43 *Reading Mercury* 16 June 1800, see also Samuel Barfield, *Thatcham Berks. and Its Manors* (1901), Vol. 2, p. 46, and A.S. Humphreys, *Bucklebury, a Berkshire Parish: The Home of Bolingbroke 1701–1715* (1932), pp. 377–8.

44 E.J. Hobsbawm and G. Rudé, *Captain Swing* (1969), pp. 134–40, 215, 311–58; *Reading Mercury* 6 December 1830, quoted by Humphreys *Bucklebury*, pp. 379–81.

45 Hobsbawm and Rudé, *Captain Swing*, p. 180.

46 Buchanan Sharp, *In Contempt of All Authority: Rural Artisans and Riot in the West of England 1586–1660* (1980), p. 257.

47 R. Tudor-Jones, *Congregationalism in England* (1962), p. 126. Jones was referring to the year 1715.

48 Shelton, *English Hunger*, pp. 34, 39.

49 J. Stevenson, *Popular Disturbance in England 1700– 1870* (1979), p. 109.

50 Hill, 'Lollards to Levellers', pp. 51–2.

51 A.G. Dickens, *The English Reformation* (1964), p. 33.

52 Hill, loc. cit.

53 Money, *Newbury*, p. 526.

54 Berks. R.O. N3/20 Quarter Sessions Journal 1666–1732 ff. 14, 16, 38, 40, 45, 55, 65, 74, 79, 80, 115, 174, 225–6, 233, 253. The earlier journals have not survived.

55 Connolly thesis, pp. 126–34.

56 P.R.O. SP.16. 177. 60. Petition of Mayors of Newbury and Reading to Council 31 December 1630.

57 P.R.O. SP.16. 192. 14.ii Report of William Hunt and Gabriel Coxe 16 May 1631.

58 *C.S.P.D. 1661–2*, p. 419, Lyon Turner, *Original Records*, loc. cit.

59 P.R.O. SP.29. 96. 129, Dolman to Lovelace 17 April 1664.

60 Connolly thesis, p. 63.

61 P.R.O. SP.16. 176.35 Gabriel Dowse to Council 6 December 1630, SP.16. 267.3. Certificate of Richard Browne 9 April 1634.

62 Connolly thesis, pp. 96–8, 106–7; Lyon Turner, *Original Records*, loc. cit.; Barfield, *Thatcham*, Vol. 1, pp. 294–300.

63 *V.C.H. Berks*, Vol. 3, p. 143.

64 Connolly, thesis, pp. 126–34; Fuller, *Worthies*, Vol. 1, p. 93; Calamy, *Memorial*, Vol. 1, pp. 290–1.

65 P.R.O. SP.29. 96. 97. Dolman to Lovelace 12 April 1664.
66 Thomson, *Later Lollards*, p. 137, *Acts of Privy Council 1592–3*, p. 268, P.R.O. SP.16.
    460. 48. Fra. Read to Rob. Read 16 July 1640.
67 Lyon Turner, *Original Records*, loc. cit.
68 Connolly, thesis, loc. cit.; Money, *Newbury*, pp. 564– 5, BL E. 419.20.
69 Sharp, *Contempt*, pp. 3, 7.
70 Peter Clark, 'The Ramoth – Gilead of the Good. Urban Change and Political
    Radicalism at Gloucester 1540–1640' in Peter Clark, Alan G.R. Smith and Nicholas
    Tyacke (eds.), *The English Commonwealth 1547–1640, Essays in Politics and Society
    presented to Joel Hurstfield* (Leicester 1979), pp. 167–87. Clark lists as other radical
    centres Northampton, Salisbury, Barnstaple, Colchester, Taunton and Coventry.
71 P.R.O. SP.29. 96. 110 Dolman to Lovelace 14 April 1664, SP.29. 96. 129. Dolman to
    Lovelace 17 April 1664.
72 Lyon Turner, *Original Records*, loc. cit.
73 Hill, 'Lollards to Levellers', p. 56.
74 Sharp, *Contempt*, p. 266.
75 Hobsbawm and Rudé, *Captain Swing*, p. 135.
76 R. and K. Dawson and K. Prewitt, *Political Socialisation* (Boston 1977), p. 121.
77 *Ibid.*, pp. 135–6.

4

Marriage, Migration and Mendicancy in a Pre-Industrial Community

B. Stapleton

Portsmouth Polytechnic

The basis of any community is its population – an aggregate of individuals living at any one time. The vital events of their lives, births, marriages and deaths were, for many if not all, the most important occasions in the histories of their families. Births and deaths represented the flows into and out of the population, the balance between them largely determining the rate at which population grew or declined. However, spatial movements the migration of people into or out of the locality, supplemented the balance between births and deaths and thereby influenced the rate of population growth or decline.

In England, in the two centuries prior to the Industrial Revolution (c.1550–1750) the flows of births and deaths and the movements of people were far from constant and, at the national level, it would be quite acceptable to divide the period into two halves. Between 1550 and 1650 there was an overall estimated surplus of births over deaths of nearly two-and-a-quarter millions, with the greatest growth occurring in the central 50 years 1575–1625. By contrast the second half of the seventeenth century saw estimated deaths exceeding births by nearly 200,000 before surpluses returned in the first half of the eighteenth century, when over 400,000 more births than deaths occurred and in the second half births exceeded deaths by nearly two millions.[1] Hence, the first century was one of population growth followed by half a century of overall decline, although that decline was heavily influenced by the impact of London which had estimated burial surpluses four times larger in the second half of the seventeenth century than in the first (408,293 as opposed to 102,944).[2] Contributing to this population decline was the trend of emigration which was a rising one, especially from the 1630s, and in the second half of the century some 240,000 people are estimated to have emigrated to America alone.[3] There was substantial emigration to Ireland as well[4] and, even though Huguenot immigrants must have offset some of this,[5] it seems that emigration was at least partly responsible for the decline in numbers and was relatively more important in its effect in the second half of the seventeenth century than the first.

Though some communities in Southern England will remain stubbornly atypical, most will fall largely into this national pattern of population change, and some noticeable effects on their populations would have been felt since the late sixteenth and early seventeeth centuries must have seen many villages teeming with children. Over half their populations would have been under 25 during the last quarter of the sixteenth century and the first quarter of the seventeenth century.[6] After that the proportion of young in the villages of England began to fall, whilst the proportions of adults and the elderly increased, until in the late 1670s and early 1680s village populations would have been the oldest in English pre-industrial demographic history.[7] However, since the number of elderly (those over 60) grew more slowly than the number of children declined, then the changing age structure would have been to the advantage of those communities experiencing it, since a higher proportion of the population in the later seventeenth and early eighteenth centuries would have been in the working age groups supporting a smaller dependent sector of children and elderly.[8] This in itself should have been beneficial to village economies, allowing slow improvements in the standard of living of English communities to become noticeable before the turn of the century, particularly since the pressure of growing population was reduced at the same time.

This changing demographic pattern would also have had its effect on the patterns of migration – not that overseas, but the flows of migrants within England which, it would appear, were vastly greater than those created by emigrants. In most English villages emigration to the colonies or Ireland would have had a negligible effect – only a handful of people would have left them at most. But the flows of individuals and families within England, and particularly local movements, would have had a more significant impact. It is still common to hear the view expressed that, before the Industrial Revolution, most English men and women were born, married and lived out their lives in the villages of their births, despite much evidence to the contrary. In the late seventeenth and early eighteenth centuries the growth of London at a pace considerably more rapid than the national population is only the most obvious manifestation of mobile English villagers.[9] However, London is an atypical example since it attracted migrants from near and far, whereas the majority of those who left their native villages did so for other communities only short distances away. It is not always easy to discover how many of those who were born into a community either stayed or moved, but it is not impossible given a reasonably unbroken and informative set of parish registers which allow a family reconstitution of the community to be undertaken. Such work has been carried out on the north-east Hampshire parish of Odiham, located equidistant between Basingstoke to the west and Farnham, in Surrey, to the east. Odiham is a sizeable parish of 7,350 acres lying on the northern scarp of the North Downs some 40 miles south-west of London, and its wide high street in which markets were held weekly lay approximately along the east–west line of the conjunction of the clay of the Thames valley to the north and the chalk of the downs in the south of the parish.

A predominantly agricultural community of over 800 persons at the beginning of the seventeenth century rising to a population of some 1,100 towards the end of that century, over 2,000 in 1811 and more than 2,800 in 1841,[10] it also possessed related industrial activities of kersey manufacture, of some importance in the sixteenth century, and tanning.

The parish registers of Odiham, form an unbroken series of marriages, baptisms and burials from 1539 to 1851,[11] and together with the non-conformist register for Odiham Independent Chapel which contains baptisms from 1795 to 1837, and burials from 1832 to 1837,[12] have provided evidence from which estimates of gross migration can be obtained. In theory those baptised in a parish and for whom no burial entry exists in the registers must have been out-migrants; those who were buried for whom no baptism entry can be traced must have been in-migrants. Enumerating such people is not, however, as simple as is sometimes implied.[13] Not all those baptised can be linked unambiguously with a named person buried, as communities often contained persons with the same first names and surnames alive contemporaneously. Where the number of those baptised equals the number of burials of those with the same names no problem exists. But where numbers are unequal and the evidence in the registers does not allow a firm attribution, then the procedure followed has been to make positive attributions for all those burials for which a matching first and surname baptism exists. Surplus burials are then regarded as in-migrants and any surplus of baptisms as out-migrants.

In the case of baptisms the period examined was 1541 to 1820. Those baptised after 1820 were increasingly unlikely to be found among the burials, which were searched up to 1890. What this exercise indicated (see Table 4.1) is that at no time during the period 1541 to 1820 was it possible to recover more than 44 per cent of those baptised from the burial registers, and in fact for the whole period from 1541 to 1700 almost two thirds of those baptised appear to have migrated from the parish. Only in the first half of the eighteenth century do less than 60 per cent of those baptised leave, before the numbers rise once more to 60 per cent and over. Thus, never less than 56 per cent of those baptised in Odiham left at some point in their lives.

The estimates of in-migration, calculated from those buried in Odiham but not having been previously baptised there, again show a remarkably

	a	b	c	F	M	%F	%M
1541 - 60	882	612	69.4	302	310	49.3	50.7
1561 - 80	810	547	67.5	275	272	50.3	49.7
1581 - 1600	822	535	65.1	279	256	52.1	47.9
1601 - 20	958	615	64.2	321	294	52.2	47.8
1621 - 40	843	530	62.8	263	267	49.6	50.4
1641 - 60	780	501	64.2	268	233	53.5	46.5
1661 - 80	644	421	65.4	230	191	54.6	45.4
1681 - 1700	604	398	65.8	211	187	53.0	47.0
1701 - 20	661	390	59.0	208	182	53.3	46.7
1721 - 40	638	357	56.0	173	184	48.5	51.5
1741 - 60	829	498	60.0	246	252	49.4	50.6
1761 - 80	928	581	62.6	292	289	50.3	49.7
1781 - 1800	1234	806	65.3	417	389	51.7	48.3
1801 - 20	1296	836	64.5	426	410	51.0	49.0
Total	11825	7627	64.5	3911	3716	51.3	48.7

a =   number of baptisms in parish registers (plus non-conformist registers for 1795-1820)

b =   number of baptisms for which no burial was registered

c =   b as percentage of a

F =   Female

M =   Male

Table 4.1 Estimates of Out-migrating Proportions of those Baptised

	a	b	c	F	m	%F	%M
1601 - 20	673	294	43.7	167	127	56.8.	43.2
1621 - 40	656	284	43.0	152	132	53.5.	46.5
1641 - 60	660	296	44.8	166	128	56.1	43.2
1661 - 80	593	253	42.6	157	96	62.0	38.0
1681 - 1700	484	197	40.7	122	75	61.9	38.1
1701 - 20	477	217	45.5	122	95	56.2	43.8
1721 - 40	570	256	44.9	152	97	59.4	37.9
1741 - 60	657	288	43.8	149	130	51.7	45.1
1761 - 80	651	271	41.6	154	117	56.8	43.2
1781 - 1800	744	291	39.1	151	140	51.9	48.1
1801 - 20	680	280	41.1	151	129	53.9	46.1
1821 - 40	916	374	40.8	193	181	51.6	48.4
Total	7761	3301	42.5	1836	1447	55.6	43.8

a =   Burials recorded in parish registers (plus non-conformist register for 1832-37)

b =   Burials recorded having no related baptism

c =   b as a percentage of a

F =   Female

M =   Male

N.B.   Between 1641-60, 1721-40 and 1741-60 the percentages of male and female migrants do not total 100. This results from a small number of wanderers whose sex was unspecified at burial i.e. 2(0.7%) 1641-60; 7(2.7%) 1721-40; 9(3.1%) 1741-60.

Table 4.2 Estimates of In-migrating Proportions of those Buried

steady flow throughout the seventeenth and eighteenth centuries (see Table 4.2). In those two hundred years over 40 per cent of those buried appear to have arrived in the parish during their lifetimes and stayed until death. However, what is interesting to note is that, when the totals of those baptised but not buried in Odiham are disaggregated by sex, there is almost always an excess of female over male migrants. When the volumes of out-migration declined, as they did from 1621 to 1640 and 1720 to 1740, these troughs are primarily the products of lower levels of female migration. Furthermore, when the sex ratio of those in-migrants buried but not baptised in the parish is examined, a constant surplus of females over males throughout the whole seventeenth and eighteenth centuries, with particularly high proportions in the late seventeenth century, is found. However, in so far as historical explanations are ever simple, there would appear to be a perfectly natural explanation for these ratios. Since the tradition in pre-industrial England, as in the twentieth century, was for most marriages to take place in the bride's parish, many brides marrying grooms from other parishes often found themselves moving to the husband's parish by virtue of his social, and especially economic, bonds. Thus the event of marriage created an increase in female migration. An analysis of Odiham in 1851 using census birthplace statements gives some supporting evidence to this assertion. What the 1,088 census residents stating non-Odiham birthplaces indicate when tabulated by age and sex is that, whereas the 203 aged under 15 produced as even a division as possible, 102 males and 101 females, and in the later teens (15 to 19) males accounted for 56 and females 51 of the 107 in-migrants (see Table 4.3), from the age of 20 onwards, females predominated in every five year age group except three, 40 to 44, 70 to 74 and 85 to 89. This resulted in a total of 437 in-migrant females to only 341 in-migrant males, clearly demonstrating that it is in the years during and after marriage that the excess of female migrants materialises. For these figures to be at all comparable with those extracted from the parish register baptisms and burials it is necessary to aggregate in-migrant males and females of all ages.

Such an aggregation produces totals of 589 females and 499 males, and results in 54.1 per cent of in-migrants being female in 1851, a percentage not at all at variance with those for the nearest 20-year period 1821–40 in Table 4.2 Since additionally, the total Odiham 1851 census population of 2,811 was composed of 1,406 males and 1,405 females it is clear that the analysis of parish register baptisms and burials is quite acceptable in indicating that women rather than men normally formed the larger proportion of the migrant population in pre-industrial England. If marriage is the key to this pattern then examination of other communities' parish registers should produce broadly similar results.

Age	Male		Female	
0- 4	25 ⎫		24 ⎫	
5- 9	31 ⎬ 102		42 ⎬ 101	
10-14	46 ⎭		35 ⎭	
15-19	56		51	
20-24	57		66	
25-29	34		47	
30-34	35		43	
35-39	39		54	
40-44	39		37	
45-49	30		35	
50-54	25		38	
55-59	27		37	
60-64	19		27	
65-69	10		20	
70-74	17		15	
75-79	4		9	
80-84	2		7	
85 +	3		2	
Total	499	(45.9%)	589	(54.1%)

Table 4.3 1851 Census: In-migrants by Age and Sex

	In-Migrant Families	Percentage of total F.R.F's	Stayers	%	Leavers, plus no. of children baptised before departure		1		2		3+	
1581-1600	143	35.6	48	33.6	95	66.4	67	70.5	17	17.9	11	11.6
1601-20	147	37.3	60	40.8	87	59.2	56	64.4	17	19.5	14	16.1
1621-40	114	33.5	54	47.4	60	52.6	38	63.3	14	23.3	8	13.3
1641-60	95	30.4	44	46.3	51	53.7	36	70.6	9	17.6	6	11.8
1661-80	96	38.9	49	51.0	47	49.0	36	76.6	5	10.6	6	12.8
1681-1700	79	35.6	46	58.2	33	41.8	20	60.6	7	21.2	6	18.2
1701-20	85	30.4	44	51.6	42	49.4	24	57.1	9	21.4	9	21.4
1721-40	113	37.0	49	43.4	64	56.6	38	59.3	8	12.5	18	28.1
1741-60	91	26.9	38	41.8	53	58.2	36	67.9	6	11.3	11	20.8
1761-80	107	27.3	40	37.4	67	62.6	46	68.6	8	11.9	12	17.9
1781-1800	150	31.8	58	38.7	92	61.3	60	65.2	17	18.4	15	16.3
1801-20	156	31.4	51	32.7	105	67.3	61	58.1	29	27.6	15	14.3
1821-40	162	29.3	54	33.3	108	66.7	81	75.0	14	13.0	13	12.0

F.R.F. = Family Reconstitution Form

Table 4.4 In-migrants – Stayers and Leavers

Analyis of the reconstituted families allows a further dimension to be added to the gross estimates of migration, though not for the population as a whole. Since family reconstitution forms are 'marriage centred' they do not reveal evidence of those who remained single for their whole lifetimes, but they can be used to reveal information about in-migrant and out-migrant couples and some at least, if not all, their children. In-migrant families are discovered by virtue of having one or more children baptised, though having no previous marriage recorded in the parish.

The most striking feature of the analysis of these families (see Table 4.4) is the high proportion whose stay in the parish was purely temporary. For the whole period from 1580 to 1840 at least 40 per cent of in-migrants having registered baptisms in Odiham departed, thus recording at least a second move in their lives. However, the proportion departing declined steadily from a peak of over two-thirds in the late sixteenth century to over two-fifths in the late seventeenth century, rising to two-thirds once again in the early nineteenth century, a trend remarkably consistent with higher numbers moving at a time when population pressure was greater, and smaller proportions migrating when population growth was much lower in late seventeenth century Odiham. It is also worth noting the high proportions of those in-migrants who departed after having recorded the baptism of only one child and, except for the early eighteenth century, over 80 per cent of all those in-migrants who left registered only one or two baptisms during their temporary stay in the parish.

Similarly, a high proportion of those who married in Odiham and subsequently left did so before any baptisms had been recorded (see Table 4.5). At all times, more than half those spouses who had been baptised in the parish had departed without registering the baptism of a single child, and in most periods the proportion was near to or over two-thirds. This evidence, would seem to corroborate the view that mobility was common among younger adults in the population.[14] Even so, some migrants clearly moved when older, and after having formed large family units; at all times there were families who had up to eight children baptised before migrating from the parish.

Nothing is known about most of these migrants except for their sex and dates of marriage, and in some cases baptism and burial dates. Most parish registers provide no information either about the ages and occupations of migrants or the distances over which they had travelled, and the registers of Odiham are no exception. However, marriage registers do supply some evidence of migration distance in those cases where the incumbent specified the parish of residence of bride or groom. Unfortunately, it is not always the case that such information was consistently provided, at least

	Total Number of Out-Migrant Families	Percentage of total FRF's	Marriage only recorded in Odiham (No baptism of spouses)	Marriage recorded and one or both spouses baptised in Odiham, plus number of children baptised before migration.						
				Total	0	1	2	3	4	5+
1581-1600	111	27.4	19	92	64	14	8	5	0	1
1601-20	85	21.6	32	53	34	14	2	0	1	2
1621-40	98	28.8	33	65	44	10	4	3	3	1
1641-60	90	28.8	38	52	37	8	1	1	2	3
1661-80	50	20.2	21	29	24	2	2	1	0	0
1681-1700	67	30.2	28	39	30	6	1	0	1	1
1701-20	75	26.8	31	44	28	6	1	5	2	2
1721-40	68	22.3	27	41	26	9	1	2	2	1
1741-60	94	27.8	41	53	37	5	3	3	1	4
1761-80	99	25.3	40	59	33	13	10	1	1	1
1781-1800	144	30.6	53	91	63	20	4	1	1	2
1801-20	153	30.8	57	96	57	18	11	2	4	4
1821-40	139	25.2	55	84	55	12	8	8	0	1

F.R.F. = Family Reconstruction Form

Table 4.5 Out-migrant Families

	<10 km	<20 km	<30 km	<40 km	<50 km	<75 km	<100 km	100+ km	Total	% of total Married
1601-20	2			1		2			5	1.2
1621-40	3	1		3		4			11	2.6
1641-60	26	3		1		3			33	10.1
1661-80	1	2	4			1			8	3.4
1681-1700	7		1						8	3.5
1701-20	16	14	6	4		1			41	18.5
1721-40	13	9	4			1			27	9.9
1741-60	14	12	9	4	2	3		1	45	12.5
1761-80	35	11	5	2		4			57	12.7
1781-1800	68	14	1	2	2	6	3	3	99	16.4
1801-20	71	10	7	3	2	9		1	103	17.1
1821-40	50	12	10	3	3	6	1	4	89	13.7
1841-50	9	9	2		1	1			22	7.6
	315	97	49	23	10	41	4	9	548	
1601-1700	39(60%)	6(9.2)	5(7.7)	5(7.7)		10(15.4)			65	100.0
1701-60	43(38.0)	35(31.0)	19(16.8)	8(7.0)	2(1.8)	5(4.4)		1(0.9)	113	99.9
1761-1840	224(64.4)	47(13.5)	23(6.6)	18(2.9)	7(2.0)	25(7.2)	4(1.1)	8(2.3)	348	100.0

Distances in kms.

Table 4.6 Marriage Horizons

before the application of Lord Hardwicke's Marriage Act[15] in the mid-eighteenth century, and the consequent introduction of printed marriage registers.

Thus, for the seventeenth and early eighteenth centuries the proportions of those married in Odiham who were stated to be from other parishes vary from 1.2 per cent of the total married between 1601 and 1620 to 18.5 per cent for the first twenty years of the eighteenth century (see Table 4.6). However, the inconsistency of the data can be most clearly shown in the mid-seventeenth century by the fortunate survival of the Interregnum register. Marriage entries in that register commence in November 1653 and end in June 1659, during which time 122 persons were married in 61 registered ceremonies. Of these brides and grooms 32 (26.2 per cent) were stated to be from parishes other than Odiham, thus providing a much higher proportion of in-migrant marriage partners than at any other time. It may well be argued that the Cromwellian Commonwealth, following on the heels of a civil war, was one of unusual mobility, but since only one other person out of a total of 328 was stated to be an in-migrant at marriage in the whole 20-year period 1641–60, the strong indication is that the Anglican registers understate the scale of migrants marrying in Odiham.[16] The fluctuating proportions of in-migrants marrying also suggest that the understatement is not in itself consistent over time. Furthermore, a statement of residence cannot necessarily be accepted as indicative of the place of baptism of the migrant. For example, almost 450 persons stated at marriage to be from Odiham have been traced in the marriage registers of other parishes in the south of England. However, the baptisms of less than half of these stated residents could be found in Odiham's Anglican registers, thus demonstrating that for those who could not be traced, at least one previous move had been made prior to the marriage ceremony. Hence, for many the distances travelled in order to marry are an indication only of the latest move in their individual cases and not of their overall movement, a not unsurprising fact since young people were frequently engaged either as servants in husbandry on annual hirings or in domestic service and thus were among the most mobile sections of a community.[17]

Analysis of the parish register entries shows that the majority of Odiham's in-migrant marriage partners travelled only short distances to be wed. In the seventeenth century 60 per cent came from less than ten kilometres (6.25 miles) away and only ten individuals had journeyed over 40 kilometres (25 miles), all of them in fact from a distance of 50 to under 75 kilometres (31.25 to 47 miles), and eight out of the ten were from London.

Discovering the size and structure of these flows of people is time consuming. Parish registers, however, can more easily provide other

	1-8 months		9 months		Total Marriages for which baptism of first child is known
	No.	%	No.	%	
1550 - 99	3	11.5	4	15.4	26
1600 - 49	27	26.2	34	33.0	103
1650 - 99	13	15.5	27	32.1	84
1700 - 49	19	17.3	38	34.5	110
1750 - 99	63	39.4	72	45.0	160
1800 - 49	132	51.2	146	56.6	258
1550 - 1849	257	34.7	321	43.3	741

The percentages and figures relate only to those marriages where the date of baptism of the first child is known.

Table 4.7 Odiham – Prenuptial Pregnancy 1550–1849

evidence about the social lives of our forebears. For example, the proportion of brides who were pregnant when married can be discovered by linking a baptism which occurred within eight months of an appropriate marriage. At Odiham the proportion of pregnant brides fluctuated over time with the general level being higher in the first half of the seventeenth century than between 1650–1750 and then rising to entirely new heights in the late eighteenth and early nineteenth centuries (see Table 4.7).

As a proportion of all brides married in Odiham in the first half of the seventeenth century, some 10 per cent had their first child baptised in under eight months after the marriage ceremony. This proportion was approximately halved in the second half of the seventeenth century before climbing to nearly 15 per cent between 1720 and 1750, to 25 per cent in the second half of the eighteenth century and about 30 per cent in the first half of the nineteenth. However, taking pregnant brides as a proportion of all brides married in Odiham may well understate the real rates of prenuptial pregnancy, since many brides who left after marriage will have been included in the total but would not have been counted as pregnant, even if they were so, by virtue of having their offspring registered in another parish.[18] If only brides who married and also had their first child baptised in the parish church at Odiham, are considered, then the ratio of prenuptial pregnancy will rise. Even so, such an approach confirms the general trend of higher proportions in the first half of the seventeenth century than the second (26 per cent and 15 per cent respectively) with the reverse being the case in the eighteenth century (17 per cent and nearly 40 per cent), and over half the brides pregnant in the first half of the nineteenth century (51 per cent). For the whole period from 1600 to 1850 over one third of all brides (35 per cent) having a first child in Odiham celebrated the baptism within eight months of the marriage ceremony.[19]

These proportions of pregnant brides are not exceptional since other communities in southern England have also recorded high levels of prenuptial pregnancy. At Colyton in south-east Devon between 1538 and 1799 over 46 per cent of brides had their first child baptised within eight months of marriage and over 60 per cent within nine months.[20] In Dorset a one in ten sample of years from the eighteenth century registers indicates that at Corfe Castle over 40 per cent of brides were pregnant and at Hawkchurch some 36 per cent were in a similar condition.[21] At Wylye, in Wiltshire 40 per cent of brides had their first child baptised within nine months of marriage and 34 per cent within eight and a half months.[22] These proportions are not greatly out of line with others since it has been indicated that about 20 per cent of brides between 1540 and 1700 were pregnant and above 40 per cent between 1700 and 1840[23] with higher levels occurring in the north than the south.

These numbers of pregnant brides are clearly indicative of widespread social attitudes which apparently condoned sexual co-habitation in early-modern England. That such views existed from early in the sixteenth century is confirmed in an extract from the *Christen State of Matrimony* published in 1543 which stated:[24]

Yet in this thygne also must I warn everye reasonable and honest parson, to beware that in contractying of Maryage they dyssemble not, nor set forthe any lye. Every man lykewyse must esteme the parson to whom he is *handfasted*, none otherwyse than for his own spouse, though as yet it be not done in the Church ner in the Streate. – After the *Handfastynge* and makyng of the Contracte ye Churchgoyng and Weddyng shuld not be differred to longe, lest the wickedde sowe hys ungracious sede in the meane season. Into this dysh hath the Dyvell put his foote and mengled it wythe many wycked uses and coustumes. For in some places ther is such a maner, wel worthy to be rebuked, that *at the* HANDEFASTING *ther is made a greate feaste and superfluous Bancket, and even the same night are the two handfasted personnes brought and layed together, yea certan wekes afore they go to the Chyrch.*

Laslett has also shown that such attitudes continued to be held throughout the sixteenth and seventeenth centuries and into the eighteenth[25] and even clearer exposition comes from the civil engineer John Smeaton who wrote of a visit to Dorset in 1756 when he went to the stone quarries at Portland to obtain materials for the building of Eddystone Lighthouse and engaged in conversation with the manager of the quarries a Mr Roper:[26]

When I was looking over the quarries at Portland, and attentively considering the operations; observing how soon the quarrymen would cut half a ton of *Spawls* from an unformed block, and what large pieces flew off at every stroke; how speedily their blows followed one another and how incessantly they pursued this labour, with a tool of from 18 to 20 pounds weight; I was naturally led to view and consider the figure of the *operative* Agent; and after having observed that by far the greatest number of the quarrymen were of a very robust, hardy form, in whose hands the tool I have mentioned seemed a mere *Plaything*; I at last broke out with surprize, and enquired of my guide, Mr ROPER, where they could possibly pick up such a set of stout fellows to handle the *Kevel*, which in their hands seemed nothing: for I observed that in the space of 15 minutes, they would knock off as much waste matter from a mass of stone, as any of that occupation I had ever seen before would do in an hour. – Says ROPER we do not go to fetch those from a distance, they are all born upon the island, and many of them have never been further upon the main land than to *Weymouth*. I told him, I thought the air of that island must be very propitious, to furnish a breed of men so particularly formed for the business they followed. – The air, he replied, though very sharp, from our elevated situation, is certainly very healthy to working men; yet if you knew how these men are produced, you would wonder the less; for *all* our marriages here are productive of children. – On desiring an explanation how this happened, he proceeded, 'Our people here, as they are bred up to hard labour, are very early in a condition to marry and provide for a family; they intermarry with one another, very rarely going to the main land to seek a wife; and it has been the custom of the island from time immemorial, that they never marry till the woman is pregnant.' But pray, says I, does not this subject you to a great number of bastards? Have not your *Portlanders* the same kind of fickleness in their attachments, that *Englishmen* are subject to? And in consequence, does not this produce many inconveniencies? None at all, replies ROPER, 'for previous to my arrival here, there was but one child, on record of the parish register, that had been born a bastard in the compass of 150 years. The mode of courtship here is, that a young woman never admits of the serious addresses of a young man, but on supposition of a thorough probation. – When she becomes with child, she tells her mother; the mother tells her father; her father tells his father, and he tells his son, that it is then proper time to be *married*.' – But suppose, Mr ROPER, she does *not* prove to be with child, what happens then? do they live together without marriage? or, if they separate, is not this such an imputation upon her, as to prevent her getting another suitor? The case is thus managed, answered my friend: 'If the woman does not prove with child, after a competent time of courtship, they conclude they are not destined by Providence for each other; they therefore separate; and as it is an established maxim, which the Portland women observe with great strictness, never to admit a plurality of lovers at one time, their honour is no ways tarnished: she just as soon (after the affair is declared to be broke off) gets another suitor, as if she had been left a widow, or that nothing had ever happened, but that she had remained an immaculate virgin.' – But pray, Sir, did nothing particular happen upon your men coming down from London? Yes, says he, our men were much struck and mightily pleased with the facility of the Portland ladies, and it was not long before several of the women proved with child: but the men being called upon to marry them, this part of the lesson they were uninstructed in; and on their refusal, the Portland women arose to stone them out of the island; insomuch that those few who did not chuse to take their sweethearts for *better, or for worse*, after so fair a trial, were in reality obliged to decamp: and on this occasion some few bastards were born: but since then matters have gone on according to the ancient custom.

It is perhaps fortunate that John Smeaton, apart from being a civil engineer, was a Yorkshireman, born near Leeds, with the sort of enquiring mind which ensured he asked a series of pertinent questions, not always put with the greatest delicacy. His conversation with Roper raises a number of points. Clearly there is the relative isolation of Portland with much inter-marriage taking place, suggesting that the island may not have contained a typical community. Secondly, there is the indication that male attitudes on the mainland, and particularly in London, were different from those in Portland, and the implicit suggestion that the behaviour of urban males was different from that of the people from rural Portland.[27] Thirdly, despite living in a nation with a patriarchial and paternalistic society,[28] Portland women demonstrated a certain level of independence by stoning out of the island those London men who had refused to marry Portland girls whom they had made pregnant. Fourthly, there is the view that Portland men being 'bred up to hard labour' were able to marry early and support a family, suggesting that age at marriage in Portland should have been lower than in England generally,[29] and also indicating that average income *per capita* may well have been higher on Portland, perhaps because of the dual economy of quarrying and marine trades (fishing and commercial shipping) with some agriculture, which existed. Lastly, it is apparent that not only were lay people aware of parish registers but also knew they could be used to indicate at least one demographic measure, the level of illegitimacy.

The surviving Anglican parish registers of Portland, however, only begin in unbroken sequence from 1694[30] although baptisms survive for the years 1660–71. From 1694 to 1780 some 2,487 baptisms are registered of which only 14 can be identified as illegitimate. Of these, nine were entered before Smeaton's conversation with Roper, rather more than the quarry manager suggested. The first occurred in 1701, the second in 1715 and a further one in 1730. The other six were in two groups of 3 in 1742–4 and 1753–5. Apart from two cases, both in 1744, the reputed fathers were named.[31] Perhaps this was possible because the mothers concerned had followed the 'established maxim' and not had a plurality of lovers. In one case it seems likely that the baby had arrived early and surprised the intending couple, since the entry for 9 November 1755 reads:

> Susannah daughter of Susannah Lane was born before matrimony was solemnized between her mother Susan and John Pearce which was on ye 31st of October and was baptised in the name of Susannah Pearce ye 9th of November.[32]

	BAPTISMS			NUMBER OF RECORDED ILLEGITIMATE CHILDREN					ILLEGITIMACY RATIOS	
DATE	Anglican	Non-Conformist (1795–1837) and Civil Registers (1837–51)	Total	Anglican Baptism Register (1538–1851)	Bastardy Papers (1637–1831)	Parish Book (1652–1831)	Parish Book (1820–35)	Civil Registers (1837–51)	Anglican Register Only	All Sources
1541–60	882			12					1.4	
1561–80	811			14					1.7	
1581–1600	815			25					3.0	
1601–20	958			19					2.0	
1621–40	843			12					1.4	
1641–60	780			11	2				1.4	1.7
1661–80	644			5	1				0.77	0.9
1681–1700	605			9*					1.3	1.5
1701–20	661			12						1.8
1721–40	638			15	3				2.3	2.8
1741–60	829			23	2				2.7	3.0
1761–80	928			41	4				4.4	4.8
1781–1800	1206	28	1234	80	12				6.6	7.4
1801–20	1220	76	1296	86	5	3	4		7.0	7.6
1821–40	1535	106	1641	76	1	3	3	3	4.9	5.2
1841–50	719	146	865	52				11	7.2	7.3
(10-year period only)										

* Includes one from Churchwarden's Accounts

Table 4.8 Odiham – Illegitimacy

This would seem to be a case of 'failed' prenuptial pregnancy rather than illegitimacy.

However, if the attitudes towards marriage expressed in the conversation between Smeaton and Roper were prevalent in Portland then it would be expected that a large proportion of the island's brides would be pregnant at marriage. Assuming Portland was a closed community and no brides left after marriage, from a sample of 11 years (approximately every tenth year) in the eighteenth century, prenuptial pregnancy affected 36 out of 70 brides, some 52 per cent. Since, as we have seen, illegitimacy levels remained very low in Portland, only 0.6 per cent in the eighteenth century to 1780, then it would appear that the tradition of marrying after a woman discovered she was pregnant was strictly adhered to. Portland's illegitimacy ratio, however, was exceptionally low, for recent studies of bastardy have shown that illegitimacy was rising in all regions of eighteenth century England.[33] Such low levels as those revealed at Portland are certainly not discovered in other parishes investigated in southern England. The lowest ratio found was 2.2 per cent at both Frome in Somerset and Tonbridge in Kent whereas Chardstock in Devon had an eighteenth century ratio as high as 6.5 per cent and the south of England has been stated to be the second most bastardy prone region after the West and North-west.[34] Even so, there were considerable variations within each region and in the south, Hampshire was regarded as a county with below average levels of illegitimacy up to and including the nineteenth century.[35] Nevertheless, at Odiham, where more detailed research has been undertaken than the unchecked sets of figures in Laslett, there was a consistent rise in the levels of illegitimacy recorded in the parish register from their lowest level of 0.77 per cent in the period 1661–80, to the early decades of the nineteenth century when the ratio reached 7.0 per cent. This rise followed a century (1620–1720) when illegitimacy levels were indeed low the trough of bastardy being reached in that 'age of permissiveness', the Restoration period (see Table 4.8).

The survival of other parish records such as parish books and bastardy papers from the 1650s, as well as utilisation of the civil registers from 1837,[36] affords a more complete picture of illegitimacy than parish registers alone provide. The result is an increase, varying from 9 per cent to 21 per cent, in the number of recorded illegitimate children in every 20-year period except one after 1640. Since there are no wildly fluctuating differences in the percentages over time and as the additional sources confirm the trend obtained from the parish registers it can perhaps be argued that using parish registers alone to measure illegitimacy can produce reasonably good ratios though at slightly lower levels than the true ones. Perhaps this demonstrates that those births not included in

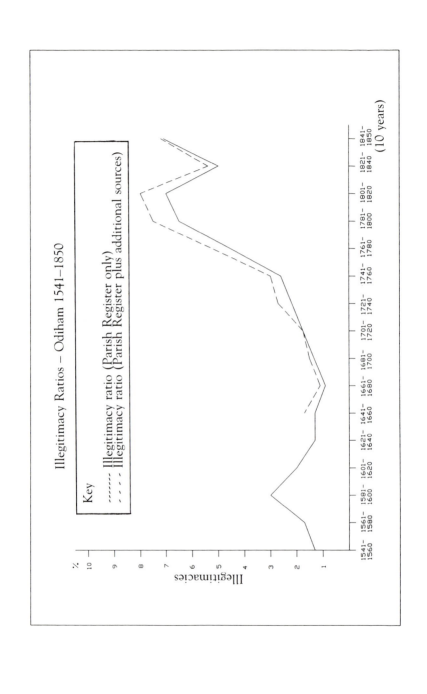

Illegitimacy Ratios – Odiham 1541–1850

Key

- - - - - Illegitimacy ratio (Parish Register only)
- - - - - Illegitimacy ratio (Parish Register plus additional sources)

Illegitimacies

% 10 9 8 7 6 5 4 3 2 1

1541-
1560
1561-
1580
1581-
1600
1601-
1620
1621-
1640
1641-
1660
1661-
1680
1681-
1700
1701-
1720
1721-
1740
1741-
1760
1761-
1780
1781-
1800
1801-
1820
1821-
1840
1841-
1850

(10 years)

parish registers have a somewhat higher representative sample of bastards than those baptisms which were included (see Graph 1). Certainly then, at Odiham, both the percentage of prenuptial pregnancies and of illegitimate births recorded follow a strikingly similar pattern, suggesting they reflect attitudes to moral behaviour which changed over time and in so doing, since illegitimacy ratios have been noted to rise and fall in inverse relationship with age at marriage,[37] indicate that age at first marriage of women at Odiham is likely to move in the same directions as that already discovered in other reconstituted parishes.[38]

However, although parish registers can be used to provide evidence of migration, prenuptial pregnancy and illegitimacy, one of their disadvantages, except in a few rare cases, is their paucity of information about the economic and social backgrounds of most of the individuals who appear in their pages. Only by taking into account other historical records is it possible to add further dimensions to the rather shadowy people which parish registers tend to reveal. This is particularly important in family reconstitution studies since fertility and mortality rates can clearly be influenced by the social class or economic status of the families concerned and the rates applicable, for example, to the nobility[39] are unlikely to be the same as those relevant to peasants living on the margins of subsistence in sixteenth and early seventeenth century England. Thus, without information about the background of reconstituted families it is impossible to determine whether changes in fertility or mortality result from the reconstituted sample being dominated by differing socio-economic groups in different periods of time.

Few parishes, however, have surviving registers reaching back to the sixteenth century which contain information in sufficient detail to allow reconstitution.[40] Even less have extant the range of parish sources, such as overseers of the poor accounts, or sets of documents, such as apprenticeship indentures or settlement examinations, which will identify occupations. It thus becomes necessary to search more widely through county records, such as quarter sessions, diocesan archives, especially probate wills and inventories, as well as national records including tax returns and central government court cases among others.[41] Although much of the evidence, when collated, duplicates already known information, especially with regard to the wealthy of any community, the exercise in multi-source linkage provided two valuable additional benefits. First, it corrected errors of attribution which may have been made in the original reconstitution using parish registers alone and secondly, additional information can be used to extend the size of the reconstitutable minority by resolving ambiguities or uncertainties. It should be added however, that in the majority of cases the attributions made in the process of family reconstitution proved to be correct.

To determine whether such an exercise could be successful, two multi-generational Odiham families were selected for comparison. One, the Mapletons, was wealthy and the other, the Lewingtons was in poverty, at least for most of its stay in Odiham. Much additional information about the families was culled from sources other than the parish registers and added to the reconstitution data (see Figs. 1–4) with the result that both families have been instrumental in demonstrating some of the problems of the methodology of family reconstitution and how the use of a wide range of sources results in modification.

Information about marriages, baptisms and burials gleaned from the Odiham parish register alone is included in Figs. 1 and 3, whereas Figs. 2 and 4 show the same families but with material added from a range of other sources including Anglican registers from other parishes. In the case of the impoverished Lewington family it is clear that proportionately less material is added. Even so, in the final generation a child James was born in 1845 to James and Caroline Lewington who, though absent from the parish register, did appear in the civil one and in consequence, apart from increasing the family's size, raised the number of pregnant brides by one! This addition, however, was not so serious a discrepancy as the errors resulting from the misallocation of children to two Mapleton fathers with the same first name (John) who were simultaneously producing families in the fourth generation of the reconstitution. Since only the father's name was given in the baptism register, once the two John Mapleton's were both married, problems relating to accurate attributions of children could obviously arise.

The first three children, who were all born to John and Katherine before the marriage of John to Elizabeth Hirst, present no difficulties (see Fig. 1). However, at the baptisms of the first of these children, Catherine, the father was described as 'junior'. The convention in these cases is that such a designation usually distinguished son from father of the same first name but in this case, somewhat oddly, John's father was called David. At the second child, Mary's, baptism the father was then stated to be of Lodge (a farm in the parish to the north of the Town of Odiham) whereas on Martha's baptism no additional information was provided. From then on the allocation of children baptised was calculated using information already given and any new evidence emerging, thus Anne was baptised in 1708 again with no additional information and in 1709 John was baptised son of John, 'Junior' of the Town of Odiham, and Penelope in 1710 to Mr John Mapleton, with Martha in 1711 producing no guiding evidence. Clearly John had to be allocated to the father already described as 'Junior' (and assuming he had moved residence) and Penelope to the other John since he was described as 'Mr'. Martha was also allocated to the same parent on the grounds that a child of the same name was already alive in the other family.

This left Anne as a doubtful case and she was allocated to John and Katherine in order to close a somewhat unacceptably lengthening birth interval. There remained four more children, Jonas, Mary and the two Elizabeths, none of whom produced any guiding information on baptism. However, Mary's (1715) allocation was determined on the same grounds as Martha's (child alive of the same name), Jonas because the birth interval created between him and John seemed more rational than that between him and the Martha baptised to John and Elizabeth in October 1711, and the two Elizabeth's partly on birth interval grounds, partly influenced by their mother's first name and additionally the second Elizabeth because the first had died (see Fig. 3).

However, such rationality (!) was shown to be demonstrably shaky by the will of the father who died in 1748 whose children were listed as Katherine (Reading) Martha (Mapleton) Penelope (Bowry) Ann (Bowry) and Elizabeth (Cox) whilst his wife was named as Katherine. Thus, Penelope and Elizabeth's transfers could be effected immediately. This automatically raised the problem of John's allocation since the interval between his baptism and Penelope's became a bare nine months. His baptism of course was that second one at which the father had been described as 'junior', but at the same time residing not at Lodge but in the Town. His transfer seemed inevitable and was appropriate also in the sense that both father and grandfather were called John and hence the father being described as 'junior' had some logicality.

Only two problem children then remained, Jonas and the first Elizabeth. It was decided to leave Jonas where he was since a birth interval between Penelope and Elizabeth of over seven years seemed too long as opposed to less than a year between him and Martha (baptised in 1711) and Elizabeth who died as an infant was also transferred to help fill the gap of over nine years now existing between the baptism of Jonas and the second Elizabeth, supposedly named after her dead sister. Incidentally, this also proved that, by accepting that the baptism description 'Mr' at Penelope's baptism had applied to the second of the John's to become a father, the wrong burial dates had been attributed to the two men (see Fig. 2).

Fortunately, the John who died in 1744 also left a will mentioning his wife Elizabeth, his son-in-law and grandson only. His other two children John and Martha, were omitted by virtue of having predeceased him, a condition also applying to Mary the daughter of John and Katherine and explaining her absence in the 1748 will. The result of this reconstruction is that two families of five and six children respectively became ones of three and eight, and all the errors emanated ostensibly from an inexplicable entry describing the first married John as 'junior', at the baptism of his first child. Ironically enough, after all the information had been pieced

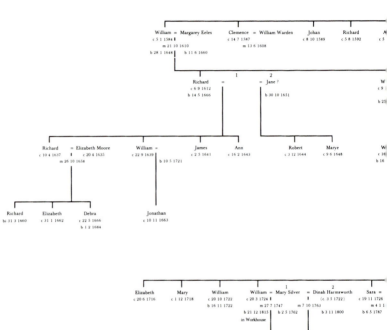

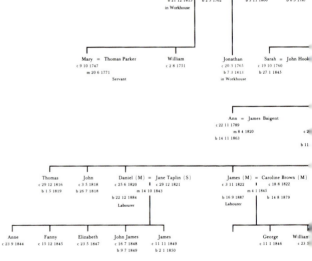

Richard LUINGTO[N]
b 16 5 1613

William = Margarey Eeles   Clemence = William Warden   Johan   Richard   A[...]
c 5 1 1584   c 14 7 1587   c 8 10 1589   c 5 8 1592   c 5
m 21 10 1610   m 13 6 1608
b 28 1 1648   b 11 6 1660

Richard =   = Jane ?   W
c 6 9 1612   b 30 10 1651   c 9
b 14 5 1666   b 25

Richard = Elizabeth Moore   William =   James   Ann   Robert   Marye   W
c 10 4 1637   c 20 4 1635   c 22 9 1639   c 2 5 1641   c 16 2 1643   c 3 12 1644   c 9 6 1648   c 18
m 26 10 1658   b 10 5 1721   b 16

Richard   Elizabeth   Debra   Jonathan
bi 31 3 1660   c 31 1 1662   c 22 5 1666   c 10 11 1663
b 1 2 1684

Elizabeth   Mary   William   William = Mary Silver   = Dinah Harmsworth   Sara =
c 20 6 1716   c 1 12 1718   c 20 10 1722   c 20 3 1724   (c 3 5 1722)   c 19 11 1726
b 16 11 1722   m 27 7 1747   m 7 10 1763   m 4 1 1
b 21 12 1815   b 2 5 1762   b 3 11 1800   b 6 5 1787
in Workhouse

Mary = Thomas Parker   William   Jonathan   Sarah = John Hook
c 9 10 1747   c 2 8 1751   c 20 3 1765   c 19 10 1760
m 20 6 1771   b 7 3 1813   b 27 1 1845
Servant   in Workhouse

Ann = James Baigent
c 22 11 1789   c 2
m 8 4 1820
b 14 11 1863   b 11

Thomas   John   Daniel (M) = Jane Taplin (S)   James (M) = Caroline Brown (M)
c 29 12 1816   c 3 5 1818   c 25 6 1820   c 29 12 1821   c 3 11 1822   c 18 8 1822
b 1 5 1819   b 26 7 1818   m 14 10 1843   m 4 1 1845
b 22 12 1884   b 16 9 1887   b 14 8 1879
Labourer   Labourer

Anne   Fanny   Elizabeth   John James   James   George   Willian
c 23 9 1844   c 15 12 1845   c 23 5 1847   c 16 7 1848   c 11 11 1849   c 11 1 1846   c 23 5
b 9 7 1849   b 2 1 1850

Dates in parentheses are estimated

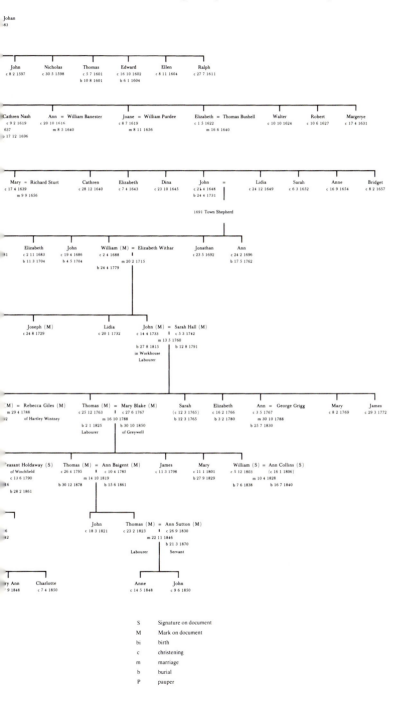

Johan
·83

John	Nicholas	Thomas	Edward	Ellen	Ralph
c 8 2 1597	c 30 5 1598	c 5 7 1601	c 16 10 1602	c 8 11 1604	c 27 7 1611
		b 10 8 1601	b 6 1 1604		

Cathren Nash	Ann = William Banester	Joane = William Purdee	Elizabeth = Thomas Bushell	Walter	Robert	Margerye
c 9 2 1619	c 20 10 1616	c 8 7 1619	c 1 5 1622	c 10 10 1624	c 10 6 1627	c 17 4 1631
637	m 8 5 1640	m 8 11 1656	m 16 6 1640			
b 17 12 1696						

Mary = Richard Sturt	Cathren	Elizabeth	Dina	John =	Lidia	Sarah	Anne	Bridget
c 17 4 1639	c 28 12 1640	c 7 4 1643	c 23 10 1645	c 2↓ 4 1648	c 24 12 1649	c 6 3 1652	c 16 9 1654	c 8 2 1657
m 9 9 1656				b 24 4 1731				

1691 Town Shepherd

Elizabeth	John	William (M) = Elizabeth Withar	Jonathan	Ann
c 2 11 1683	c 19 4 1686	c 2 4 1688	c 23 5 1692	c 24 2 1696
b 11 3 1704	b 4 5 1704	m 20 2 1715		b 17 5 1762
		b 24 4 1779		

Joseph (M)	Lidia	John (M) = Sarah Hall (M)
c 24 8 1729	c 20 1 1732	c 14 4 1733 c 5 3 1742
		m 13 5 1760
		b 27 8 1815 b 12 8 1791
		in Workhouse
		Labourer

(M) = Rebecca Giles (M)	Thomas (M) = Mary Blake (M)	Sarah	Elizabeth	Ann = George Grigg	Mary	James
m 29 4 1788	c 25 12 1763 c 27 6 1767	(c 12 3 1765)	c 16 2 1766	c 3 5 1767	c 8 2 1769	c 29 3 1772
·2 of Hartley Wintney	m 16 10 1788	b 12 3 1765	b 3 2 1780	m 30 10 1788		
	b 2 1 1825 b 30 10 1850			b 25 7 1830		
	Labourer of Greywell					

·easant Holdaway (S)	Thomas (M) = Ann Baigent (M)	James	Mary	William (S) = Ann Collins (S)
of Winchfield	c 26 4 1795 c 10 4 1785	c 11 3 1798	c 11 1 1801	c 5 12 1803 (c 16 1 1806)
c 13 6 1790	m 14 10 1819		b 27 9 1829	m 10 4 1828
46	b 30 12 1878 b 15 6 1861			b 7 6 1838 b 16 7 1840
b 28 2 1861				

John	Thomas (M) = Ann Sutton (M)
c 18 3 1821	c 23 2 1823 c 26 9 1830
	m 22 11 1846
	b 21 3 1870
Labourer	Servant

·ry Ann	Charlotte	Anne	John
9 1848	c 7 4 1850	c 14 5 1848	c 9 6 1850

S	Signature on document
M	Mark on document
bi	birth
c	christening
m	marriage
b	burial
P	pauper

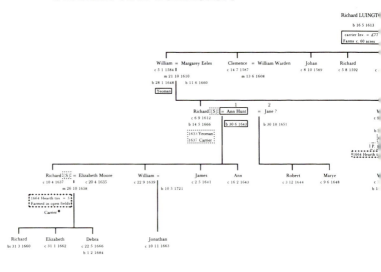

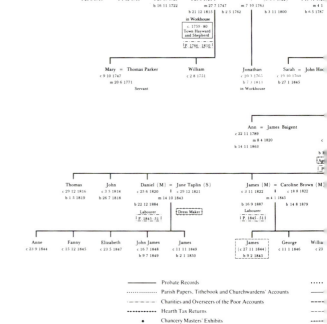

	Probate Records
....	Parish Papers, Tithebook and Churchwardens' Accounts
– – – – –	Charities and Overseers of the Poor Accounts
••••••••••••	Hearth Tax Returns
•	Chancery Masters' Exhibits

Dates in parentheses are estimated

han

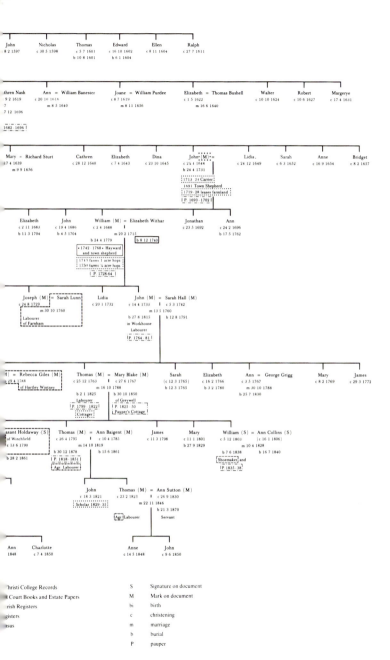

John
8 2 1597

Nicholas
c 30 5 1598

Thomas
c 5 7 1601
b 10 8 1601

Edward
c 16 10 1602
b 6 1 1604

Ellen
c 8 11 1604

Ralph
c 27 7 1611

thren Nash
9 2 1619
7
7 12 1696

Ann = William Banester
c 20 10 1616
m 8 5 1640

Joane = William Purdee
c 8 7 1619
m 8 11 1656

Elizabeth = Thomas Bushell
c 1 5 1622
m 16 6 1640

Walter
c 10 10 1624

Robert
c 10 6 1627

Margerye
c 17 4 1631

1682 1696

Mary = Richard Sturt
47 4 1639
m 9 9 1656

Cathren
c 28 12 1640

Elizabeth
c 7 4 1643

Dina
c 23 10 1645

John (M) =
c 21 4 1648
b 24 4 1731

Lidia,
c 24 12 1649

Sarah
c 6 3 1652

Anne
c 16 9 1654

Bridget
c 8 2 1657

1713 24 Carrier
1691 Town Shepherd
1719 28 leases farmland
P 1693 - 1702

Elizabeth
c 2 11 1683
b 11 3 1704

John
c 19 4 1686
b 4 5 1704

William (M) = Elizabeth Withar
c 2 4 1688
b 24 4 1779   m 20 2 1715

Jonathan
c 23 3 1692

Ann
c 24 2 1696
b 17 5 1762

b 8 12 1740

1742 - 1768 • Hayward
and town shepherd
1743 farms 1 acre hops
1759 farms ¼ acre hops
P 1728-64

Joseph (M) = Sarah Lunn
c 24 8 1729
m 30 10 1760
Labourer
of Farnham

Lidia
c 20 1 1732

John (M) = Sarah Hall (M)
c 14 4 1733   c 5 3 1742
m 13 5 1760
b 27 8 1815   b 12 8 1791
in Workhouse
Labourer
P 1764 81

1) = Rebecca Giles (M)
29 4 1788
of Hartley Wintney

Thomas (M) = Mary Blake (M)
c 25 12 1763   c 27 6 1767
m 16 10 1788
b 2 1 1825   b 30 10 1850
Labourer   of Greywell
P 1799 1822   P 1825 - 50
Cottager   Pauper's Cottage

Sarah
(c 12 3 1765)
b 12 3 1765

Elizabeth
c 16 2 1766
b 3 2 1780

Ann = George Grigg
c 3 5 1767
m 30 10 1788
b 25 7 1830

Mary
c 8 2 1769

James
c 29 3 1772

asant Holdaway (S)
of Winchfield
c 14 6 1790

b 28 2 1861

Thomas (M) = Ann Baigent (M)
c 26 4 1793   c 10 4 1785
m 14 10 1819
b 30 12 1878   b 15 6 1861
P 1818 - 1851
Agr Labourer

James
c 11 3 1798
b 27 9 1829

Mary
c 11 1 1801

William (S) = Ann Collins (S)
c 5 12 1803   (c 16 1 1806)
m 10 4 1828
b 7 6 1838   b 16 1 1840
Shoemaker and
P 1835 - 38

John
c 18 3 1821
Scholar 1829 35

Thomas (M) = Ann Sutton (M)
c 23 2 1823   c 26 9 1830
m 22 11 1846
b 21 3 1870
Agr Labourer   Servant

Ann
1848

Charlotte
c 7 4 1850

Anne
c 14 5 1848

John
c 9 6 1850

hristi College Records
Court Books and Estate Papers
rish Registers
gisters
sus

S   Signature on document
M   Mark on document
bi   birth
c   christening
m   marriage
b   burial
P   pauper

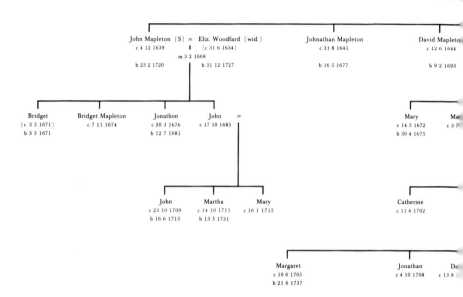

Jonathan MA

b 21 1 168

John Mapleton (S) = Eliz. Woodfard (wid.)	Johnathan Mapleton	David Mapleto
c 4 12 1639 (c 31 6 1634)	c 31 8 1641	c 12 6 1644
m 3 2 1668		
b 23 2 1720 b 31 12 1727	b 16 5 1677	b 9 2 1693

Bridget	Bridget Mapleton	Jonathon	John =	Mary	Ma
(c 3 5 1671)	c 7 11 1674	c 20 3 1676	c 17 10 1685	c 14 5 1672	c 3 7
b 3 5 1671		b 12 7 1681		b 30 4 1675	

John	Martha	Mary	Catherine
c 23 10 1709	c 14 10 1711	c 16 1 1715	c 11 6 1702
b 16 6 1713	b 13 5 1731		

Margaret	Jonathan	Da
c 10 6 1705	c 4 10 1708	c 13 9
b 21 6 1737		

Dates in parentheses are estimated

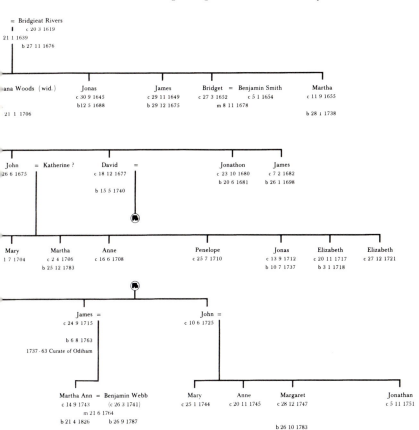

```
=  Bridgieat Rivers
I     c 20 3 1619
21 1 1639
      b 27 11 1676
```

```
ana Woods (wid.)    Jonas           James           Bridget  =  Benjamin Smith      Martha
                    c 30 9 1645     c 29 11 1649    c 27 3 1652    c 5 1 1654        c 11 9 1655
                    b12 5 1688      b 29 12 1675    m 8 11 1678
21 1 1706                                                                           b 28 1 1738
```

```
John  = Katherine ?      David      =              Jonathon         James
26 6 1675                c 18 12 1677               c 23 10 1680    c 7 2 1682
                                                    b 20 6 1681     b 26 1 1698
                         b 15 5 1740
```

```
Mary      Martha      Anne           Penelope          Jonas        Elizabeth      Elizabeth
1 7 1704  c 2 4 1706  c 16 6 1708    c 25 7 1710       c 13 9 1712   c 20 11 1717   c 27 12 1721
          b 25 12 1783                                 b 10 7 1737   b 3 1 1718
```

```
James =                    John =
c 24 9 1715                c 10 6 1725

b 6 8 1763
1737 - 63 Curate of Odiham
```

```
Martha Ann = Benjamin Webb        Mary         Anne          Margaret        Jonathan
c 14 9 1743    (c 26 3 1741)      c 25 1 1744  c 20 11 1745  c 28 12 1747    c 5 11 1751
           m 21 6 1764
b 21 4 1826    b 26 9 1787                                   b 26 10 1783
```

S	Signature on document
c	christening
m	marriage
b	burial
NW	North Warnborough

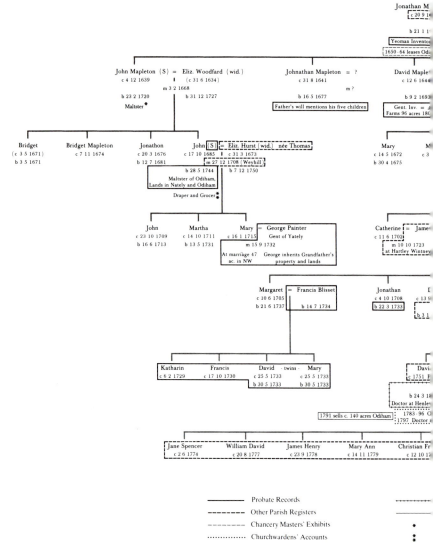

Probate Records

- - - - - - - - Other Parish Registers

- - - - - - - - Chancery Masters' Exhibits

. . . . Churchwardens' Accounts

Dates in parentheses are estimated

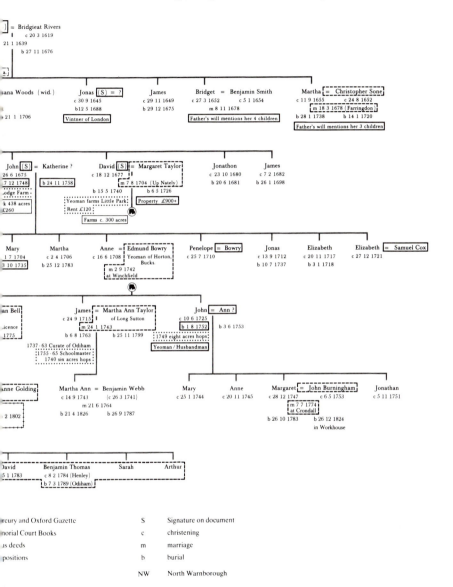

rcury and Oxford Gazette   S   Signature on document

norial Court Books   c   christening

us deeds   m   marriage

positions   b   burial

NW   North Warnborough

together, the marriage date of John and Katherine has remained unknown. Additionally, doubts about the dates of death of six adults with
the same first and surnames were resolved, thus expanding the information
about marital fertility, mortality and completed family size.

However, the totality of information about the two families provides
some interesting comparisons, apart from the obvious fact that evidence
about them comes from differing sources. First, 18 names additional to the
44 in the Odiham parish registers have been added to the Mapleton family
from registers in other parishes whereas only three (plus one from the civil
register) have been added to the 113 named Lewingtons in the Odiham
registers; 29 per cent as against 2.6 per cent. This evidence would seem to
imply that the wealthier were likely to be more mobile and had wider
marriage horizons than the poor, a conclusion strengthened by the fact
that the Mapletons arrived later in the parish than the Lewingtons and
had departed before the end of the period of study, whilst the Lewingtons
were still present in 1851.

Secondly, though both families commenced in apparently similar ways
as yeoman farmers, the Mapletons' agricultural activities were clearly on a
larger scale than those of the Lewingtons, and their subsequent history
diverged remarkably, the Mapletons retaining a middle class status and
moving into the professions – medicine and the clergy – and their lands
being apparently mainly leased out, whilst the Lewingtons, after Richard
the great grandson and heir of the first Richard (see Fig. 3) disappeared
from view, were continued by the younger grandson William's
descendants. William appears to have inherited at least part of the
carrying business run by his grandfather, but no land, and is seen to be in
straitened financial circumstances by his exemption from Hearth Tax from
1664 to his death. Every succeeding generation then appears to have been
in increasing difficulties and the ages at which they begin to receive
charity are a clear indication of the existence of a multi-generational
deepening poverty trap. William was 52 years old when he first received
relief in 1664, his son John 45 and his grandson William 40. The last two
Lewingtons to receive assistance were David and James both in 1845 and
they were then aged respectively 25 and 23!

Not all the factors which influenced the history of these two families are
known. For the Mapletons it is virtually certain that the property of
Jonathan's grandson John (maltster, clothier and landholder), would have
passed down to his only surviving child Mary and through her to the
Painter family since George Painter, the son inherited his grandfather's
property. This could help to explain why the professions became attractive
to the descendants of David Mapleton, particularly since David's elder
brother John had the largest family to inherit his wealth. It does appear
that for both families the continuation of the line through younger sons

had differing effects on the family fortunes. However, the Lewingtons clearly fared worse and this may be due to the fact that the average completed family size of the Mapletons was 5.3 children while that of the Lewingtons was (over the period up to 1772 when both families were simultaneously in Odiham) 8.0; and whilst seven of 37 (19%) of the Mapleton children died before the age of 15 only six of 57 (10.5%) of the Lewington's did. Thus, larger families with lower child mortality would certainly increase the strain on the family budget. Furthermore, when the ages at death of adults are calculated the Mapleton average was 48 and that of the Lewington's was 59.2, an increase of over 11 years.

The fertility or mortality of individual families like these could, of course, be affected by genetic factors, but if they prove typical then they demonstrate the curious paradox that the poor experienced not only higher fertility rates but also lower child mortality and a later age at death than their wealthier contemporaries in at least one community in pre-industrial England.

But increasingly it could not have been large families which caused their dependence because they arrived in poverty at ages too low for them to have had large numbers of children.[42] Certainly the first generation of Lewingtons to be recorded in poverty would seem to have had a family of nine children at home. But of the last eight Lewington conjugal families to receive relief one had four children, one three, one had two children, two had one and three had none when they first became dependent.

In many ways the Lewington's experience in particular is a microcosm of that affecting Odiham paupers in general. Despite contemporary views, such as those of Malthus,[43] who conveyed the impression that the poor were all able bodied with ever growing families, the reality at Odiham was substantially different. Throughout the whole 200 years, from 1650 to 1850, at least two-thirds of those becoming dependent did so when they had produced only three children or less (see Table 4.9) and in the last century, 1750–1850, over three-quarters had three children or less when first receiving relief. Not inconsiderable numbers began to need relief before the first child was born. However, the arrival of the first infant resulted in almost one-third having to seek relief between 1650 and 1750 and not quite a half between 1750 and 1850, a proportion which rose to nearly two-thirds in this latter century by the time two children had been born.

Clearly this evidence does not suggest that large families were the cause of poverty although many who became dependent did continue to have children. Thus, of those between 1800 and 1849 who had no children when first in receipt of relief although almost a quarter remained childless, perhaps because they were infertile couples, the other three-quarters had from one to fourteen children whilst still dependent on relief. Similarly, of those who became dependent on charity or overseers distributions when

No. of Children	1650-99			1700-49			1750-99			1800-49		
	No.	%	Cumul. %	No.	%	Cumul. %	No.	%	Cumul. %	No.	%	Cumul. %
0	15	22.7		5	13.9		22	16.9		44	23.2	
1	4	6.1	28.8	7	19.4	33.3	39	30.0	46.9	48	25.4	48.6
2	13	19.7	48.5	11	30.6	63.9	22	16.9	63.8	27	14.2	62.8
3	12	18.2	66.7	7	19.4	83.3	17	13.1	76.9	26	13.7	76.5
4	7	10.6	77.3	5	13.9	97.2	14	10.8	87.7	21	11.1	87.6
5	4	6.1	83.3	1	2.8	100	9	6.9	94.6	8	4.2	91.8
6	8	12.1	95.5	0			2	1.5	96.1	3	1.5	93.3
7	2	3.0	98.5	0			4	3.1	99.2	10	5.2	98.5
8	0			0			1	0.8	100	2	1.5	100
9	1	1.5	100	0			0			0		
TOTAL	66	100	100	36	100	100	130	100	100	189	100	100

Includes children under 15 only. Those 15 and over deemed to have left home or be contributing to family incomes.

Excludes widows.

Examples are from families where both date of marriage and date of death are known.

Table 4.9 Numbers of Children at First Receipt of Relief

they had only one child most continued to have further children, the largest family being of twelve in total. Of this group half had up to and including five children and half between six and twelve children demonstrating that, although substantial numbers of children were not the cause of poverty, many had large families subsequently. It would seem therefore, that what caused poverty was the loss of any casual or continuous earnings which a wife received, so that a couple had to survive on the husband's income alone. Hence two mouths had to be fed perpetually from one income. Once a child had arrived the position was worsened since three mouths were dependent on one income. Clearly for many, wages were so close to the margins of subsistence that any change in family circumstances such as the onset of pregnancy or the arrival of a baby was such that the probability of survival without resort to parish relief was impossible and, bearing in mind the increasingly younger age of dependency on relief, the situation must have deteriorated in the century 1750–1850.

This raises the question of the economic background of the paupers and some evidence has survived of their occupations.[44] In the first half century, 1650–99, of 47 paupers for whom occupational information has survived almost a third (32.0 per cent) were small farmers (husbandmen) and the majority of the remainder were small craftsmen such as weavers, sheremen, saddle-tree makers, tailors and shoemakers who made up nearly two-fifths of the total (38.3 per cent). Much smaller proportions were labourers (unspecified) or engaged in dealing, building and transport occupations (see Table. 4.10).

From 1700 to 1749 the information is too limited to make very useful comparisons. It does hint at a crisis in the building trades, perhaps because of the limited population growth of this and the previous half century which must have seen a downturn in the demand for new buildings for domestic purposes and it also suggests the continuing decline of small farmers and craftsmen.

Much more evidence becomes available in the second half of the eighteenth century and especially in the first half of the nineteenth. What the occupations reveal is that the economic structure of the community was changing. Dominating the paupers of the period 1750–99 was the labourer – over half of the occupationally identified paupers fell into this category. A few more small farmers (five) also sought relief. These would appear to be the last of their kind in Odiham since when the enclosure of the open fields and commons took place in 1791[45] not a single husbandman was listed. Nearly 1,600 acres were enclosed of which almost 1,200 went to absentee landlords. Only eight yeoman farmers resident in Odiham were named. Most of the agricultural land was leased to tenant farmers, hence it seems likely that many of the unspecified labourers were

	1650-99		1700-49		1750-99		1800-49	
	No.	%	No.	%	No.	%	No.	%
1. Agriculture	(17)	36.2	(3)	15.0	(22)	20.6	(82)	37.1
Ag.Lab.					5	4.7	81	36.7
Husbandman	15	32.0	2		5	4.7		
Yeoman					3			
Town Shepherd or Hayward	1		1		4			
Gardener	1				4		1	
Shepherd					1			
2. Industrial Service								
Labourer	5	10.6	3	15.0	56	52.3	90	40.7
3. Building	(3)	6.4	(7)	35.0	(4)	3.7	(14)	6.3
Bricklayer	1				4		7	
Carpenter	1		1				4	
Joiner			1					
Glazier							2	
Thatcher	1		3				1	
Brickmaker			2					
4. Manufacturer	(18)	38.3	(5)	25.0	(19)	17.8	(26)	11.8
Weaver	2						2	
Feltmaker	1							
Shereman	2							
Stocking frame w.k.					5		1	
Blacksmith			1				2	
Brasier	1							
Basket Maker							1	
Cooper	1				2			
Turner	1							
Saddle tree maker	2				1		1	
Sawyer			2		1		6	
Wheelwright							2	
Currier							1	
Tanner	1				1			
Breeches maker					1			
Shoemaker	3		2		4		7	
Tailor	2				1		3	
Hatter					1			
Miller					1			
Baker	1				1			
Upholsterer	1							

	1650-99		1700-49		1750-99		1800-49	
	No.	%	No.	%	No.	%	No.	%
5. <u>Transport</u>	(1)	2.1					(2)	0.9
Railway Lab							1	
Turnpike Rd Lab							1	
Carrier	1							
6. <u>Dealing</u>	(3)	6.4	(1)	5.0	(2)	1.9	(2)	0.9
Victualler					1			
Butcher	2		1				1	
Corn Chandler					1			
Grocer							1	
Higler	1							
7. <u>Public Service & Prof.</u>	-		(1)	5.0	-		(2)	0.9
Ale taster			1					
Post boy							1	
Soldier							1	
8. <u>Domestic Service</u>	-		-		(4)	3.7	(3)	1.4
Gamekeeper							1	
Servant					4		1	
Sweep							1	
TOTAL	47		20		107		221	

The occupational classifications are modified from those devised by W.A. Armstrong 'The Use of Information about Occupation' in E.A. Wrigley (ed) *Nineteenth Century Society: Essays in the Use of Quantitative Methods for the Study of Social Data.* (Cambridge, 1972), pp. 191–310.

Table 4.10 Occupations of Paupers

in practice landless agricultural ones employed by the tenant farmers. This view is supported by the higher proportion of specified agricultural labourers between 1800 and 1849. Most of these have been identified from the 1841 and 1851 census returns[46] which indicated whether a man was an agricultural labourer or not.

Thus, in this 200-year period, it seems that, in the first century, poverty was dominated by declining small farmers and craftsmen and in the second by increasing numbers of landless agricultural labourers. No indications of the earnings of small farmers and craftsmen have survived to demonstrate why some became paupers. Falling grain prices in England generally and Hampshire in particular[47] from the late 1660s certainly would have reduced incomes and caused small farmers economic difficulties. As for agricultural labourers, it is generally accepted that their incomes failed to keep pace with prices between the later seventeenth and mid-nineteenth centuries.

At Winchester, just over 20 miles south-west of Odiham (33 km) labourers' wages were 12d (5p) per day for the whole of the period from 1654 to 1710[48] and between 1690 and 1730 agricultural labourers' wages in the southern county of Sussex were also stated to be 12d[49] per day. Over a century ago, Thorold Rogers indicated that such wages would result in an annual income for labourers of between £14 and £15 based on earnings of 6s (30p) a week and accounting for holidays.[50] By the 1760s he agreed that wages had risen to 1s 2d per day or 7s (35p) a week and approximately £17 per annum.[51] This increase in money wages was accompanied by a downward drift of prices, thus ensuring an increase in real wages in the century between 1650 and 1750,[52] a factor perhaps reflected in the lower proportion identified in poverty in the period 1700–49.[53]

From the mid-eighteenth century to the mid-nineteenth, it is generally agreed, however, that agricultural labourers' wages, among many others, declined in real terms.[54] This decline was substantial. Snell indicates that agricultural labourers' money wages rose by about 50 per cent between 1741–5 and 1806–10 whilst average prices rose some 185 per cent.[55] It is no surprise, therefore, that large numbers of agricultural labourers were among those receiving relief in Odiham.

Married couples could often only have been surviving on the casual work of wives and thus the loss of a partner's earnings would have been sufficient to tip the balance to below the subsistence margin, especially since many labourers then had no land on which to grow food to sustain themselves particularly in the frequent bad harvest years of the Napoleonic-war period. Hence, both the changing rural economic and social structure as well as the adverse movement of real wages were instrumental in ensuring that increasing numbers of agricultural workers became dependent on relief in the later eighteenth and early nineteenth centuries.

The change from a rural peasantry to a rural proletariat was clearly one which was accompanied by increasing problems of poverty for many in southern England.

Notes

1 Figures derived from E.A. Wrigley and R.S. Schofield, *The Population History of England 1641–1871: A reconstruction*, p. 167.

2 *Ibid*. p. 168.

3 H.A. Gemeny, 'Emigration from the British Isles to the New World 1630–1700: inferences from colonial populations', *Research in Economic History*, v (1980), Table A5, p. 215.

4 Carew Reynel, 'The True English Interest', in J. Thirsk and J.P. Cooper, *Seventeenth Century Economic Documents*, p. 758.

5 Robin D. Gwynn, *Huguenot Heritage: The History and Contribution of the Huguenots in Britain*, (1985), p. 35.

6 Wrigley and Schofield, *op.cit.*, pp. 528–9.

7 *Ibid*.

8 *Ibid.*, and Barry Stapleton, 'Age Structure in the Early Eighteenth Century', *Local Population Studies*, 34, (1985), pp. 27–34.

9 E.A. Wrigley, 'A Simple Model of London's Importance in Changing English Society and Economy 1650–1750', *Past and Present*, 37, (1967), pp. 44–70.

10 The population figure for the late seventeenth century is estimated from the Compton Census of 1676, William Salt Library, Stafford, M S Salt 33, and also the Hearth Tax of 1665, PRO Exchequer K R Lay Subsidy Rolls, E179/176/565; for 1811, PRO C2/49 and 1841, PRO HO/107/395.

11 H.R.O. 47M81/PR1–12; 16–17; 19–20.

12 P.R.O. RG 4/723.

13 T.H. Hollingsworth, 'Historical Studies of Migration', *Annales de Demographie Historique*, (1970), pp. 92–3. A more detailed analysis of Odiham's migration patterns can be found in Barry Stapleton, 'Migration in Pre-Industrial Southern England: The Example of Odiham', *Southern History*, Vol. 10 (1988), pp. 47–93.

14 R.S. Schofield, 'Age-Specific Mobility in an Eighteenth Century English Parish', *Annales de Demographie Historique*, (1970), pp. 261–74 and P. Clark, 'The Migrant in Kentish Towns 1580–1640' in (eds.) P. Clark and P. Slack, *Crisis and Order in English Towns 1500–1700*, (1972), pp. 117–63.

15 26 Geo. II, c33 (1753).

16 It is also possible that with the need to be wed in the presence of a Justice of the Peace the market town of Odiham happened to be where such a man was available locally, thus couples came from neighbouring communities to be married there. See Dorothy McLaren, 'The Marriage Act of 1653: Its influence on the Parish Registers', *Population Studies*, 28, No 2, (1974), pp. 319–27. I am grateful to Dr Joan Thirsk for reminding me of this article.

17 P. Laslett, *Family Life and Illicit Love in Earlier Generations*, (1977), pp. 50–101 and Ann Kussmaul, *Servants in Husbandry in Early Modern England*, (1981), pp. 46–69.

18 Additionally, some brides went to the parish of residence of their respective mothers for the latter days of their confinement and consequently had children baptised in a parish away from that of their residence. This would have reduced still further the proportion of pregnant brides. Similarly, since baptism was delayed in some cases, the gap between marriage and baptism was extended resulting in a further potential loss of pregnant brides.

19 It is possible that these figures overstate the level of pre-nuptial pregnancy since those brides who remained infertile or who had no children would be omitted from this calculation.

20 Laslett, *The World We Have Lost*, (2nd edn.), (1971), p. 148.

21 The transcriptions of the Corfe Castle and Hawkchurch registers are in the Dorset Record Office, Dorchester. I am grateful to Simon Collins-Dryer for providing me with his collected data.

22 Laslett, *op. cit.*, p. 148.

23 P.E.H. Hair, 'Bridal Pregnancy in Rural England in Earlier Centuries', *Population Studies*, 20, (1966), pp. 233–43 and 'Bridal Pregnancy in Earlier Rural England further examined', *Population Studies*, 24, (1970), pp. 59–70.

24 *The Christen State of Matrimony*, 1543, p. 43b, quoted in John Brand *Observations on Popular Antiquities*, 2 vols., (1813), Vol. II, p. 20.

25 Laslett, *op. cit.*, pp. 147–54, and 3rd edn., (1983), pp. 168–73.

26 J. Smeaton, *A narrative of the building and a description of the construction of the Edystone Lighthouse with stone*, 1791, Book II, p. 65n.

27 However, see Laslett, *Family Life*, pp. 146–7, for the view that urban, and especially London, illegitimacy ratios were low.

28 For these views see Laslett, *World We Have Lost*, (2nd edn.), pp. 3–4; 17–19. K. Wrightson, *English Society 1580– 1680*, (1982), pp. 57–65 and R.W. Malcolmson, *Life and Labour in England 1700–1780*, (1981), pp. 151–2.

29 Because of intermarriage on Portland it is not possible to undertake a family reconstitution of the population which could have revealed some evidence of the age at marriage.

30 Portland Parish Registers were analysed in the chuch at Easton. They are now at the D.R.O., PE/PTD RE 1/1–3.

31 Perhaps the lack of a reputed father's name in the two cases in 1744 is indicative of the occasions when London men were responsible for the pregnancies.

32 D.R.O./PE/PTD RE 1/3.

33 Laslett, *Family Life*, pp. 102–59, and Peter Laslett, Karla Oosterveen and Richard M. Smith, *Bastardy and its Comparative History*, (1980), pp. 1–65 and 86–140.

34 Laslett, *Family Life*, pp. 133–48.

35 *Ibid.* pp. 146–8.

36 I am most grateful to the Registrar General for granting access to the civil registers, and the Superintendent Registrar at Aldershot for providing facilities for their analysis.

37 Peter Laslett and Karla Oosterveen, 'Long-term trends in Bastardy in England', *Population Studies*, 27, (1973), p. 256.

38 E.A. Wrigley and R.S. Schofield, 'English Population History from Family Reconstitution, Summary Results 1600–1799', *Population Studies*, 37, (1983), pp. 157–84.

39 T.H. Hollingsworth, 'A Demographic Study of the British Ducal Families', *Population Studies*, 11, (1957), pp. 4–26, and 'The Demography of the British Peerage, supplement to *Population Studies*, 18, (1964).

40 See E.A. Wrigley (ed.), *An Introduction to English Historical Demography*, (1966), pp. 96–159, for exploitation of English parish registers for family reconstitution purposes.

41 For the complete list of sources used in the family reconstitution of Odiham see B. Stapleton, 'Sources for the Demographic Study of a Local Community from the Sixteenth to the mid-Nineteenth Century', *The Journal of Regional and Local Studies* 4, (1984), pp. 1–26.

42 Information about recipients of charitable relief in Odiham has been obtained from the accounts of three charities, those of Frances Clarke, widow (founded 1609), Lady Elizabeth Gurney (founded 1638), and Henry Smith (founded 1641). The sources survive from 1654 in the Odiham Churchwarden's Account Books, and have been used to estimate poverty levels. The Account Books are now in the Hampshire Record Office H.R.O. 47m 81/PW 1–2 and 60–1, 4 vols.

43 T.R. Malthus, *An Essay on the Principle of Population*, Royal Economic Society Facsimile of the 1798 edn., (1926), pp. 72–3 for example.

44 Occupational information was gleaned from a wide range of sources. For the full list see Stapleton, 'Sources', *The Journal of Regional and Local Studies*, Vol. 4, 1984, pp. 1–26.

45 H.R.O. Odiham Enclosure Award, 1791.

46 P.R.O. H.O./107/395 Census of G.B. 1841 and H.O./107/1681 Census of G.B. 1851.

47 See B.R. Mitchell and P. Deane, *Abstract of British Historical Statistics*, (Cambridge 1962), pp. 486–7 for Winchester prices and J. Thirsk (ed.), *The Agrarian History of England and Wales*, Vol. V, II, 1640–1750, (Cambridge, 1985), p. 6 for English prices.

48 London School of Economics and Political Science, Beveridge Collection W.5. I am most grateful to the Trustees for allowing me access to the collection.

49 Thirsk, *Agrarian History*, Vol. V, II, p. 877.

50 J.E. Thorold Rogers, *Six Centuries of Work and Wages*, revised edn., (1886), pp. 397–8.

51 *Ibid.* p. 404.

52 See Thirsk, *Agrarian History*, Vol. IV, p. 4 for indication that labourers' real wages rose by about 11 per cent between 1640 and 1750.

53 This lower proportion is to some extent a result also of less satisfactory surviving sources in Odiham since for some years names of recipients of relief were not given.

54 See, for example, K.D.M. Snell, *Annals of the Labouring Poor*, (Cambridge 1985), pp. 23–49 and especially p. 34; Henry Phelps Brown and Sheila V. Hopkins, 'Seven Centuries of the Prices of Consumables compared with Builders' Wage-rates', originally published in *Economica*, 23, (1956), p. 92, and reprinted in Phelps Brown and Hopkins, *A Perspective on Prices and Wages*, (1981), pp. 12–59; and Thorold Rogers, *Six Centuries*, pp. 479–89, 510–11.

55 Snell, *Annals*, p. 34 and Phelps Brown and Hopkins, *Seven Centuries*, p. 30.

5

Labour Consciousness and Industrial Conflict in Eighteenth-Century Exeter

University of Southampton

To historians wishing to describe eighteenth-century England in terms of a "classless hierarchy", certain actions and attitudes of manufacturing workers present some difficulties. Professor Perkin, for example, admits that, "class feeling was nearer to the surface in industrial relations" than it was in other social and political relationships. Although capitalism in the sense of production for the market by wage earners employed by capitalists was "as old as the old society", there had been an increasing proletarianisation:

> the worker became a proletarian working for a capitalist. Since men do not have to be taught where their economic interest lies, mutually hostile combinations frequently resulted.[1]

Perkin accepts that workers combining into local trade clubs provide the "ultimate roots of the modern working class movement", but insists that "the roots are not the thing itself". Occasional resentment produced "local, sporadic, temporary combinations", while in between times "the workers' organisation, if it survived at all, relapsed into a cross between drinking club and friendly society, often frequented by independent craftsmen and small masters, which was the average trade club". More widespread and permanent trade unionism such as among the felt hatters, the London tailors, the Spitalfields silk weavers, the West of England clothworkers, or the framework knitters of the East Midlands, proved the rule, for they existed often with the recognition or connivance of the law to uphold the paternal system of industrial regulation. Professor Perkin considers the passing of the Combination Acts of 1799 and 1800 as "a step in the direction of class industrial relations", although even they came about as an "afterthought" prompted by William Wilberforce when a bill specific to combinations of millwrights was passing through. As such, he sees the Combination Acts as "only the last of some 40 acts for particular industries or localities". In fact there were very many fewer specific acts.

Perkin is repeating a common misunderstanding here, but his view is true to a long-standing orthodoxy deriving from Dorothy George which has played down the significance of the Combination Acts and which has only just begun to be revised.[2]

In a perceptive survey R.J. Morris has questioned the description of the eighteenth century as "classless", pointing to the widespread existence of workers' combinations and of strike activity in the many industries where labour and capital had become distinct, he concludes that although the evidence is fragmentary, it is enough to leave a question mark against the "classlessness" of the eighteenth century.[3] Edward Thompson's influential patrician/plebeian model of eighteenth-century social relations seems to pay little attention to the urban journeymen and he is content to accept the argument that artisans "evinced the 'vertical' consciousness of the 'Trade' (rather than the 'horizontal' consciousness of a mature industrial working class").[4] But need the consciousness of many groups of journeymen be described in either way? Evidently they could not have had the "mature" consciousness which came with those workers formed by industrial capitalism, but neither can they be conveniently placed as a group only evincing a "vertical" consciousness. After all, whatever was true of the lower orders generally, for many artisans the characteristic form of conflict was the industrial dispute with their employers.

Until recently historians had seriously underestimated the occurrence of industrial disputes in the eighteenth century. Where they once talked of dozens, they now must accept hundreds. Robert Malcolmson's social history is perhaps the first general survey to recognise this: "It appears however, that industrial conflicts were much more widespread than has sometimes been allowed". Even so Malcolmson is still content to place such disputes very largely within a traditional, paternalist framework of popular rights:

> of the right to a basic subsistence; of the right to have their interests considered and taken account of by the established authorities; of the right to resist the "arbitrary will of employers".[5]

In his generally excellent book, Malcolmson does not really consider the "aggressive" strike nor the use of collective strength to improve conditions or advance wages, rather than simply to resist the impositions of employers. Yet both kinds of combination clearly existed, we have the strong testimony of Adam Smith for that,[6] and as historians pay increasing attention to early trade unionism, it is no longer safe to assume that "most" eighteenth-century labour disputes were of one kind rather than the other.[7] This study examines three different disputes in eighteenth-century

Exeter in an attempt to identify appropriate ways of describing the consciousness of urban journeymen.

The Shipwrights in 1766

At Topsham, the point of the salt-water reach on the Exe, ship-building on a small scale took place utilising some of the Scandinavian and Baltic imports which came through the port. In 1766, a year of high prices, the master shipwrights of the port were attempting to force wage-cuts and deteriorating conditions of work on their journeymen. This attempt led to an agreement among some of the latter, not to accept work from any master on the new worsened terms. Eleven of them signed a remarkably formal document to this effect. They bound, under default of "twenty pounds of lawful British money", not only themselves but their "Heirs, Ex[ecut]ors and Administrators and Assignees" to an agreement which was to last "for so long a time as any three of us shall be living and capable of working and labouring as a Journeymen Shipwright".[8]

Two grievances were clearly set out in the preamble: reduction of wages, and lengthening of hours, while a third – curtailing of beer allowances – appeared later. The formal legal appearance of the document reinforced a language redolent with phrases of "rights", and "privileges" confirmed by timeless custom and observance. The masters were seeking to deprive the journeymen of their "Ancient Rights and Privledges (sic)" by reducing wages which had been "from time immemorially paid" and by imposing "new burthens" in lengthening the working-day beyond what had been "usual and customary for Journeymen Shipwrights to work and labour". The journeymen bound themselves to accept no work for less than the "full sum" of 2s 6d a day, "being the usual and accustomed wages". Nor were they to accept any less than "the usual allowance" of liquor. So far as hours were concerned they would work no longer than 6 a.m. to 6.15 p.m. in the summer, with half an hour for breakfast and an hour for dinner. In the winter months (November to 1 March) the same hours except for a dinner break shortened by fifteen minutes. (As the agreement was drawn up in December, when the masters would have had little scope to extend the day, it may well have been the meal breaks which were at issue.)

Why did the master-shipwrights seek to lower wages in 1766? That was, after all, a year in which resistance might have been especially expected. In their preamble, the journeymen claimed that the reduction would bring them to "the greatest distress" and render them "totally unable to provide for themselves and families". On their "usual" wages which probably averaged out at 12s 6d to 15s a week, they would have been well enough off at most times, but 1766 was a year of exceptionally high food prices.

Wheat prices had been rising steadily since 1762 when the Exeter price had been 29.92s the Winchester quarter. By 1765 it had reached 40.17s, and then leapt to 50.23s in 1766. The price was then at the level it had reached in 1756, following which the City's first recorded eighteenth-century food riot had taken place. Not surprisingly food riots again broke out in Exeter and its district in 1766. One incident took place at Topsham, where the shipwrights lived and worked, only a matter of weeks before the agreement was signed, when a corn cargo was seized and sold at low prices by a crowd who had marched out from Exeter. Wage cuts were being attempted at a time when even level earnings would have meant a substantial fall in living standards.[9]

The employers were probably seeking advantage from a slackening in the labour market after the ending of the Seven Years War. Small scale ship-building on the Exe was not directly affected, but the shipwright establishment at Plymouth Naval Dockyard was being reduced from its peak in 1763 when it had reached more than 600, and there can have been no shortage of skilled men in south Devon.[10]

There is no difficulty in fitting the skilled-worker consciousness revealed in the Agreement into well-established models which stress defensive and, more specifically, reactive attitudes. It is "labour consciousness" of a sort, for its perception of a separation of interest is clear, but its theme is betrayal: the breaking by the masters of the time-honoured customs of the trade. The document, if exceptional, is so for its form rather than its content.

The Woolsorters in 1787

Twenty years later a well-documented dispute in Exeter between the journeymen woolsorters and their employers would seem to reveal a different form of consciousness which was neither defensive nor reactive. At the beginning of February 1787 a woolstapler was approached by one of the three journeymen woolsorters in his employ. Times, he was told, were so hard that the journeymen could not support their families on their wage of 9s a week and unless it was increased to 10s 6d, they would leave his service at the end of the week. This they accordingly did on the next Saturday when their demand was refused. At the beginning of the following week the four journeymen employed by another woolstapler came into his counting house, asked for a rise to 10s 6d and left immediately on his refusal. The same evening seven journeymen quit the service of a third employer. The three masters straightaway laid information of illegal combination against the fourteen journeymen, who, they said, were members of a club and had "entered into Combination with others for the purpose of raising their wages". Warrants were issued and within twenty-four hours ten of the fourteen had been taken to either the Southgate or the Bridewell and committed for one month by the summary jurisdiction of the magistrates under the 1727 statute prohibiting combinations of woollen workers.[11]

Within a week they were freed. They had solicited their employers to intercede and this they had done under condition that the journeymen publish an apology recognising the illegality of their action, as "a warning to others of the same business" and that they return to work at the old wages until at least mid-summer. The whole dispute, then, lasted only a week, and seemed to involve only fourteen journeymen. However, because depositions were taken and survive along with other documents on the dispute, it is possible to understand the background to the event in unusual detail. The woolsorters were indeed members of a "club". They were among the forty members of the "Union Society": their name for the Exeter branch of the Woolstaplers Society which had been established in London, two years earlier in 1785 and had 478 members over England. (It seems that woolsorters at times called themselves "journeymen wool-staplers".) The formation of the national club may well have been a formalisation of previously looser tramping arrangements, for this was the purpose for which funds were claimed to have been formed. Certainly the establishment seems to have given a measure of confidence to the Exeter men, for one boasted to a reluctant joiner, that he had better stick to his present employer, for the Union could "prevent his being employed in this City, or in any part of the kingdom by sending letters to all the Towns in England where the woolsorting business is carried on". It seems, however, most likely that the City's forty members had been meeting in the Blue Boar's Head Tavern for some years before the establishment of the national society, for not only is it clear that they had long controlled entry to the trade, but they had also won wage increases since 1764, when they had been paid 6s a week plus a shilling for taking home wool to cut off the pitch marks. In 1765 wages rose to 7s basic plus the shilling, followed by 8s (plus the shilling) in 1768–9 and a basic 9s in 1770 for work carried out on their employers' premises, being no longer required to earn the last shilling by taking work home. This steady increase of wages was quite against the trend for the City's workers, who, especially the weavers, had been suffering falling wages from the middle of the eighteenth century. It had been "won" by the journeymen, for the leading employer referred to the men as having "advanced their wages" in 1765 and stated that in 1768 the men "were dissatisfied and rose their wages" and in 1770 "again advanced their wages".

The printed regulations issued in 1785 did not initiate the woolsorters' control over apprenticeship which was the basis of their exceptional wage bargaining success. According to one society member, it existed "for the purpose of regulating the trade". No member would work for any master who "shall take an apprentice or journeyman contrary to their will, or secret rules". In particular they intended to keep out woolcombers, who in many cases worked for the same employers, and whose knowledge of raw wool would have been a basis for easy adaption to a trade where wages were comparable, but where hours were considerably shorter. The structure of the trade was that a population of around fifty journeymen were divided among perhaps eight or nine employers on whose premises they worked, performing an essential role in the preparatory stages of the serge manufacture. Were they in the real sense skilled? They do not seem to have had any rhetoric of skill or "mystery", but the ability to judge, select and match different wools was certainly one which needed experience and knowledge. In pointing out that in Gloucester women were employed as sorters at only 4s a week, one of the employers does not seem to have been denying the required abilities, but emphasising that the work was "easy" in the sense of requiring no wage-compensation for hard physical labour.

For some time before February 1787, the journeymen had been preparing to make a wage demand for 10s 6d a week, an increase of almost 20%. A woolsorter who did not join the Society, deposed that he had been pressured to do so for two months before the turn-out, but had refused, "apprehending the true meaning of [?] association was to form some plan against the interest of their masters" and that "they probably would raise their wages or refuse to work on some frivolous pretence". The forty members paid 1d a week "towards the support of the travelling labourers, only in the same trade", but were in fact building up a strike fund which they judged, at the beginning of 1787 when it had reached £8.00, to be sufficient "for maintaining the turn-outs". At 40d a week it would have taken almost a year to raise this sum, assuming there had been no calls upon it for tramping or other expenses. It would seem that the journeymen had been building up their strike fund from the founding of the national society in 1785.

One sorter, trying to persuade a colleague to support the "turn-out", responded, when asked how he would live, that "the Club would engage to pay him 10s 6d for this week", and that he "would have wages from the Club until he was again employed". Clearly £8.00 would not have supported a full turn-out of forty men for very long, and it seems small wonder that the journeymen had nicknamed their fund "the loaves and fishes"! In fact the Union Club was neither intending to bring out all its members at one time, nor expecting to have to stay out for long. Professor W.G. Hoskins, in a brief account of the dispute, notes that only "about a dozen" sorters struck (in fact, it was precisely fourteen) and asserts on this basis that "Most apparently refused to come out on strike" and labels the fourteen "militant".[12] Reading the documents with a little understanding suggests a very different explanation. The turn-outs were to follow the strategy, well known in several trades by the late eighteenth century, of the "rolling strike". Only three shops were intended to turn-out at the beginning:

> This informant having heard several shops had turned out on account of the Club asked . . . what shop was to turn out next, to which he replied it is not as yet determined by them, meaning as he understood by the Club. . . .[13]

The strategy also involved the choice of moment. "If they persevered a fortnight . . . the Masters would be obliged to comply with their Demands, and that now was the time to turn out and get their price." The arrested men had stated to the justices that they had thought the "large stocks of wool on hand *would insure* them their demand". In their retrospective assessment of the course of events, the employers also referred to them as taking place in February last "when the Masters had great quantities of wool on their hands to be sorted".

The journeymen had been confident of success: they had the funds, the support and the moment. They further must have had among their number those with happy memories of the masters' giving in to wage demands on earlier occasions. They seem to have been taken totally by surprise when their employers resorted so promptly to the law – which indeed they could have done when faced by the earlier demands. Why did they do so in 1787? As we shall see their later inclination was to agree to pay almost as much as the men demanded. Among the requests for legal opinion, depositions, notices etc. which make up the documentation, there was no expression of hostility or even bitterness from either side. It seems to have been the case that the employers were concerned with the appearance of what they considered a tighter and deeper form of union among their employees. This is suggested by their insertion of an advertisement into the same issue of the *Exeter Flying Post*, which carried the journeymen's apology, offering constant employment to any journey-men woolsorters, "provided they do not belong to or are members of any Combination, Society or Club".[14] A month after the dispute they met and issued a sheet of printed resolutions. They had met they said because of "some *recent* combinations among their workmen" (their stress), and were unanimously agreed that "Combinations among Labourers may be very prejudicial to them and also to the Masters". They instanced a fine of 5s imposed for violation of a Union Bye-Law as an example of an illegal act, as well as their "very reprehensible conduct" in unlawfully directing woolsorters to leave the service of a master who took an apprentice "prohibited in their System of Club-Laws". This long-standing point of contention was emphasised in their specific assertion of the right to bind someone who had served his time as a woolcomber. If faced by combination in future, then the employers pledged themselves to mutual assistance.

At this meeting they also bound themselves not to pay more than the old wage of 9s a week, but that was evidently not their major concern. For among the papers is a letter from the leading employer seeking legal opinion on securing a regulation of wages from the City's justices at the next sessions. They intended to offer at the court a wage of 10s a week throughout the year, without any increase in hours. They wanted the regulation "in order to prevent the like Combinations of the Journeymen Woolsorters in future". Legal opinion was that a rate could be set under the powers of 5 Elizabeth extended by 1 James c.6. and that the application could hope for success if someone experienced in the trade testified "that the price of labour has increased near fifty per cent within these twenty years without sufficient cause".[15]

A motion for a wage table for the woolsorters was put at the mid-April Sessions, the employers' counsel arguing that such a regulation was needed "to preserve the peace and commerce of the nation". The discussion was adjourned until 30 April and then again until 19 May, but no record of its implementation exists.[16]

How can the consciousness of the journeymen woolsorters be described? The masters do not appear to have made any attempt to reduce wages, increase hours or otherwise worsen the conditions of labour. Indeed in the cited utterances of the striking journeymen there is no note of recrimination against either employers in general or any particular employer. It seems evident that we cannot place the consciousness evidenced in 1787 alongside that of the journeymen shipwrights in 1766 for it was neither defensive nor reactive. One of the striking journeymen had asserted that "sooner than work for 9s a week he would go home to the workhouse", while others had complained that "times were hard". Was the attempt then, one at increasing wages in the face of a rising cost of living? If so, then it was not a short-term response to a recent price-rise. The turn-outs had begun early in 1787 whereas the price of wheat in Exeter in 1786 had been at 42.5s the quarter the lowest of the decade, lower than the 44.85s of 1770 when the sorters had secured their last advance. Real wages seem to have suffered a little from 1780 to 1782 for wheat had been at its lowest in a thirty-year period in 1778 and 1779 and had then risen by a third to 1780, futher increasing over the two following years to a peak of 52.9s in 1782, higher even than in the food-riot year of 1766. From that peak prices came slowly, but steadily down to 1786. Had the journeymen then received the extra 1s 6d in 1787, it would have seemed a genuine increase in their standard of living.[17]

Adam Smith accepted the disposition of workmen to "combine in order to raise . . . the wages of labour". In his account he begins by describing *defensive* combinations, but continues:

> workmen . . . sometimes . . . without any provocation . . . combine of their own accord to raise the price of their labour. Their usual pretences are, sometimes the high price of provisions; sometimes the great profit which their masters make by their work.

The generally pessimistic tone of this passage in *The Wealth of Nations*, is qualified to an extent elsewhere in that work:

> Half-a-dozen woolcombers, perhaps are necessary to keep a thousand spinners and weavers at work. By combining not to take apprentices they can not only engross the employment, but reduce the whole manufacture into a sort of slavery to themselves and raise the price of their labour much above what is due to the nature of their work.[18]

The local irony of 1787 is that there existed a tightly organised group of journeymen who occupied a strategic position in the chain of serge production, prior even to that of the woolcombers (whom they particularly excluded from their trade), whose conditions of employment they bettered. There seems little doubt that this was achieved through "Union" – the locally preferred word to "Society". How can we describe the woolsorters' form of labour consciousness, for it was clearly that, other than as "a trade union consciousness"? Indeed in Adam Smith's usage it must be defined as an *offensive* trade union consciousness.

Weavers and Combers in 1726

Events in Exeter, Taunton, Tiverton and other towns engaged in the serge manufacture which came to a head in early 1726 (late 1725 O/S) are much better known, even if a failure to separate them adequately from events in the woollen cloth districts of the west country has produced a degree of misunderstanding. Failing to note that the petitions, since 1707, and the evidence collected by the Commons committee which led to the Act of 1726 prohibiting combinations among woollen workers and containing the important wage-fixing clause, all came from Devonshire and the adjacent parts of Somerset, Cole and Filson wrote of ephemeral combinations of "country weavers" which were "unlike" the local trade clubs of artisans and accordingly unable to maintain a continuous existence i.e. less like proper trade unions.[19] They were wrong. The organisation of weavers and combers in the serge towns *was* based on well-established trade clubs, and the evidence for continuous existence is indisputable. In 1707 the weavers at Taunton were reported to have a club with "a common Seal, tipstaff and Colours, which they displayed at Pleasure and meet as often as they think fit, at their Club-house, being an Inn at Taunton". At Tiverton the combers were organised at least as early as 1700. Petitions to Parliament reveal that by 1717 clubs of weavers and combers were an established matter of concern at Exeter, Taunton, Tiverton and Bradninch, and their activities produced the Proclamation of 1718 against "unlawful Clubs, Combinations etc" (later "lawless") among combers and weavers, who:

> illegally presumed to use a Common Seal, and to act as Bodies Corporate, by making and unlawfully conspiring to execute certain Byelaws or Orders, whereby they pretend to determine who had a right to the Trade, what and how many Apprentices and Journeymen each man should keep at once, together with the prices of all their Manufacturers, and the manner and materials of which they should be wrought.

Journeymen who were out of work because their masters had refused their demands were supported by the clubs. Riots had occurred with serges being cut from looms, houses broken into and prisoners set free. Although the Proclamation refers to the problem as existing "in several parts of the Kingdom", it especially picks out Devon and Somerset. Petitions to Parliament in 1726 from Exeter, Tiverton, Bristol and Taunton repeat the allegations of 1717. That from Taunton describes the clubs as having existed "for some years past" and, significantly, as having "assumed a power to raise their wages". That from Exeter states that both wool combers and weavers had "refused to work".[20]

In fact although there was a grievance expressed from Taunton about masters paying in truck,[21] the events of 1725–6 in the south-west were not really defensive or reactive: they were an attempt at employing both union and crowd action to advance wages. The basic approach was to make a wage demand, and if it were refused to turn-out, no weaver or comber taking the places of those who thus struck. Workers who accepted work on the old terms were intimidated: one at Taunton was "carried upon a Coolstaff because he fetched Mr Myner's work contrary to the orders of the Club". Indeed, over the last months of 1725 and the early ones of 1726 crowd theatre was much in evidence in the streets of Exeter and the other serge towns. At Crediton a mob, headed by a "Captain", threatened masters if they refused to advance wages, and paraded the town carrying aloft a piece of serge cut from the loom of one of the refusing masters. At Callington a master-weaver was cool-staffed, and others threatened with the same. At Taunton the town clerk attempting to read the riot act was treated to the ritual indignity of having his wig removed and dirt put upon his head. One employer at Exeter agreed to increase his weavers' wages although, he insisted, they had been willing to continue working at the old rates, "the Club threatened if they did so to pull them out of the house, and coolstaff them".[22]

"Pull them out of the house": the phrase is significant. The weaving of serges was not organised under a putting-out system. The master weavers employed journeymen on their premises, but there was nevertheless little prospect for most journeymen of becoming masters themselves. The employment structure in other words much more resembled that of, say, the London tailoring trade, than that of the proto-industrial rural textile manufactures. Merchant capital in the Exeter district, except at Tiverton, kept aloof from the manufacturing processes. The master weavers were best described as prosperous upper-middling men. They were organised at Exeter into the Company of Weavers, Fullers and Shearmen incorporated in 1490 which still managed to exercise a considerable degree of control over the serge manufacture throughout the eighteenth century. The master weavers became a hereditary caste for the capital requirements of the manufacture were high enough to freeze mobility, but not so high as to define the master weavers in the same terms as the "gentlemen clothiers" of Gloucestershire. Indeed "clothier" was not a label in common use in the serge districts because of the separation of merchant and manufacturing capital. When we read of rioting journeymen coolstaffing a master, we know we are in a different world of industrial and social relations than those which characterised the woollen broad cloth districts. It is hard to imagine the great clothiers of the western counties, men who sometimes did not even know the number of weavers to whom their wool was put out, being the subjects of such an *overt* infliction of indignity, although they might well have received letters like those sent to the master weavers which threatened to "burn their houses, kill their horses, and cut down and deface their orchards".[23]

Clearly numbers involved, and the crowd at Taunton was said to have numbered about a thousand, are the most evident difference between the incidents of 1725–6, the shipwrights dispute of 1766 and the woolsorters of 1787. But we should not blind ourselves to similarities. As in the case of the woolsorters, turn-outs were to take place when wage demands were refused and those who turned out were to be supported from the funds of a union which long pre-existed the dispute. Further timing was planned: "they generally begin in the Spring, when there is the greatest demand for goods, and most plenty of work". There was no talk of *defending* ancient rights and privileges against attack from employers, although the legitimacy conveying power of ensigns, flags and seals strongly suggest a degree of continuity with guild traditions. The petition from the weavers of *Wiltshire and Somerset* of 1718 in which they described themselves as "poor" and "distressed" and complained of an "oppressive combination" of clothiers cutting wages by lengthening the warping bar "contrary to law, usage and custom from time immemorial" and by imposing "illegal and arbitrary" deductions from wages, has, however, no real echo from the serge districts at this period.[24] Possibly we should think of an overlapping of forms of consciousness, but something which could be described as "trade-union consciousness" is clearly there.

There is, however, other important evidence which helps explain why the Exeter and district populace were so riotous in the winter of 1725–6. This is provided by the series of wheat prices available for the city:

Table 5.1   *Exeter Wheat Prices 1721–25*

Date	Shillings per Winchester Quarter
1721	29.36
1722	30.69
1723	29.05
1724	34.57
1725	41.04[25]

In fact the movement of cereal prices shows over 1725 that sort of abrupt increase, 38% above the average for 1721–3, which later in the century would have precipitated food riots in the area. Food riots do not, however, seem to have occurred in the Exeter district until 1756.[26] Thereafter they regularly did so, and, as Dr Swift, has shown, persisted as a form of protest until those of 1854 provided the last English example of the genre.[27] In his examination of food riots in Devon from 1790 to 1810, John Bohstedt finds woollen workers "the most prominent group". He further notes their "militant tradition", but also the decline of the industry. He concludes that their participation in food riots after 1790 represented:

industrialization run backwards, that is a shift from associational to communal collective action. Strikes gave way to food riots as Devon's woollen industry unravelled. A formerly powerful organised labour force could no longer stave off industrial disaster, but their militant tradition undoubtedly contributed leaders, experience, and pride to the communal food riots of 1795 and 1801.[28]

That is stirring stuff and there is some quality in the insight, but if there is a watershed in the consciousness of the weavers and combers from "offensive" to reactionary, it took place long before the food riots of the 1790s. By the middle of the eighteenth century the great days of the serge manufacture were over. Hoskins suggests that weavers wages then around 9s week had fallen to 8s by 1787 and 7s in 1791, which last level had actually been fixed at Quarter Sessions and renewed up to 1800. In fact, despite brief interludes of relative recovery, the labour market never again so advantaged workers as it had done in the first quarter of the eighteenth century.[29]

Presumably the Statutory prohibition of combinations of woollen workers had some short term effect, for no industrial riots were recorded in 1727 though cereal prices then were extraordinarily high and well above those even of 1725. But in the longer term it is not the absence of industrial disputes which characterises the long decline of the manufacture, for they continued: it is rather their changing nature. In terms of Adam Smith's distinction they became defensive not offensive (with, of course the noted exception of the woolsorters in 1787). Indeed those which have been recorded all seem to have been in reaction to employer action. Woolcombers at Tiverton in 1720 rioted against the use of ready-combed Irish yarn, and in 1738 marched with the weavers there as a protest against merchants who did not give a price for goods whereby a poor may can live". One *dealer* was "horsed on a staff" in this incident. The Tiverton combers struck against the use of Irish wool again in 1749. This time battling with the town's weavers who were waiting to work on it, the latter coolstaffing one of their own number who sympathised with the combers and refused to weave the Irish yarn.[30] (In fact weaver reaction to Irish yarn was not entirely predictable. It was not simply a matter of reverting to self interest after their combined actions of the 1720s. At Cullompton in 1787 it was said that a "combination of weavers" was still preventing its use. This was, however, an outlying centre, and it is possible that the income of weaving households there depended upon the spinning earnings of the women, whereas very little spinning was done in Exeter itself.)[31] Unease among Taunton's weavers in 1764 was said to have been occasioned by the intent of a combination of employers to cut wages.[32]

Conclusion

From such shifting sands of evidence as these three disputes provide, any conclusions about how we should describe the consciousness of eighteenth-century skilled (in the real or self-perceiving sense) manufacturing journeymen must be tentative. Clear investigation of the "combination histories" of more groups would help, for example of the calico-printers so assured in their collective strength when they moved from London to Lancashire in 1783 that their employers called them "gentlemen journeymen" and complained of their ability to gain "most extravagant wages". Although they lost a strike in 1785 when the trade was on a downswing, they made effective use of the rolling strike during the upswing of 1788–90. Their success, however, intensified the employers' search for effective machine-printing and for alternative hand-methods employing less-skilled labour.[33] By the early nineteenth century the once proud journeymen were desperately, but vainly petitioning for statutory regulation of the trade. Here too, the shift from "offensive" to "defensive" trade unionism is part of the internal history of a trade.

When a group of journeymen was on the "defensive" it was most likely to invoke notions of the "community of the trade" as a vertical consciousness group within which men and masters respected their reciprocal obligations. ". . . We are social creatures, and cannot live without each other; and why should you destroy community?" was the question addressed to their employers by the journeymen woolcombers of Norwich during a dispute in 1752.[34] As I have suggested elsewhere, the harmony of this form of "community" was capable of renewal if temporarily broken by dispute. Broken perhaps by, as the Wiltshire weavers termed them in 1739, "unmasterlike masters". As the poem entered in a rate book after the bitter dispute involving London silkworkers in 1773 expressed it:

> May *upright* masters still augment their treasure,
> And journeymen pursue their work with pleasure.[35]

Journeymen cabinet makers issued a book of prices in 1788, below which they were not prepared to accept work. They denied they were dictating new terms to their employers, stating rather that they were seeking to "conciliate mutual regard – to be treated as men possessing an ingenious art".[36] Community in this sense refers to what Maxine Berg has called the "moral community" of the skilled trades the basis of their "corporate, collectivist and solidarist idiom" and as, Robert Malcolmson has argued of their rejection of a narrowing definition of rights that considered only their freedom to sell their labour on the open market.[37] It also defined a frontier between the skilled and the unskilled: into which later category women were very generally placed.

They were not so from the other important sense of "community". Dr Berg remarks on a "striking difference" between the cultural and community basis of rural or family-based manufacture and that of the urban crafts:

The custom and community which impinged upon the work unit of domestic industry, particularly on the women, was one which moved in quite different directions, out to a plebeian culture based on community ties between families and neighbours, not on the ties established between workers in a journeymen's association.[38]

"Association" versus "Community"; *Gemeinschaft* versus *Gesellschaft?* Belonging versus joining . . . the famous distinction of Ferdinand Tonnies has always had a disarming simplicity which has disguised the difficulty of applying it to real cases.[39] Robert Southey, it may be recalled, feared from Methodism that it "familiarised the lower classes to the work of combining in association", yet Robert Colls has recently described the relationship of Primitive Methodism to the north-eastern mining communities as "organic and instinctive".[40]

Perhaps more fundamental is to respect "community" – for we can hardly do without the word, because of its basis in *place* reinforced by family, kinship and neighbourhood relations rather than as a social system to which association was an alien form. Of course in some uses it means much more than a network of horizontal relationships which can come to reinforce class solidarities, but allows for a horizontal consciousness in which reciprocation between social classes takes place. That is the sense in which Bohstedt understands it in *Riots and Community Politics*. And it is one which identifies the "space" within which Edward Thompson's patricians and plebs interact. It is also a space into which industrial disputes sometimes enter: Gentry, not necessarily as an official "magistracy", for example, being called upon for support or arbitration. Adrian Randall's work on the industrial strife of 1765–6 and the food riots of 1766 in the Gloucestershire woollen districts confirms the existence of a "community of shared values and expectations" incorporating beliefs and attitudes inexplicable by purely economic considerations underlying *both* forms of protest.[41] Dr Randall asserts this not only against the "compartmental" approach to protest, but also against Rodney Dobson's precocious stress on the existence of a skilled worker perception of labour as a commodity which could be bargained with, as a step towards a more "modern" system of industrial relations. Among the groups of London artisans, tailors, compositors, hatters and the like which Dobson mostly studied, one can sense an arena of interaction within which employers and workers to some extent perceived their roles and the moves which were open to them. Possibly even Dobson's suggestion of "conflict resolution" based upon mutual recognition of bargaining strength, is applicable to some eighteenth-century industrial situations.[42] Perhaps as much may have been suggested in applying Adam Smith's sense of "offensive" combination in two of my selected case studies, in indicating long and careful preparation before embarking on strikes, including choosing the moment of maximum advantage, and in pointing to deliberate strategies in industrial action. My conclusion is a qualified one: there is evidence enough of what can be fairly described as "trade union consciousness" among eighteenth-century journeymen in a number of trades, yet I doubt whether any group had jumped with both feet into a "system of industrial relations". The language of times of confidence and labour-advantage did not persist when times changed.

The existence of a "trade union consciousness" should not be pushed aside into an *all-embracing* concept of "moral economy". Rather we should recognise the parallel existence of different forms of worker-consciousness in the eighteenth century. Indeed we could try harder to enter the world of the *urban* workers of the eighteenth century. In a sense, research priorities in recent years have tended, to stress the rural nature of eighteenth-century England. Yet it is not only the case that the population of England surged by 133% over the "long-eighteenth century, while that of France grew by only 39% and that of the Dutch Netherlands stagnated, but it is also the case that the urban population increased both absolutely and relatively. Between 1700 and 1800 the rural agricultural population increased by only 11%, the rural non-agricultural population increased by around 40%, while the urban population almost trebled. Let us stress the significance of this, because there are those, who want to insist that eighteenth-century England was a typical "ancien regime" society. The urbanisation of English society in the eighteenth century was, in European terms, exceptional.[43] Over-zealous proto-industrialists should pay greater heed to the fact that the percentage of the English population living in towns of 10,000 or more inhabitants rose from 13.4% in 1700 to 24% in 1800, whereas the percentage for north and west Europe excluding England *fell* from 12.8 to 10%. Put in another way: 57% of the net European urban gain over the first half of the eighteenth century, and 70% over the second half was taking place in England. Nor should we over-ascribe this to the Bath gentry–leisure–culture syndrome. Five of the ten largest provincial towns in 1775 owed their size primarily to manufacturing: Birmingham, Norwich, Manchester, Sheffield and Leeds. Of the other five only Bath had no really significant level of manufacturing, for Liverpool, Bristol, Newcastle and Plymouth all did. Nor does the "top ten" include urban manufacturing centres like Nottingham, Coventry, Leicester, Exeter or Colchester nor a host of expanding towns in the West Riding or Lancashire. We need not labour the point, Dr Corfield has amply justified her claim that: "The proliferation of specialist industrial towns in the course of the eighteenth century constituted . . . one of the most distinctive and novel elements in the urban transformation."[44] Our eighteenth-century historiography could, I think, do with that stirring which Gary Nash's *Urban Crucible* provided for the other eighteenth-century English-speaking world across the Atlantic.[45]

Notes

1 H.J. Perkin, *The Origins of Modern English Society 1780–1880* (1969), p. 31.
2 *Ibid.* pp. 32–3; J.G. Rule, "The Formative Years of British Trade Unionism: An Overview", in J.G. Rule (ed.), *British Trade Unionism 1750–1850. The Formative Years*, (1988), pp. 11–12.
3 R.J. Morris, *Class and Class Consciousness in the Industrial Revolution 1780–1830*, (1979), pp. 17–18.
4 E.P. Thompson, "Eighteenth-Century English Society: Class Struggle without Class", *Social History*, III, no. 2, 1978, pp. 134, 144. Thompson, however, considers the issue more fully in *Customs in Common*, (1991), pp. 57–63. See the discussion in J.G. Rule, *The Labouring Classes in Early Industrial England, 1750–1850*, (1986), pp. 383–4.
5 R.W. Malcolmson, *Life and Labour in England 1700– 1780*, (1981), pp. 113, 126.
6 Adam Smith, *Wealth of Nations*, 1776, (ed.) E. Cannan, 1904, paperback edition, (1961), I, pp. 74–5; see the discussion in J.G. Rule, *The Experience of Labour in Eighteenth-Century Industry*, (1981), p. 147.
7 C.R. Dobson, *Masters and Journeymen. A Pre-history of Industrial Relations 1717–1800*, (1980), lists 333 labour disputes in England, but see J.G. Rule, *Experience of Labour*, p. 148.
8 The only evidence on this dispute is a single document in the Devon County Record Office, 146 B/add 21.
9 The Exeter grain price series is in B.R. Mitchell and P. Deane, *Abstract of British Historical Statistics*, (Cambridge, 1962), pp. 486–7; W.G. Hoskins, *Industry, Trade and People in Exeter 1688–1800*, (Exeter, 1968), p. 138.
10 G. and F.L. Harris, (eds.) *The Making of a Cornish Town. Torpoint and Neighbourhood through Two Hundred Years*, (Exeter, 1976), p. 22.
11 My account of this dispute is based on the bundle of documents relating to it in the Devon County Record Office: Misc. Legal Papers Box 64.
12 Hoskins, *Exeter*, pp. 54, 60–1.
13 *Misc. Legal Papers, Box 64, Deposition of John Wood.*
14 *Exeter Flying Post*, 22 Feb. 1787.
15 5 Elizabeth c.14, usually known as the Statute of Artificers of 1563 had two main features: the requirement of serving a seven-year apprenticeship to trades and the empowering of magistrates to fix wages at Quarter Sessions. The first of these was repealed in 1814 and the second in 1813. 1 James I, c.6 was passed in 1603 to re-inforce the wage fixing power.
16 *Exeter Flying Post*, 18 April, 19 May 1787.
17 Mitchell and Deane, op. cit. pp. 486–7.
18 Adam Smith, *Wealth of Nations*, I, pp. 74–5, 141.
19 G.D.H. Cole and A.W. Filson (eds.), *British Working Class Movements. Select Documents 1789–1875*, (1965), pp. 82–3, 86–8.

20 Journals of the House of Commons, XV, p. 312, 26 Feb.1707; XVIII, p. 715, 1717; XX, p. 598–9, 3 Mar. 1725; p. 602, 7 Mar. 1725, p. 627, 19 Mar. 1725; p. 647, 31 Mar. 1726.

21 *Ibid.* XX, p. 627.

22 *Ibid.* XX, p. 647.

23 For the Gentlemen Clothiers of the west of England broadcloth districts see: E.A.L. Moir, "The Gentlemen Clothiers: a study of the organisation of the Gloucestershire Cloth Industry 1750–1835" in H.P.R. Finberg, (ed.), *Gloucestershire Studies*, 1957.

24 *Commons Journals*, XX, p. 627; Public Record Office, SP 35/14 f. 132.

25 Mitchell and Deane, op. cit., pp. 486–7.

26 No earlier riot is noted in A. Charlesworth, (ed.), *An Atlas of Rural Protest in Britain 1548–1900*, (1983).

27 R. Swift, "Food riots in mid-Victorian Exeter, 1847–67", *Southern History*, II, 1980, pp. 101–28.

28 J. Bohstedt, *Riots and Community Politics in England and Wales 1790–1810*, (Harvard, 1983).

29 Hoskins, *Exeter*, p. 56.

30 M. Dunsford, *Historical Memoirs of Tiverton*, 1790, pp. 226, 228, 230.

31 Hoskins, *Exeter*, p. 56.

32 *Exeter Mercury*, 11 May 1764.

33 *Facts and Observations, to prove the Impolicy and dangerous Tendency of the Bill now before Parliament, for limiting the number of Apprentices, and other restrictions in the Calico Printing Business. Together with a Concise History of the Combination of the Journeymen*, (Manchester, 1807); M. Berg, *The Age of Manufactures 1700–1820*, (1985), pp. 76, 84, 172, 279.

34 Quoted in: R.W. Malcolmson, "Workers' Combinations in Eighteenth-Century England", in M. and J. Jacob (eds.), *The Origins of Anglo-American Radicalism*, (1984), p. 149.

35 See. J.G. Rule, *Experience of Labour*, p. 209.

36 Preface to London cabinetmakers' Book of Prices, 1788, Modern Records Centre, University of Warwick.

37 Berg, *Age of Manufactures*, p. 159; Malcolmson, "Workers' Combinations", p. 153.

38 Berg, *Age of Manufactures*, pp. 160–1.

39 For a discussion of Tonnies ideas on "community" see Rule, *Labouring classes*, pp. 155–6.

40 Robert Southey, *The Life of Wesley*, 1893 edn. p. 522; R. Colls, *The Pitmen of the Northern Coalfield. Work, Culture and Protest, 1790–1850*, (Manchester, 1987), p. 169.

41 See Adrian Randall, "The Industrial Moral Economy of the Gloucestershire Weavers in the Eighteenth Century", in Rule, *British Trade Unionism*, pp. 29–51.

42 C.R. Dobson, *Masters and Journeymen*, Chap. 10.

43 See especially: E.A. Wrigley, "Urban Growth and Agricultural Change: England and the Continent in the Early Modern Period", in R.I. Rotberg and T.K. Rabb (eds.), *Population and History. From the Traditional to the Modern World*, (Cambridge, 1986), pp. 123–68.

44 P.J. Corfield, *The Impact of English Towns 1700–1800*, (Oxford, 1982), p. 22.

45 Gary B. Nash, *The Urban Crucible: Social Change, Political Consciousness, and the Origins of the American Revolution*, (Harvard, 1979).

6

Rite, Legitimation and Community in Southern England 1700–1850: the Ideology of Custom[1]

R. W. Bushaway
University of Birmingham

I

In 1759 Oliver Goldsmith published an elegant defence of custom in preference to written laws. 'What, say some, can give us a more contemptible idea of a large state, than to find it mostly governed by custom; to have few written laws, and no boundaries to mark the jurisdiction between the senate and people?'[2] He boldly asserted that 'Custom, or the traditional observance of the practice of their forefathers, was what directed the Romans, as well in their public as private determinations. . . . So that, in those times of the empire in which the people retained their liberty, they were governed by custom; when they sunk into oppression and tyranny, they were restrained by new laws, and the laws of tradition abolished.'[3] Goldsmith saw this abolition all around him in mid-eighteenth-century England as the 'multiplicity of written laws' marked English life with the 'sign of a degenerate community'.[4] In contrast to many of his contemporaries, Goldsmith did not accept that 'every nation is free in proportion to the number of its written laws',[5] that is, where the measurement of freedom was made against a rapidly expanding Statute Book.

This essay sets out to consider popular custom in southern England during the eighteenth and early nineteenth centuries, not as a separate and unconnected form of behaviour, but as a feature of life located in a particular social context in which reference was made implicitly or explicitly to a coherent ideology. It is argued that part of the problem for historians in recovering this ideology lies with the way popular custom has been studied in the past.

Social historians first studied popular custom as an element of the wider popular cultural experience of the labouring poor in the eighteenth and nineteenth centuries. The particular emphasis of these studies was their concern with patterns of leisure and popular culture in contrast to the experience of the workplace. Bob Malcolmson's pioneering study concluded that popular recreations were transformed by contact with the significant economic and social forces arising from the Industrial Revolution. He writes:

> Traditional recreation was rooted in a social system which was predominantly agrarian, strongly parochial in its orientations, marked by a deep sense of corporate identity. . . . In the new world of congested cities, factory discipline, and free enterprise, recreational life had to be reconstructed – shaped to accord with the novel conditions of non-agrarian, capitalistic society.[6]

In his study of leisure in the Industrial Revolution, Hugh Cunningham stressed the importance of the process by which leisure was transformed and in which the working class should not be seen as 'passive consumers' but as active participants.[7]

Only in more recent studies has popular custom emerged more clearly as a dynamic force to be considered in its own right. The recent collections by Eileen and Stephen Yeo, Bob Storch, my own work, and earlier publications by Alun Howkins and others have concentrated on popular custom as a terrain which was hotly contested by working people and the rural elite.[8] Popular custom was not a separate and disconnected feature of social life in eighteenth- and nineteenth-century England, rather it was the essential underpinning for a holistic structure of values, beliefs, mechanisms and forms which both derived from and had implications for the rural labouring poor's view of relationships in the village. It is this mental world which is characterised here in terms of an ideology of custom.

In referring to an ideology of custom, the phrase is not used in the orthodox Marxist sense of false consciousness or illusion. As Engels wrote in 1893:

> Ideology is a process accomplished by the so-called thinker consciously, it is true, but with a false consciousness. The real motive forces impelling him remain unknown to him; otherwise it simply would not be an ideological process. Hence he imagines false or seeming motive forces. Because it is a process of thought he derives its form as well as its content from pure thought, either his own or that of his predecessors.[9]

A useful application of the term, suggested by Antonio Gramsci, is more relevant to eighteenth-century English society. 'One must therefore distinguish', he wrote, 'between historically organic ideologies, those, that is, which are necessary to a given structure, and ideologies that are arbitrary, rationalistic, or "willed". To the extent that ideologies are historically necessary they have a validity which is "psychological"; they "organise" human masses, and create the terrain on which men move, acquire consciousness of their position, struggle, etc.'[10] The notion of ideology as a 'terrain' of struggle is particularly significant for the study of custom and ritual in Hanoverian and early Victorian England. As Bob Storch commented on popular ritual: 'There is nothing particularly useful about spending valuable research time discovering the last date a maypole appeared in a Swaledale village – unless that bit of information is made to speak to some wider questions'.[11] In reconstructing the ideology of custom, the historian should address questions of social function, change and continuity, support and opposition, control and conflict. Maypoles were, for example, often stolen and their appearance in the village could indicate divisions among social groups in the community. One Somerset schoolmaster complained on 2 May 1737 that, 'This day the Rabble of the town being headed by John Ward set up a may pole near my school which gave great disturbance, they having stole the tree from one Addams.' Ward referred to the 'may pole' as the 'flora pole' and said that 'it did suggest and tell him many future things'.[12] This example illustrates the social context of a particular local custom in the eighteenth century and suggests that the action was not universally welcomed in the community. Clearly, motives were involved for the participants which went beyond those of leisure or the indulgence in quaint and picturesque practices for their own sake. This event was both dynamic and defiant exceeding simple concepts of popular custom which imply survivalism or immutability.

The folklorist, Dr E.C. Cawte, has defined the concept of 'custom' as 'set form' which can vary with country or social class but is constant.[13] William Sumner described his concept of 'folkways' in similar terms:

> If asked why they act in a certain way in certain cases, primitive people always answer that it is because they and their ancestors always have done so. . . . The frequent repetition of petty acts, often by great numbers acting in concert or, at least, acting in the same way when face to face with the same need . . . produces habit in the individual and custom in the group.[14]

Custom's legal basis should be stressed as it is this which underpinned the labouring poor's defence of popular customary activity. Charles Calthrope considered the nature of custom in relation to copyhold tenure in a series of lectures published in 1635. 'Custom', he wrote, 'is where by continuance of time, a Right is obtained concerning divers persons in common'.[15] Its 'true measure', he continued, '. . . is where a custom, or usage, or other things have been used, so long as a man's memory cannot remember the contrary. That is, when such matter is pleaded, that no man then in life, hath not heard anything, nor know any proof to the contrary'.[16]

At Merdon manor near Hursley in Hampshire the force of custom was brought into sharp focus at the end of the seventeenth century in a bitter dispute between the tenants and the Lord of the manor.[17] Their customary rights had been usurped by a former Lord of the manor, Richard Maijor. When the manor passed to the Cromwells by marriage, the tenants determined to regain their lost rights. In an action at the Court of Chancery, which began in 1692 and was not completed until 1705, their customary rights were restored. Matthew Imber printed some eighty copies of the Chancery decision, having personally translated Chancery hand, and these he distributed to the surviving tenants as a permanent record of their rights. This decision became a bench mark which was to sustain the legal basis of custom until its challenge in the second half of the eighteenth century. Imber stated that the decree:

being written in Chancery-Hand, and part thereof being in Latin, and therefore cannot be read or understood by many of you; I have therefore abstracted the said Decree, and presented the same to every one of you, that you and your successors may upon all occasions rightly know the customs of the said manor, and thereby avoid such things as might create such great Disputes and Expenses, as you and your friends have lately undergone.[18]

What the case revealed was the mechanism by which customs were retained. Part of the tenants' evidence was based on 'divers ancient custom books and particulars of the customs [which] had been kept, taken, and past from Generation to Generation'.[19] Indeed, one of the misdemeanours about which the tenants complained was the 'concealing the Ancient Presentments, Court Books, Rolls, and other manuscripts, relating to the customs . . .'.[20] The case was brought before it was too late so that '. . . the testimony of Ancient witnesses who were alive and could prove the same' was available to Chancery and could be preserved '*in perpetuam rei memoriam*'.[21]

The Lord of the manor vigorously opposed the tenants' case and alleged that '. . . the defendants combining together to introduce new Customs, prejudicial to the interest of Mr Cromwell . . . and to enlarge the Ancient Customs beyond what had been used time out of mind . . .'[22] were the abusers and innovators. He argued that some of the customs so introduced were 'unreasonable'. He also pointed to the events of Richard Maijor's Lordship as evidence that the rights had no customary base. The Court recited the customs found to be true and stated that they now stood:

absolutely ratified and confirmed by the Decree and Authority of this Court, to be observed and performed by all the said parties the Lord and

Customary Tenants of the said Manor, their heirs and successors for ever.[23]

The case was so long at trial that both Cromwell and some twenty of his litigious tenants had died by the time it was concluded.

It should be remembered that, although the legal interpretation of custom, when applied, often referred to the practices of manor administration and to land tenure, the notion was a powerful agent of legitimation for the poor's activities in a wider cultural context. The term 'customary society' has been used elsewhere to denote the perceived reciprocal relationship between groups in the English village in the eighteenth and nineteenth centuries.[24] This took the form of a contractual framework within which, in the view of the rural labouring poor, the structurally superior (farmers, landowners, parish clergy, lord of the manor) accepted certain duties and responsibilities for the structurally inferior (tenants, smallholders, cottagers and squatters, wage labourers and the poor) and in return received due recognition of their structural status, and compliance or cooperation with their enterprises and decisions. This relationship was not perceived of as having a foundation on the notion of deference nor did it recognise any place for paternalist gestures. It was governed by reference to custom.

Much of the contractual framework which underlay 'customary society' had been carried forward from the Middle Ages – the manor and manorial administration, the church and liturgical ritual, and, in the case of small towns, the borough and the customs of the corporation.[25]

Custom governed many aspects of life in the rural community, not merely the narrow legal area of tenure and common rights with regard to property. Custom can be discerned in the organisation of work; the network of popular beliefs, leisure, social relationships and value systems. Richard Gough's early eighteenth-century 'soap opera', the *History of Myddle*, begins by describing the physical location of the boundaries of the parish of Myddle and includes a statement as to the customs of the lordship of Myddle.[26] His role in recording local custom and usage was precisely the feature of customary law criticised, in the mid-eighteenth century, by some jurists who wished to see legal practice firmly based on the certainties of statute law controlled by a professional elite. It was these jurists whom Oliver Goldsmith sought to challenge in 1759. This was not merely an intellectual debate between lawyers about the law, but an ideological debate concerning people, politics and the nature of property. The later decades of the eighteenth century witnessed the concerted undermining of custom by a combination of forces which defined new ideologies of work discipline based upon the wage and which led to new developments in capital intensive farming and industrial processes, enclosure, and emparkment. These ascendant ideologies were assisted by the moral impact of evangelicalism and the intellectual force of rationalism and resulted in new social divisions which distanced master and man and saw an increasingly inequitable division of wealth. Custom would have no place in this world.

In the second half of the eighteenth century, the structurally superior withdrew from their responsibilities for the structurally inferior and opposed their initiatives or decided no longer to participate in them. The Somerset rector, William Holland, for example, recorded on 29 May 1807, 'Today is Club Day at Stowey and I was invited to walk in the Procession but did not as I do not much relish the noise and tumultuous proceedings. Mr Starkey preached. Thomas is gone to view the bustle'. He had preached the Club sermon in previous years but was opposed to such features as women's races which he regarded as 'almost indecent'.[27] Custom was a barrier to the new ideology of wealth based upon private property and was consciously dismantled so that emparkment, the strengthening of the game laws, and the removal of customary rights such as wood gathering and gleaning could proceed.

The legal definition of custom contained the root of its vulnerability. As Calthrope wrote:

> Custom although it doth chiefly consist of continuance of time and usage, yet it doth further require seven other necessary properties, incident for the maintenance of a good custom.[28]

He stated that custom must be reasonable, certain, in accordance with Common right, on good consideration, compulsory, without prejudice to the King, and of profit to the claimant.[29]

It was towards the proof of certainty that much eighteenth-century criticism was directed. Calthrope pointed to this central weakness when he wrote of custom that '. . . incertainty in all cases maketh confusion' and '. . . that without some kind of certainty, neither law nor custom can be good'.[30]

Custom, then, was understood by both the labouring poor and the rural elite, during the Hanoverian and early Victorian period, as having a legal basis. Custom was not merely synonymous with force of habit nor was it an antique cloak for invalid or irrational popular actions. Custom was the medium for the continuity and record of collective memory in the local community and defined its internal relationships and its perception of the external world. It is for this reason that Richard Gough set down what he knew of the disputed location of a certain Billmarsh Green, adjacent to Myddle:

All that I can say is, that when the inhabitants of Myddle parish do walk their boundaries, they take their small common wholly within their bounds; and when the parishioners of Broughton do walk their boundaries, they take it, and a little croft that lies between it and the barn at Billmarsh within their bounds. But the tythes of the croft are paid in Myddle Parish. But all Billmarsh was formerly a common, and it should seem that this Green was left out of it when it was inclosed, for all other places make heyment from Billmarsh, except this Green.[31]

It was of crucial importance to Gough's contemporaries that custom should preserve a certain and authentic record of what was common and what was not as the process of enclosure was completed.

The annual custom of parish or manor boundary walking, particularly at Rogationtide, acted as the medium of record and could, as in the case of Myddle, highlight disagreements between parishes and their differing perceptions of events in the lives of their inhabitants. By the early nineteenth century a correspondent of the antiquary, John Brand, felt impelled to justify boundary walking:

You will no doubt think this a very rude and primitive way of perpetuating evidence, but experience has proven it not to be a bad one.[32]

'Proven experience' was no longer seen by that date as an adequate justification for the maintenance of such popular customs in the eyes of the rural elite. In the case of the boundary walking of the parish of Kidderminster in 1818 notice was published in the parish church for three Sundays prior to the perambulation. Notices were also sent to adjoining parishes and the perambulation was accomplished in stages. The first stage began on 18 May with a prayer and a verse from a psalm at the church. The procession moved off at nine o'clock in the following order:

Town Crier, Javelin men, Band of Music, Vicar and two senior churchwardens, Minister and two junior churchwardens, parish and vestry clerks, inhabitants.[33]

The parish banner was also carried. At various points on the perambulation the party met with representatives from neighbouring parishes where the boundaries met and the gospel was read. A detailed record was kept which included a note of all changes since the last perambulation. Refreshments were taken at various places including the local public house and the house of a member of the local gentry. Significantly, the record kept noted the impact of enclosure. For example:

from Shatterfoot Toll Gate the Kidderminster Parish goes down the whole of the Turnpike Road to a field above the road that leads to Birch Wood, it then goes into and takes part of a field which has been Enclosed by John Knight Esquire as waste land out of the Turnpike Road and continues going down the said new Enclosure, close to some oaks which stood in the hedgerow before the said Enclosure was made.[34]

The parish boundary walking at Kidderminster was popular custom in action. Custom was, therefore, ideological and, in consequence, political as it was a powerful agent of legitimation for the activities of the labouring poor during the eighteenth and early nineteenth centuries. Opponents of custom were under no illusion as to its strength even when deployed in defence of seemingly barbaric and morally reprehensible behaviour. 'Custom is too powerful', wrote a pseudonymous Hampshire correspondent in 1773, '. . . to be overcome by reproof or exhortation only'.[35] His letter to the local newspaper was a lengthy and impassioned plea to respectable Hampshire society to use its utmost vigour and influence in opposing and suppressing the notorious but popular Shrovetide sport of 'throwing-at-cocks' or 'cock-squoiling'. By challenging the role which custom played in legitimating such annual calendar activities in late eighteenth-century southern England, he joined the debate between those who wished to see the regularisation of popular culture by the application of statute law, particularly in what they perceived to be indeterminate areas, and those who saw custom as part of the framework of the local community and as a defence for the poor and powerless against the onslaught of propertied men.

Custom linked together components of local community cultural life and reflected, on the one hand, the symbolism of social cohesion in which the rural labourer was able to maintain certain popular rights, and, on the other, provided opportunities for socially critical and disruptive behaviour, which in some cases, could establish a popular cultural environment for more orthodox movements of social protest such as food rioting in the late eighteenth century and the Captain Swing disturbances of 1830–1.[36] Popular customary collective activity sought to defend such rights as gleaning, fuel gathering, access to recreational and ritual venues, and annual non-institutionalised largesse collections from Christmas boxes to harvest levies. The latter were described by less generous contributors as 'civility money',[37] that is a financial payment to ensure compliance with the prevailing social hierarchy throughout the year. Part of this defence consisted of investing popular rights with ceremonial and ritual often adapted from older forms or other festivals. New statute laws, such as those against wood theft in 1766 and legal judgements, such as that which defined gleaning as an illegal practice in 1788 were used to extinguish the legitimacy of specific popular customary rights and to undermine the powerful notion of custom itself in order that the law of propertied men might prevail.[38] The young Marx noted this process, particularly with regard to what he described as 'the alms of nature'. During the Sixth Rhine Province Assembly, an urban deputy opposed the provision by which the gathering of berries was treated as theft. The customary nature of this activity was clear as Marx recorded:

> He spoke primarily on behalf of the children of the poor, who pick these fruits to earn a trifling sum for their parents; an activity which has been permitted by the owners *since time immemorial* and has given rise to a *customary right* of the children. This fact was contested by another deputy, who recorded that in his area these berries have already become articles of commerce and are dispatched to Holland by the barrel.[39]

Marx commented:

> In one locality, therefore, things have actually gone so far that a customary right of the poor has been turned into a monopoly of the rich.[40]

A similar process occurred in late eighteenth-century England with regard to wood gathering and gleaning.

'They literally get their fuel "by hook or by crook", whence, doubtless, comes that very old and expressive saying, which is applied to those cases where people will have a thing by one means or another.' The securing of sufficient quantities of wood for fuel to provide warmth, for cooking and, occasionally, for manufacturing purposes, remained a major preoccupation for a great number of labouring families throughout the eighteenth and nineteenth centuries. This had also been the case for their forebears in the late Middle Ages when custom provided both the means and the measurement for legitimate taking of wood. This is the meaning of the phrase 'by hook or by crook' – implements permitted in the gleaning of the woodland – as was recognised by William Cobbett in 1822.[41] Indeed, some fifty years after Cobbett wrote those words, a song of the National Agricultural Labourers' Union could still immortalise and, by implication, condemn the actions of 'Squire Puddinghead' who gloated that:

> If Polly Brown but takes a stick
> from Farmer Giles' fences,
> I fine her twopece as its worth,
> and fourteen bob expenses.[42]

Woodtaking was opposed, not because of the actual value of the wood, but from the desire to protect the exclusivity of private property. Previous generations of 'Squire Puddingheads' had prosecuted numerous 'Polly Browns' for similar offences. That the poor 'would have the thing' remained a constant theme of rural life for the greater part of two centuries during which the wrath of the propertied was visited upon the poor with varying degrees of harshness and severity. It is the customary context which informed the action of the poor in gathering wood, regardless of precise changes in law in which new statutes were created and the custom of wood collecting was redefined as the crime of wood theft. It is wood taking which illustrates the terrain of conflict between the propertied and the poor even after the changes in the law in the eighteenth century.

Records of summary convictions for wood offences survive in Wiltshire from 1752–1801.[43] They are not representative of the county and probably survive from the work of a small number of magistrates. Yet evidence is provided of the nature and continuity of wood theft in the second half of the eighteenth century. Of the offenders 33 per cent were women and 45 per cent of the total committed the offence in their parish of birth or residence. Only 14 per cent of offences were stated to have been committed in a parish other than the one in which the offender lives. The occupations given by offenders were 39 per cent 'labourer', 5 per cent 'weaver' and only 2 per cent as 'yeoman' or 'gentleman'. In 17 per cent of cases no occupation or status was specified. A family relationship connecting groups of offenders was indicated in 19 per cent of cases. The months of December to March were those in which the majority of offences (68 per cent) occurred, whereas only 19 per cent of offences occurred from April to July and 13 per cent from August to November. Of all the cases 48 per cent were first offences. Of witnesses or complainants 21 per cent were stated as the owner of the property where the offence was committed. Similarly, 11 per cent refer to the witness or complainant as 'gentlemen' and 11 per cent as 'yeomen' and 13 per cent of witnesses or complainants were agents of the owner (woodward, keeper, bailiff, agent, steward, servant, warrener). Only 3 per cent of cases record that the witness or complainant was an agent of the law (constable, magistrate). These figures indicate that woodtaking was seasonal, that offenders were mainly poor people and that offences were mainly committed in the offender's own parish. The propertied or their agents were often involved in bringing offenders before the magistrate and a significant number of women and children, often in family groups, were responsible for woodtheft. There is little evidence of a 'blackmarket' in wood and, in most cases, when motivation is suggested, the wood was stolen for fuel.

Wood collection was seen as a legitimate activity by poor people and was defended by reference to an ideology of custom. New and ascendant ideologies defined the practice as criminal yet it remained widespread. 'Many people', it was noted in Hampshire in 1773, 'have been committed this week to the common Bridewell for making it their daily practice to tear hedges, a practice very frequent and prejudicial to the farmers.'[44] In this case, wood gathering was directly linked to hedge breaking which was seen as more threatening because of its implications for the legitimacy of enclosure. In 1770 and 1771 an advertising campaign in Berkshire sought to discredit wood gathering and attack the legitimation of custom.[45] Even the common practice of gathering nuts was frowned upon because it jeopardised the integrity of private property and disturbed game preserves. Campaigns were conducted against 'nutters' in the local press in southern and eastern England in the late eighteenth century. It remained a theme of those who sought to oppose apparently innocent rural pursuits. Richard Jefferies was still obliged to condemn the custom at the end of the nineteenth century:

> men and boys in the winter come stealing into the wood where the blackthorn thickets are for sloes . . . Those they gather they sell, of course; and although the pursuit may be perfectly harmless in itself, how is the keeper to be certain that, if opportunity is offered, these gentry would not pounce upon a rabbit or anything else? Others come for dead wood, and it does on the face of it seem hard to deny an old woman who has worked all her days in the field a bundle of fallen branches rotting under the trees . . . But if the keeper admits the old woman shivering over her embers in the cottage to pick up these dead boughs, how can he tell what further tricks others may be up to? The privilege has often been offered and as often abused, until at last it has been finally withdrawn – not only because of the poaching carried out under the cloak of picking up dead wood, but because the intruders tore down fine living branches from the trees and spoiled and disfigured them without mercy.[46]

The attack on specific calendar customs and other customary activities should not merely be viewed as an attack by the propertied on certain manifestations of popular culture seen as disruptive or morally-unacceptable leisure activities. When wassail singers at Grampound in Cornwall visited the houses of the village 'to drink the King's health, as the custom has been',[47] their activity was reinforced and legitimated by reference both to supposed royal sanction and to custom. Their credentials were authenticated in the second verse of their song, which ran:

> In a friendly manner this house we salute
> For it is an old custom, you need not dispute

> Ask not the reason from where it did spring
> For you very well know it's an old ancient thing.[48]

Their orderly behaviour, expressed in a later line, 'with our jolly wassail and our hats in our hand' was dependent upon clear recognition of their undisputed customary right to visit the village and levy, albeit in a respectful manner, a customary winter dole. It was not symbolic of deference. The function of the dole itself was clear when the wassailers sang that they 'hope your civility to us will be proved'. The relationship between the wassail singers and their neighbours at Grampound was a customary one and the giving of the dole was not seen as voluntary but as the expected and undeniable response to a popular right exercised once a year.

II

Popular custom, then, had an ideological and legal basis in eighteenth-century England which made it a dynamic element in the relationship between the labouring poor and the rural elite. John Brand, in 1795, justified the study of popular antiquities in terms of the political nature of this relationship. He wrote:

> The people, of whom society is chiefly composed, and for whose good all superiority of Rank, indispensably necessary as it is in every government, is only a grant, made originally by mutual concession, is a respectable subject to every one who is the Friend of Man.[49]

This Painite statement suggests that the methodology adopted in the study of popular custom should be based upon an analytical understanding of its political implications. The problem of methodology is the reason why popular custom has only recently been studied in the wider context of village life. Earlier students of popular custom adopted the approach of the antiquary. The forerunner of folklore studies was referred to as popular antiquities, to be distinguished from the study of natural antiquities.[50] From the outset, popular custom was considered to be apart from, and separate to, the normal experience of life, often viewed solely as the vestige or survival of older ways which were indeterminate in time and not infrequently to be condemned on moral grounds. John Brand continued:

> Vulgar rites and popular opinions . . . may be said to lose themselves in the mists of Antiquity. They have indeed travelled to us through a long succession of years, and the greater part of them, it is not improbable,

will be of perpetual observation: for the generality of men look back with superstitious veneration on the ages of their forefathers, and authorities that are grey with time seldom fail of commanding those filial honours claimed even by the appearance of hoary age.[51]

Brand's predecessor, Henry Bourne, wrote in 1725 that 'ceremonies and opinions, which are held by the common people, such as they solely or generally observe. For tho' some of them have been of national and others perhaps of universal observance, yet at present they would have little or no being, if not observed among the vulgar.'[52] The earliest collectors of popular antiquities thought of customs as surviving from an indeterminate past when wider support was once enjoyed. Popular custom was not seen as having a contemporary relevance, except in terms of leisure, for its participants. The study of popular antiquities was pursued from a similar methodological standpoint throughout the nineteenth century when, from a discussion of appropriate nomenclature, the term 'folklore' was adopted. Many nineteenth-century folklorists continued to view their subject matter as primitive survivals and from a social Darwinist perspective in which the relentless progress of humanity could be observed. Andrew Lang, for example, writing in florid style, thought that:

> The natural people, the folk, has supplied us, in its unconscious way, with the stuff of all our poetry, law, ritual; and genius has selected from the mass, has turned customs into codes, nursery tales into romance, myth into science, ballad into epic, magic mummery into gorgeous ritual. . . . The student of this lore can look back and see the long trodden way behind him, the winding tracks through marsh and forest and over burning sands. He sees the caves, the camps, the villages, the towns where the race tarried, for shorter times or longer, strange places many of them, and strangely haunted, desolate dwellings and inhospitable. But the scarce visible tracks converge at last on the beaten ways, the ways to that city whither mankind is wandering.[53]

The principal aim of much of this work was collection and comparison and a process of fragmentation and separation of popular custom took place. Popular custom was seen as a separate area of social life and, even within folklore studies, component specialisms such as folk song and folk dance were further split off. The folk song and dance revival of the early twentieth century emphasised this process to the extent that it could later be seen as a movement first to preserve and then to restore to the 'folk' their own long-lost culture in order to enrich their culturally barren lives. This view was still prevalent in the 1960s:

When families were forced by economic circumstances, during the Industrial Revolution, to go to live in the manufacturing towns, they left their cultural pattern behind. Luckily, at the beginning of this century, when The Folk Song Society was attempting to restore the cultural heritage to the English Folk, the Board of Education was seeking for means whereby to meet the needs of culturally-deprived children.[54]

The importance of the work of collection during the revival period cannot be denied but it contributed to the further fragmentation of the study of popular custom and was influenced by the moral and social concerns of the collectors themselves. A further methodological problem to add to that of the fragmentation of popular custom, was the habit of some nineteenth-century antiquaries of building on earlier collections occasionally by slavish and unauthenticated repetition.[55]

The view of popular custom as mere survival does not admit the possibilities of change and transformation within the context of contemporary society or the dynamic application of custom in the defence of popular rights. It is in this latter sense that Antonio Gramsci argued for the study of folklore as important to the understanding of the mechanisms of social structures. He defined 'folklore' as a:

> view of the world and of life, in great measure implicit, of certain strata (determinate in space and time) of society, in opposition (here, too, mostly implicity, mechanical, objective) to the 'official' views of the world (or, in a wider sense, of the cultural parts of a particular society) that have occurred through history's development. . . . We can only understand folklore as a reflex of the conditions of cultural life of the people.[56]

Popular custom is, therefore, innovative and dynamic and its study uncovers the conflicts and tensions of normally-concealed relationships in eighteenth- and nineteenth-century English village life. The historian of popular custom should attempt to establish the social and economic context of the material and to delineate a chronology which examines the continuity or discontinuity of particular popular customary activities. Change, transformation, suppression or withdrawal of support by groups in the community should be charted. It is essential to adopt a methodological approach to popular custom which recognises its centrality, locates it within a holistic structure and identifies it as part of the process of social change and not as some distant and unchanging baseline in the past which has only antique relevance to the present.

III

In what areas did an ideology of custom inform the actions of the labouring poor in Southern England in the eighteenth and early nineteenth centuries? Firstly, it was an essential means of legitimating the local calendar. The passage of events in time was the thread of continuity which connected the individual experience of the labouring poor and their families. The local calendar was composed of many different types of repeated experience: of work, of leisure, of the church, of parish or manor administration, and of the local established gentry families. It provided a frame of reference for the expression of the labourers' perception of the prevailing social hierarchy. Calendar customs were not merely a collection of social occasions which occurred in any one year, and which were found to a greater or less extent, in most other places. Forms of popular customary activity might well be common to specific generic groups but each local calendar was seen as being particular to the individual community. The national stereotypes of some popular customs arose in the later nineteenth century and were dependent upon the development of mass communications particularly the railways and popular newspapers. The assimilation of local popular cultural variety into large conglomerate national stereotypes was a recent development. The process of rejection, selection, and approbation which the Victorian middle class applied to specific popular customs from the middle decades of the nineteenth century was, in itself, a major contributor to the development of national and acceptable (at least by bourgeois criteria) sterotypic calendar customs. One of the key developments in the construction of a national calendar was Queen Victoria's 1887 Jubilee. It is noticeable that local fetes and parades, whilst drawing on local experience and older customary forms, particularly Whit festivals, took on a national uniformity. A description of events at Turvey, typical of many other local celebrations, serves to illustrate this:

> At eleven o'clock a procession was formed at the Buckinghamshire end of the village and proceeded to perambulate the streets in the following order:- The Gentry and Committee and Stewards led the way, followed by the New Leicester Brass Band in their picturesque uniform, the Turvey Drum and Fife Band in their bright scarlet capes came next . . . then came the several Benefit Clubs and Societies with their banners and insignia . . . the boys and staff of the Bedfordshire Reformatory came next walking four abreast; and a large number of the inhabitants, male and female, falling in with commendable regularity, closed the procession.[57]

In this case, older elements of parish boundary walking, village club processions and Whitsun rituals were present.

A Thanksgiving Service and village tea took place later in the day. By 1887 the underpinning of the local calendar by reference to custom had been weakened. The middle decades of the nineteenth century saw an onslaught on popular calendar customs which, in many cases, led to their disappearance or drastic remodelling. As Flora Thompson wrote of Lark Rise's customary calendar:

> But these modest festivals which had figured every year in everybody's life for generations were eclipsed in 1887 by Queen Victoria's Golden Jubilee.[58]

Despite previous lack of local interest in the Royal family, Flora Thompson wrote that:

> there was going to be a big 'do' in which three villages would join for tea and sports and dancing and fireworks in the park of a local magnate. Nothing like it had ever been known before.[59]

The form was not determined by local initiative. This was state culture. She continued:

> The newspapers were full of the great achievements of her reign: railway travel, the telegraph, Free Trade, exports, progress, prosperity, Peace: all these blessings, it appeared, were due to her inspiration. Of most of these advantages the hamlet enjoyed but Esau's share; but, as no one reflected upon this, it did not damp the general enthusiasm.[60]

Such national festivals eclipsed the local calendar.

Earlier national celebrations had taken place, particularly to mark military and naval victories and the accessions of monarchs, but these had been celebrated within the local community and without the sense of participation in a national event which could supplant specific local calendar events in importance.[61] Before 1887, local customary calendars had been of great significance. As was noted in southern England in the late nineteenth century:

> The elder men, nevertheless, yet reckon by the feast-day; it is a fixed point in the calendar, which they construct every year, of local events. Such and such fair is calculated to fall so many days after the first full moon in a particular month; and another fair falls so long after that. An old man will thus tell you the dates of every fair and feast in the villages

and little towns ten or fifteen miles round about. He quite ignores the modern system of reckoning time, going by the ancient ecclesiastical calendar and the moon.[62]

This reckoning of time was a customary one.

Secondly, custom preserved and defined the physical limits of the parish or manor in regular Rogationtide perambulations. This physical delineation also provided a mental map for local inhabitants of the limits of community. Those within the boundary were a part of a particular moral world and those without were outsiders. This process, reinforced by custom, defined and limited the in-group. Many popular calendar customs either reinforced the perception of local community boundaries or adhered to them openly or clandestinely. The annual mapping of the community which took place at Rogationtide was essential to the maintenance of those calendar rituals which emphasised popular solidarity. Mummers, mayers, wassailers, Shrovetide football players, St Thomas's dolers, harvest workers claiming largesse, Whitsuntide-Benefit Club processions, would all make use of the mental map of the local community for their annual visits. Custom reinforced this moral world, defining those who it was legitimate to visit and those who were outside the community. The annual perambulation, sometimes referred to as 'processioning', was, in some cases referred to as 'possessioning', thereby revealing the moral function which the custom had for many of its participants.[63] 'Possessioning' had the important function that it provided an annual record of commons and common rights in the parish or manor. The discontinuance of the parish bounds walk was designed to wipe popular memory so that rights and customs associated with open fields and commons before enclosure would be forgotten or could only be recollected in a hazy and, therefore, legally indefensible way. The practice had, in earlier times, been legitimated both by reference to the Church, in particular to the Book of Homilies, and to manor administration in the form of the customary manorial courts. The *Elizabethan Book of Homilies* upheld Rogationtide perambulations, and parishioners, great and small, were enjoined to:

> be content with our own, and not contentiously strive for others, to the breach of charity, by any encroaching one upon another, or claiming one of the other further than in ancient right and custom our forefathers have peaceably laid out unto us for our commodity and comfort.[64]

Such justification was founded upon custom and did not fit the individualist, *laissez-faire* philosophies of late eighteenth-century proprietors who saw self-aggrandisement through enclosure as the true 'spirit of the age' and not the maintenance of custom.

Emparkment and the protection of private property required a general questioning of the relevance of custom and customary practice when it might lead to ambiguity or provide a barrier to the designs of the propertied. At Tring, for example, in the early eighteenth century:

> There was an eminent contest here between Mr Guy, and the poor of the parish, about his enclosing part of the common to make him a park; Mr Guy presuming upon his power, set up his pales, and took in a large parcel of open land, called Wiggington Common; the cottagers and farmers opposed it, by their complaints a great while; but finding he went on with his work, and resolved to do it, they rose upon him, pulled down his banks, and forced up his pales, and carried away the wood or set it on a heap and burnt it; and this they did several times, till he was obliged to desist; after some time he began again, offering to treat with the people, and to give them any equivalent for it: But that not being satisfactory, they mobb'd him again.[65]

The motive force which lay behind the action of the poor at Tring in this contest was their belief that Mr Guy's actions were illegitimate and that their open defiance was a legitimate attempt to re-establish the original position in the face of the innovating development of emparkment. The account of the conflict at Tring was described by its author as an instance of 'the popular claim in England; which we call right of commonage, which the poor take to be as much their property, as a rich man's land is his own'.[66] What, then, connects the persistence of wood gatherers in the face of legal prohibition and the actions of anti-enclosers in defiance of the intimidation of local landowners presuming upon their power? In one sense, it is the force of economic necessity which impelled the labouring poor to employ what means were available to them for their survival. Yet these were also acts of popular solidarity founded on the belief that their actions were legitimated by reference to custom. Both woodtakers and anti-enclosers defied the ideology of private property which was to transform England in the second half of the eighteenth century. The notion of custom, which linked the actions of taking wood and hedge breaking, was consciously attacked and its manifestations were increasingly opposed by the propertied.

Thirdly, custom would be renewed and deployed in defence of the rural labourer's rights, and it remained an important bulwark throughout the eighteenth and early nineteenth centuries. Popular custom was not peripheral to the labouring poor during this period, as might be suggested by those who regarded its manifestations as economically-valueless survivals of an older way of life. Such customary rights remained central to the economy of the labouring poor and were potent sources of conflict with the landed elite. The stereotype of the criminal wood stealer was imposed on the image of the wood gatherer and offenders were to be prosecuted and punished, to the utmost severity as transgressors of new statute law.[67]

Fourthly, the right to collect annual doles of various forms was defended by custom during this period. The conflict over the maintenance of such annual doles in the early nineteenth century can sometimes be followed in the pages of the Parliamentary Reports of the Charity Commissioners, who no longer accepted the legal validity of custom but were only prepared to admit charitable distributions where supported by written record. At Piddlehinton in Dorset it was the practice for the Rector to give annually, on old Christmas Day, a pound of bread, a pint of ale and a mince pie to every poor person in the parish. This was recorded by the charity commissioners as an 'ancient custom' in 1837[68] and one inhabitant recalled that the distribution took place until 1841 when it was first discontinued by the new Rector Revd Thomas T. Carter.[69] He was an old Etonian in his first parish and Piddlehinton would have seemed to Carter to have been in the Dark Ages. His first object was the restoration of the church and his style was soon apparent to his parishioners:

> The removal of the gallery was a terrible grievance, and so was the breaking up of the choir, to make a fresh beginning . . . but the main body of the people bore all this very well.[70]

The Christmas pies were substantial and were baked, together with the bread, at a large, purpose-built oven at the Rectory.[71] Carter was unhappy that the dole went to the poor from miles around and also to parishioners who were by no means in need. He offered to substitute the dole with a distribution of blankets to the deserving poor to the same value.[72] Even wealthy parishioners opposed this scheme and demanded the continuance of the dole as of right and threatened to withhold tithe payment if Carter proceeded with his plan. Carter detected in this opposition 'a kind of democratic independence of spirit'[73] which might lead to violence or anarchy. It should be remembered that these events took place only a decade after the Captain Swing disturbances when another example of rural labourers' democratic independence of spirit was evident. Having taken legal advice he discontinued the custom.[74] Carter wrote to Eton College, who held the gift of the living, and argued that 'persons of bad character, illegitimate children etc., were benefited indiscriminately with the most respectable' and that, on some past occasions, violence had occurred.[75] Carter continued giving the dole to those he regarded as deserving cases, but refused to give the dole to those who claimed it of right. As a result four of the principal farmers refused to pay their tithes until the 'rights of the parish' were restored.[76] Carter published a defence of his actions and the dole was not revived. He left the parish shortly afterwards on health grounds. He was installed as rector at Clewer in 1844 and resigned the living at Piddlehinton. Many years later he recorded:

> After I had been some while at Clewer, once on a Christmas Day a large parcel arrived, and at the bottom of a heap of rags and straw appeared a mince pie.[77]

That parishioners might show democratic independence in defence of customary rights was not a welcome development to the more powerful elements of village society by the mid-nineteenth century. Such custom, in their view, was bad custom. Carter thought the Christmas dole to be 'most hurtful'.[78]

A similar argument was used by the proponents of enclosure to justify their attack on the poor's economy of wastes and commons. One such writer recorded in 1798 that Commons were:

> a real injury to the public; by holding out a lure to the poor man – I mean of materials wherewith to build his cottage, and ground to erect it upon; together with firing, and the run of his poultry and pigs for nothing. This is . . . temptation sufficient to induce a great number of poor persons to settle upon the borders of such commons. But the mischief does not end there; for having gained these trifling advantages, through the neglect or connivance of the lord of the manor, it unfortunately gives their minds an improper bias, and inculcates a desire to live . . . without labour, or, at least with as little as possible.[79]

The phrase 'without labour' signifies 'without waged labour' that is independent of the need to work for the wages of neighbouring farmers and proprietors. 'Doleing' customs denied the donor the opportunity to discriminate between the worthy and unworthy claimants of the dole. Claimants of customary doles usually identified themselves by association with the particular calendar date and declared themselves to be customary visitors. In effect, the claimants were independent of the normal ties of social control in which the regular exercise of charity was under the authority of an established hierarchy in the rural community.

In some places, custom continued to be a defence against the propertied, particularly more independent working communities such as forest villages, mining towns, fishing villages and small weaving communities.

Custom was an ideological concept and the attack on custom mounted in the late eighteenth and early nineteenth centuries was also seen in ideological terms. The attempt to undermine the potency of custom was a direct assault on the component parts of customary society. Attempts to suppress popular calendar customs and ceremonies, to undermine their validity, to question their morality, to challenge their sources of support, to deny access to customary venues and to break up their continuity were part of a coherent process.

The culture of the labouring poor in southern England during the eighteenth and early nineteenth centuries was not composed of a collection of disconnected 'folk' survivals but was a consistent structure of values, beliefs and rights which formed the framework of their lives. Custom enabled working people to adopt assertive positions, to take initiatives and provided a dynamic by which they could affect the process of social change. Custom allowed working people in the eighteenth and early nineteenth centuries to take on aggressive, assertive, combative, socially-critical and threatening roles. Confronted in this way, the rural elite became increasingly unambiguous in its attitude to popular custom, recognising that its potency and legitimacy, for the poor in particular, limited their freedom of action and brought into question ascendant individualist philosophies. The folklorist, George Lawrence Gomme, attempted to define 'folklore'. He wrote:

> Folklore consists of customs, rites and beliefs belonging to individuals among the people, to groups of people, to inhabitants of districts or places; and belonging to them apart from and oftentimes in definite antagonism to the accepted customs, rites, and beliefs of the State or the nation to which the people and the groups of people belong. These customs, rites, and beliefs are mostly kept alive by tradition. . . . They owe their preservation partly to the fact that great masses of the people do not belong to the civilisation which towers over them and which is never of their own creation.[80]

This definition, in essence, identifies the nature of the terrain of conflict contested by official and unofficial cultures in rural southern England in the Hanoverian and early Victorian period. During the second half of the eighteenth century, the terrain was disputed at law and was largely won by the opponents of custom by 1850.

Notes

1 Versions of this essay have also been given at the AGM Conference of the Folklore Society in 1984 and at the University of Birmingham at a conference on 'Crime, Perquisites and the Customary Economy in England, 1650–1850' which took place in

1986. I should like to thank the organisers for inviting me to present this work and to those who attended for their useful comments. I particularly wish to thank Professor John Rule whose support and encouragement have greatly assisted me and who first stimulated and guided my interest in popular custom. Any errors remain my responsibility. Since this essay was written E.P. Thompson's eagerly awaited volume *Customs in Common* (1991) has been published.

2 Oliver Goldsmith 'Custom and Laws Compared' in *The Bee*, No. VII (Saturday 17 November 1759). Reprinted in Oliver Goldsmith *The Citizen of the World and the Bee*, (ed.) Austin Dobson (1934), p. 414.

3 Ibid.

4 Ibid. pp. 414, 416.

5 Ibid. p. 414.

6 Robert Malcolmson *Popular Recreations in English Society, 1700–1850* (Cambridge, 1973), pp. 170–1.

7 Hugh Cunningham *Leisure in the Industrial Revolution* (1980), p. 185.

8 Eileen and Stephen Yeo (eds.) *Popular Culture and Class Conflict, 1590–1914* (1981); Robert D. Storch (ed.) *Popular Culture and Custom in Nineteenth-Century England* (1982); Bob Bushaway *By Rite: Custom, Ceremony and Community in England, 1700–1880* (1982); Alun Howkins *Whitsun in 19th Century Oxfordshire* (Oxford, 1973); Ruskin College History Workshop Pamphlets No. 8; See also C.E. Searle 'The Cumbrian Customary Economy in the Eighteenth Century' *Past and Present*, No. 110, February 1986, pp. 106–33.

9 Engels to F. Mehring, July 14 1893, published in *Karl Marx and Frederick Engels: Selected Works* (1973), p. 690. See also Raymond Williams *Key words: A vocabulary of Culture and Society* (1976). Entry under 'Ideology', pp. 126–30.

10 Quintin Hoare and Geoffrey Nowell Smith (eds.) *Antonio Gramsci: Selections from the Prison Notebooks* (1973), p. 377.

11 Storch *Popular Culture*, p. 17.

12 Somerset Record Office. John Cannon's diary. DD/SAS C/1193/4. Entry for 2 May 1737. I am indebted to the writer John Fletcher for drawing my attention to this reference.

13 E.C. Cawte *Ritual Animal Disguise: A Historical and Geographical Study of Animal Disguise in the British Isles* (1978), p. 1.

14 William G. Sumner *Folkways: A study of the Sociological Importance of Usages, Manners, Customs, Mores and Morals* (1906. Reprinted Dover 1959), p. 3.

15 Charles Calthrope *The Relation Betweene the Lord of a manor and the Coppy-Holder His Tenant* (first published London 1635. Reprinted The Manorial Society, London, 1917), p. 14.

16 Ibid. p. 15.

17 For an outline account of the dispute at Merdon Manor, see D.L. Peach *The History of Hursley Park* (Hursley, 1974), pp. 20–2. I am grateful to Philippa Stevens who first drew my attention to this case.

18 Matthew Imber *The Case, or An Abstract of the Customs of the Mannor of Merdon* (1707), pp. 5–6.

19 Ibid. p. 10.

20 Ibid. p. 21.

21 Ibid. p. 24.

22 Ibid. p. 30.
23 Ibid. p. 80.
24 Bushaway *By Rite*, pp. 22, 182, 231.
25 See recent work on town rituals including: Peter Borsay 'Ritual, Popular Culture and the English Town *c*. 1660–1800'. Paper presented at the Social History Society Conference on Popular Culture at Chester in 1981. Abstract printed in *Social History Society Newsletter* Spring 1982, p. 3, and Borsay '"All the World's a stage": Urban Ritual and Ceremony 1600–1800' in *The Transformation of English Provincial Towns* (ed.) Peter Clark (1985); David Cannadine 'Civic Ritual and the Colchester Oyster Feast' *Past and Present* No. 94, February 1982, pp. 107–30; Mervyn James 'Ritual, Drama and Social Body in the Late Medieval English Town' *Past and Present* No. 98, February 1983, pp. 3–29; Charles Phythian-Adams 'Ceremony and the Citizen: The Communal Year at Coventry 1450–1550' in *Crisis and Order in English Towns 1500–1700: Essays in Urban History* (eds.) Peter Clark and Paul Slack (1972); James G. Kilmartin, 'Popular Rejoicing and Public Ritual in Norwich and Coventry 1660–1835' (unpublished PhD Thesis, University of Warwick, 1987).
26 Richard Gough *The History of Myddle* (ed.) David Hey (1981), pp. 29–30, 64–7
27 *Paupers and Pig Killers: The Diary of William Holland, A Somerset Parson, 1799–1818* (ed.) Jack Ayres (1986). Entry for Friday 29 May 1807, p. 145. Holland had preached the sermon at the Club Day in 1800, see entry for Thursday 29 May 1800 (p. 35). On that occasion he described the Club Day in much more supportive terms, although he did not like the women's races.
28 Calthrope *The Relation Betweene*, p. 17.
29 Ibid. pp. 17–18.
30 Ibid. p. 24.
31 Gough *Myddle*, p. 63–4.
32 British Library. Additional Mss. 41313 FF 83–4. Letter from Robert Studley Vidal to John Brand, dated 31 July 1805 from Cornborough.
33 Perambulation of the boundaries of North Westside of the Parish of Kidderminster, by the Vicar, Minister, churchwardens and other inhabitants on 18th Day of May 1818. Kidderminster Public Library. Bound Mss. on open shelves. *Descriptive Particulars of the Boundaries of the Parish of Kidderminster* FF 1–2. I am grateful to Dr Len Smith who pointed me to this source.
34 Ibid. F 10.
35 *Hampshire Chronicle*, 15 February 1773. Letter against the Shrovetide custom of throwing at cocks, signed 'Humanus'.
36 Bushaway *By Rite*, pp. 107–66 and pp. 167–206 for a more detailed consideration.
37 Joseph Haslewood's annotated copy of John Brand *Observations on Popular Antiquities* (ed.) Sir Henry Ellis (1813). See interleaved note in Vol. 1 between pp. 447 and 448.
38 See Bushaway *By Rite*, pp. 207–37 for a fuller account of the development of legal sanctions against wood gatherers.
39 Karl Marx and Frederick Engels *Collected Works*, Vol. 1 (1975), p. 234.
40 Ibid. pp. 234–5.
41 William Cobbett *Rural Rides* (1973), p. 59.
42 John Miller 'Songs of the labour movement' in *The Luddites and Other Essays* (ed.) Lionel M. Munby (1971), p. 133.

43 Wiltshire Record Office. Summary Convictions Records for Offences against Timber, 1740–1803. For the work of a Wiltshire justice and the extent to which woodtakers were prosecuted earlier in the eighteenth century see *The Justicing Notebook of William Hunt 1744–1749* (ed.) Elizabeth Crittall (Devizes 1982), Wiltshire Record Society, Vol. XXXVII, 1981.

44 *Hampshire Chronicle* 14 June 1773.

45 *Reading Mercury* 23 April, 3 and 17 December 1770, 16 and 30 September, 18 November 1771, 17 August 1772. I wish to thank Ms Avril Leadley for drawing my attention to these references.

46 Richard Jefferies *The Gamekeeper at Home* (1910), pp. 137–9.

47 Paul Jennings *The Living Village: A Picture of Rural Life drawn from Village Scrapbooks* (1972), pp. 99–102.

48 Roy Palmer *Everyman's Book of English Country Songs* (1979), pp. 234–7.

49 John Brand *Observations*, Vol. 1, xx–xxi.

50 See Bushaway *By Rite*, p. 14.

51 Brand *Observations*, vii.

52 Preface to Henry Bourne *Antiquitates Vulgares* (Newcastle upon Tyne 1725) quoted by John Brand *Observations*, xvi.

53 Andrew Lang *Adventures Among Books* (1905), p. 37. Lang's essay was first published in 1872 in *Scribner's Magazine*. For a recent discussion of the persistence of survivalism see Georgina Boyes 'Cultural Survivals Theory and Traditional Customs' *Folk Life: Journal of Ethnological Studies* Vol. 26, 1987–8.

54 *English Dance and Song*, Vol. XXX, Autumn 1968, No. 3. Article by Ken Stubbs 'Singing and Playing in Schools', p. 77.

55 Bushaway *By Rite*, pp. 16–18.

56 Antonio Gramsci 'Observations on Folklore' in Alastair Davidson *Antonio Gramsci: The man, His ideas* Australian New Left Review (1966), p. 86.

57 Revd G.F.W. Mumby *Former Days at Turvey* (1908), pp. 86–7.

58 Flora Thompson *Lark Rise to Candleford* (1973), p. 261.

59 Ibid. p. 262.

60 Ibid.

61 See, for example, an account of celebrations at Stamford in 1789 on the announcement of the King's recovery from illness in *The Torrington Diaries: A selection from the Tours of the Hon. John Byng* (ed.) C. Bruyn Andrews and abridged in one volume by Fanny Andrews (1954), pp. 141–2. Byng was highly critical of such displays and referred to them as 'pompous treats' and 'insults on poverty'. In 1794, he witnessed further celebrations for Lord Howe's victory, see p. 497.

62 Richard Jefferies *Wild life in a Southern County*, (first published London 1879, reprinted Nelson nd.), p. 110.

63 See, for example, the boundary dispute between the Hampshire parishes of Hurstbourne Tarrant and Vernham Dean in 1784 where the terms 'processioning' and 'possessioning' are used interchangeably by witnesses. Hampshire Record Office Quarter Sessions Records. QMP/2. Minutes of Proceedings, Michaelmas 1782–Easter 1784. Epiphany Sessions 1784 FF 171–9.

64 *Certain Sermons or Homilies Appointed to be Read in Churches in the Time of Queen Elizabeth of Famous Memory* (1890). 'An Exhortation to be spoken to such Parishes where they use their perambulations in Rogation week for the oversight of the bounds

and limits of their town', pp. 527–8.

65 Daniel Defoe *A Tour Through England and Wales* (1928), Vol. II, pp. 15–16.

66 Ibid. p. 16.

67 For a detailed treatment of wood theft and the prosecution of offenders in the Hampshire parish of Eling see Bushaway *By Rite*, pp. 219–25.

68 Parliamentary Papers. 29th Report of the Commissioners for Inquiring concerning charities, Vol. xxi (1835), p. 108.

69 John Symonds Udal *Dorsetshire Folk-Lore* (Hertford, 1922, reprinted Toucan Press 1970), p. 117.

70 Thomas Thellusson Carter *Life and Letters* (ed.) W.N. Hutchings (1903), p. 19.

71 Udal *Dorsetshire Folk-Lore*, p. 117.

72 Carter *Life and Letters*, p. 19. The pies were baked by a baker from Dorchester and the ale was brewed at the Rectory.

73 *The Piddle Valley Book of Country Life* (ed.) Muriel Pike (1981), p. 21.

74 Carter *Life and Letters*, p. 19.

75 *The Piddle Valley Book*, p. 22.

76 Ibid.

77 Carter *Life and Letters*, p. 19.

78 Ibid.

79 William Marshall *The Review and Abstract of the County Reports to the Board of Agriculture* (York 1818), Vol. 5: Southern and Peninsular Departments, p. 116, which quotes John Middleton *General View of the Agriculture of Middlesex* (1798).

80 George Lawrence Gomme, article on Folklore in *Encyclopaedia of Religion and Ethics* (ed.) James Hastings (Edinburgh, 1913), p. 57.

7

Popular Protest and Social Crime: the Evidence of Criminal Gangs in Rural Southern England 1790–1860

R. Wells
Brighton Polytechnic

Introduction

The burgeoning poverty problem in the rural South achieved scandalous proportions during the intense and prolonged post-Napoleonic war agricultural depression. Low prices for farm produce, the tardy and inadequate reductions of rent from high wartime levels, and the increasing real costs of national and local taxes, generated a considerable shrinkage of cereal acreages combined with less intensive farming, to have a devastating and prolonged impact on entire rural communities from 1815 until the later 1830s. During this period, farmworkers, as the notorious victims of low pay, under-and unemployment, were joined by many craftsmen, and the situation was further aggravated by scores of bankruptcies among smaller farmers, together with the relative impoverishment of hundreds of larger agrarian capitalists. Rapid demographic growth was the final poverty-inducing ingredient. The operations of the old poor law expanded hugely, with the resultant conflicts between ratepayers with opposing interests, and between poor-law authorities, the Bench, and claimants, to turn it into a theatre for continuous altercation laced with perennial social protest.[1] Society-security administration figured strongly in the Captain Swing rising of 1830.[2] Many southern counties were among the most pauperised in the country, with Sussex invariably at the top of lists compiled on the criteria of *per-capita* poor law expenditure. The attempt to sanitise the rural economy, by the enforcement of *laissez-faire* economic principles through the radical, utilitarian Poor Law Amendment Act of 1834, which illegalised the payment of all non-medical relief to able-bodied males, constituted a major break with the past, despite widespread practical modification of the law through minor evasive tactics.[3] The resultant traumatic shock experienced by working people galvanised an episodic riotous response in the South, followed by more enduring covert protest, including arson against the properties of the new Poor Law Guardians. Initially at least, most farmers retained their customary policy of minimising winter-time employment, and seasonal mass lay-offs remained the norm. In most villages, farmers discriminated against unmarried workers, who were assumed to be able to spin out peak summer and harvest wages, across the remainder of the year, supplemented by any casual earnings. Labour requirements were met from the employment of married men. This exposed thousands to the seasonal, and others to the perennial, threat of incarceration in the punitive and hated new work-houses whose deterrent objective succeeded, in conjunction with other factors, in vastly inflating the already serious vagrancy problem in the southern countryside.[4]

The Swing and anti-Poor Law riots, together with what successive generations of contemporaries from the later eighteenth century to the 1860s, interpreted as repetitive crime waves, highlighted the antiquated systems of police. Most rural parishes relied on the infamously inadequate services of unpaid amateur constables, annually elected by vestries, though a minority experimented with paid officers, a system given statutory blessing by the 1833 Lighting and Watching Act. The policing of boroughs varied greatly, but at their best, they comprised a tiny force of salaried men, a situation which improved unevenly and slowly in such towns as adopted the 1835 Municipal Corporations Act. The permissory Rural Constabulary Acts of 1839–40 allowed counties to create profes-sional forces, but their adoption was bitterly resisted, and achieved in only a minority of Southern counties, including Hampshire and East Sussex.[5]

Much recent historiography has addressed the subjects of crime and popular protest, and the resultant volume of publications is too vast to review here. Both topics have been sufficiently researched to permit major syntheses, of crime by Jim Sharpe and Clive Emsley, and of popular disturbances by John Stevenson.[6] 'Social crime', loosely described as acts proscribed by law, but thought neither immoral nor warranting pun-ishment by considerable sectors of the community, notably poaching and the theft of articles historically embraced by crumbling customary rights, especially waste and woodland products, has been sensitively discussed by John Rule.[7] Popular protest in its overt and commonly riotous forms, across a huge range of topics, has been variously analysed, and of late more covert forms, notably incendiarism, the sending of threatening letters, animal maiming and malicious damage, have been shown to have become permanent features of the early nineteenth-century countryside. The paramount feature of these studies, is that open and secretive modes of protest were widely supported especially by working people, in response to factors over which they had little, if any, control, and were therefore legitimate expressions which regularly succeeded in achieving some redress of grievances.[8] Certain aspects of contemporary criminology, have been investigated by historians, and rejected in the case of Victorian identifica-tions of a criminal class,[9] but there has been no systematic study of criminal gangs despite their recurrent contemporary identification over this period, and their centrality to early Victorian debates over crime, public order and police.

From time immemorial, organised crime had evoked great fears. The 'formidable gang' led by the Clapson brothers in the mid-1790s, allegedly 'at least 36 strong', included 'the noted Jigg', 'so long a terror to the neighbourhood in which he resided'. Squire Fuller's detachment of Yeomanry Cavalry was called out to surround the house in which he was detected, and his arrest followed his being felled by a 'naked sword'; his, and the Clapsons' subsequent transportation was hailed as a great deliverance by the affluent in rural Sussex.[10] The appearance of metropolitan 'black legs' at provincial fairs generated somewhat lesser, but repetitive anxieties, revealed for example in the Mayor of Reading's 1810 resort to 'hand bills . . . cautioning the public'; this served to deter some villains from attending the fair, but they decamped on stolen horses.[11] The present essay seeks to analyse organised crime, principally that committed in the rural South, to re-examine historians' apparent penchant for categorisations like 'social crime', 'popular protest', and indeed the notion of 'rural crime' itself.

The West Firle Gang

The neighbouring villages of West Firle and Glynde, in the vicinity of Lewes, were among the most 'closed' in the South. West Firle (population, 1811, 551; 1821, 644) was virtually totally owned by the resident Lord Gage. Glynde, (population 1811, 203; 1821, 250) contained only 1,100 acres, of which 1,000 were farmed by John Ellman, the epitome of a thrusting, entrepreneurial, and socially aspirant big-farming tenant, whose success was symbolised by his son's eventual elevation to the county Bench.[12] One criminal association active in this district in the last years of the war before 1815, was led by Joseph Attree, a thirty-four-year-old journeyman blacksmith, employed at West Firle. Three of Ellman's workers, his twenty-three-year-old groom Samuel Horsecraft, and two labourers Henry and William (aged thirty in 1815) from the deviant Kenward family,[13] and sawyer William Wood, comprised the other known members of this criminal fraternity. They all poached locally. Rabbits were the principal target; they were usually snared, and this, together with the need to steal a gun, from Ellman, which they intended to return, probably reflects 'close' village prohibition of firearm possession by proletarians. They also regularly fished Gage's 'Garden Pond', pillaged his vegetables, and even raided his cucumber frames. More serious crimes were facilitated by Attree's skills; when he picked locks and made replacement keys for owners who had lost the original, he often

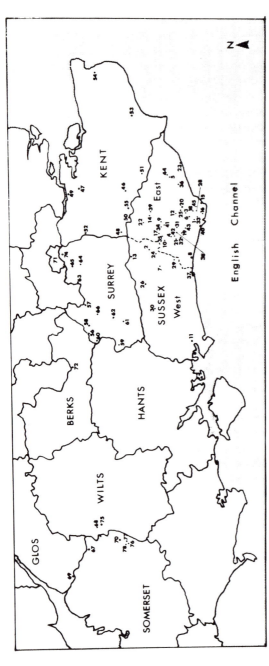

Locations in Southern England Mentioned in This Essay

made a duplicate for himself. He thus had access to at least the parish 'Coal Hole', Gage's substantial pigeon-house, and Ellman's wine cellar.[14]

Stolen rabbits, alcohol, pigeons and coal, were consumed in this group's families. Horsecraft even had his share of six pigeons 'baked at Stephens the Baker's'. But stolen goods were also sold. Customers for pigeons included Lewes postman Tinsley who supplemented his income by 'buying pigeons for Shooting Matches', and Lewes 'pieman' Worsell who took rabbits, which Attree on occasion also hawked round Lewes pubs. Two of his brothers worked as cellarmen in different Brighton hotels, and were ideally placed to fence 'a Brace or two' of carp, periodically brought over by Attree.

Although this fraternity were cautious, with Horsecraft occasionally rejecting Attree's suggestions for targets about Ellman's establishment, they had a number of narrow escapes. Horsecraft feared that 'he would be transported' about Christmas 1813, when Ellman offered a reward for the stolen gun, and Attree was almost detected when removing the wires from snared rabbits. Attree's undoing followed his boasting to Thomas Howard, one of Gage's labourers, whom Attree wished to recruit; Howard joined, but at the instigation of Gage's gamekeeper whom he informed. Howard went on a number of pond, garden and pigeon-house raids in the summer of 1815. On the gang's arrest Horsecraft cracked, and in October was admitted King's Evidence, but the lack of corroborative evidence led to charges being preferred against only Attree and William Kenward for theft, and Worsell for receiving. The former two received seven-year transportation sentences, but the latter was acquitted, and joined a long tradition of receivers found not guilty by juries hostile to the evidence of approvers against those not directly responsible for theft. Interestingly, Gage also attended this Quarter Session to formally qualify as a magistrate.

Stanton Collins and the Alfriston Gang

Alfriston, nestling in the Cuckmere Valley's penetration of the South Downs, was a moderately sized village, with a relatively gently rising population from 590 in 1811 to 648 and 694 in 1821 and 1831. In 1820, its 2445 acres were principally owned by five non-residents, Lady Burlington, Lords Gage and Cavendish, General Chowne and Thomas Harben, and let to substantial farmers. Several Downland farms extended beyond the parish boundaries.[15] One major tenant, and the largest ratepayer, Henry Pagden, also owned the Great Tithe. Residential and commercial property, including two or three farmhouses, were owned by tradesmen, including the various branches of the prosperous Brooker family, who invested the profits principally from shopkeeping, in residential property during the late eighteenth century. Tradesmen domiciled elsewhere, including the Collins family, made parallel investments. In 1807, Charles Collins rented premises, which he bought in 1816, for his butchering business. John Collins, a Brighton draper, also invested in a house. So too did butcher James Collins, since 1794 of Chiddingly, some eight miles distant, who purchased the honeycombed and ramshackle amalgam of buildings known as the Market Cross, in 1815. James's sons, Stanton and Steven, were born in 1796 and 1805 respectively. Stanton was probably apprenticed to Charles in the 1810s, and in 1822 took over and rented these premises, prior to buying the Market Cross from his father. In 1824 the father handed over the Chiddingly business to Steven, thereby establishing both sons in the butchering trade. Stanton erected new business premises on adjacent land in 1826–7, raising the capital by mortgaging the Cross to his father for £500.[16]

Economic divisions were underpinned by religious affiliations. Since the seventeenth century, the village had hosted a strong dissenting element, reflected in the ambitious construction in 1801 of a 400-seat Congregational Chapel destined for a stormy future. Only one Alfriston farmer, John Bodle, was a Chapel worshipper, and support derived principally from tradesmen, with some farmworkers, from Alfriston and neighbouring villages. John Newman was an original trustee; in 1799 he went into a partnership in a tanning business with twenty-one-year-old Charles Brooker, who soon broke his family's Anglican allegiances, and was eventually appointed to the ministry and a trusteeship. In 1810 he married his partner's sister, Elizabeth. Brooker was involved in various rifts, including the 1811 decision to exclude visiting preachers from the Countess of Huntingdon's Connection, and the 1812 contested appointment of George Betts as pastor. Betts's ministry was also troubled, notably by his 1825 refusal to marry Brooker to his deceased wife's sister, Ann. The couple were married, but under Anglican auspices, and although Ann was buried in the Chapel on her premature death in 1827, another dispute exploded in 1831 with Brooker locking Betts out of the building, in an episode which terminated in riot charges brought at the Assizes. This 'foolish business' in the estimate of an Anglican vicar who attended court, at least produced 'some amusing . . . cross questioning'. A substantial proportion of the congregation seceded and worshipped in the Seven Croft Barn during the 1830s, leaving Brooker and the new pastor to dominate the Chapel, until this rump split fatally in 1839, when Brooker again used his powers as trustee to lock-out his opponents. Despite these ruptures, some loyalties survived. Labourer William Ford, who joined in 1807, benefited from charitable collections in the 1810s, and 'Died in the Lord' in 1838, having responded positively to censure over the conduct of a beershop which he ran in the last years of his life. John Thorncraft, an Arlington farmworker, was another early communicant who continued into the 1830s, surviving censure for heavy drinking in the 1820s. Thorncraft's four children were all baptised in the Chapel, including son Samuel in 1809.

Some tradesmen retained Anglican loyalties. Stanton Collins's two children were baptised as Anglicans, and in 1820 he voted for a controversial rate to repair and extend the church. However, farmers comprised the backbone of the Anglican congregation, symbolised by that branch of the Brooker family who graduated into farming during the war years, when William took the tenancy of the sixth largest farm in the parish. Churchwarden from 1801 to 1811, and again in 1825, William transferred the farm lease to son James in 1819, who survived a change of owners in 1822, and took – in partnership – an additional farm in 1823. James's son, Charles Springate, was farming his own land on his early death in 1850, and all his six children were baptised Anglicans. Parish officers were drawn from both sides of the religious divide. Anglicans William and Charles Brooker senior both served as overseers in 1813, and the former again in 1816; in 1825 Charles junior served with his trading partner Newman. Property owned jointly by William and Charles senior was rented to the parish from 1801 to house paupers, and in 1827 the vestry rented part of the Market Cross from Collins, for subletting to impoverished farmworkers. Alfriston housed a disproportionate number of labourers as their numbers were swelled 'by the residence there of labourers working for farmers in adjoining [Downland] parishes there being very few cottages' available in the latter. Many labourers were also in receipt of allowances in-aid-of wages.[17]

But, if members of both the trading and farming sectors of the community thus exploited the old poor law, the post-war agricultural depression generated conflicts beween 'the trades' and the farmers, which principally derived from the latter – both inside and outside the parish – driving poor rates up through minimising employment in general, with mass lay-offs during the winters, and also paying derisory wages. During one typical February, according to a hostile observer, the labourers:

> were all without Employment, loitering about in listless and destructive Idleness and receiving relief . . . beyond the wages given to independent labourers in some parts . . . the population discontented & the paupers laugh at the honest labourer when they see him doing his utmost to keep off the Parish, telling him what a fool he is to work himself to Death . . . when they can get just as much from the Parish.

Nevertheless, harsh decisions by cost-conscious vestries were universal, and expanded the poor law as a theatre for three-dimensional conflict between, farmers and tradesmen, and claimants with both, the latter 'terming' parish officials 'their Enemies'.[18]

Alfriston's geographical location gave the village superb advantages for smuggling, and its eighteenth-century notoriety as a centre for contraband was broadened in the early nineteenth century by the scale of crime and protest. In 1831 the press said its 'population abounded with smugglers, poachers and bad characters', and in 1834 the vicar noted that Alfriston was 'famous for disaffection . . . for years a scourge to the Neighbourhood'. In February 1824, Henry Pagden asserted that along with all farmers he had 'for some Time past lost divers Quantities of Oats, Barley and Peas', and a press report the following year related that the district was infested by 'plunderers' who stole clothing, implements, and anything edible from farm premises; farmworkers, including Pagden's, were also victims, losing jackets and even lunchboxes. Charles Brooker repeatedly suffered at the hands of shoplifters. Thieves targetted Anglican churches; copper piping was stolen at Alfriston, and at nearby Folkington even the 'large copper sundial' disappeared. A prosecuting society, founded during the war, and supported principally by Downland farmers from several parishes, struggled futilely against successive crime waves. Minor successes were scored against petty thieves, including the one month hard labour term served by the seventeen-year-old Samuel Thorncraft for the theft of seven apples from major farmer Ade in 1826.[19]

Arson in the district assumed serious proportions in the 1790s and, before the end of the war, Downland farmers who introduced threshing machines were threatened with incendiarism. The trough of the depression in 1822, and a peak year for incendiarism, included among its victims farmers who used threshing machines at adjacent Folkington and Jevington. In October 1829, another machine owner, farmer and tithe proctor Rogers of neighbouring Ardingly, ignored threatening letters against its use, and a massive fire, started in different places, consumed thirteen hay and wheat ricks, and the barn containing the offensive technology. Although the rector subsequently ascribed the start of Captain Swing in Sussex to this incident, the Alfriston district was not an epicentre of that revolt.[20] In the autumn of 1830, the nearest mass mobilisations occurred six miles away to the north and east, at Laughton and Eastbourne. But arson was again employed against threshing machine owners at nearby Berwick and East Dean. However, it is symbolic that a fugitive Swing rioter from Ninfield, a Wealden Swing centre, sought sanctuary at Alfriston, and on his arrest was 'rescued on the road', with the terrified constable forced to unlock the handcuffs. Alfriston farmworker William Pearson was acquitted of the rescue at the Assizes.[21]

Smuggling remained a further volatile ingredient. Tradition has it that Congregationalist leaders condemned participation, and in April 1815 a party of Seaford fishermen stoned the Chapel; the fact that the sole prisoner brought before the Bench easily found sureties of £100 suggests that these men were smugglers, and Chapel leaders opted for a public apology, rather than advancing legal proceedings. Stanton Collins was reputedly a leading smuggler, and tradition again has it that this was the source of serious antagonism between him and the younger Charles Brooker. The hard evidence on this score eludes, but antagonisms certainly derived from Brooker's resort to litigation in 1825 over the alleged rape by Collins, of a girl employed by him under the vestry's auspices. Brooker, as overseer, together with Newman and churchwarden William Brooker, were the responsible parish officers at the time, whereupon 'many determined young men . . . were heard to vent the most violent threats and express the greatest disgust' at these officers' conduct. All of their properties were the targets of nocturnal attacks, but the rewards offered by the prosecution society drew blanks. Committal proceedings against Collins foundered on evidential problems, whereupon the dispute was transferred to inter-personal innuendo exchanged in the columns of the county press. The Brookers launched prosecutions against Collins's friend, William Adams of The George, who was fined heavily and subsequently imprisoned, for repeated licensing offences early in 1826, successes which stimulated further attacks on the Brookers's properties.[22]

Whatever Collins's involvement in smuggling, in the 1820s he emerged as the organiser of an extensive criminal fraternity. He dealt in stolen corn, the Lewes brewer Chitty being one regular customer, and Collins also fenced rustled sheep. Much intelligence of appropriate targets came from farmworkers, some of whom, including Sam Thorncraft, had permanent employment, and who regularly liaised with Collins at The George. Several of these men were convicted criminals, including Thorncraft, William Pearson and George Huggett; others, like Lewis Awcock, John Reeds and William Adams's son, Robert, were not. A typical raid occurred on 20 April 1831 after Huggett and Pearson inspected the Revd Capper's tithe barn at Arlington to see 'if there was any booty worth having'. On discovering oats, they repaired to The George, and Collins subsequently provided the cart for the theft of twenty-eight bushels valued at £3. A similar robbery executed by Collins and Robert Adams at Litlington netted twelve bushels of barley, which they took to Collins's brother-in-law, miller John Gorringe of Horsebridge, some six miles from Alfriston. Gorringe was clearly a prosperous rogue who employed several men, including one who had been tried recently for thieving from a previous employer.[23] Gorringe's employees were suspected members of Collins's fraternity, and the miller himself was 'not much surprised' to be called up at 1 a.m. one night to receive goods stolen by Collins. On 11 November 1831, an itinerant jeweller staying overnight in the village, was robbed of his entire stock of 481 items valued at over £200. These were but some of a spate of thefts enumerated by the press in 1831 under the headline 'Depredations . . . prevailing at Alfriston'.[24]

The terrorist tradition established in the 1820s was maintained but not restricted to affluent targets. Labourer Sawyers had his beehives thrown into the Cuckmere, and shoemaker Boniface's house was stoned. The parsonage barn, rented by two farmers, including the dissenter Bodle, was fired in October 1831, and huge corn stocks destroyed. Thorncraft thought little of taking days off from his employment of 'several years' with farmer Ade of Ardingly to spend at beerhouses. Although suspected of allegiance to Collins, Thorncraft blandly asserted that Ade '"knows better than to discharge me"', and on one occasion flourished a steel 'that was what he set the barns and hovels on fire with'. Collins himself became more brazen in the tense atmosphere prevailing in the immediate aftermath of the Swing revolt, and even one of his defence witnesses subsequently admitted that Collins's 'Character has been blackened of late'. In plebeian circles he achieved folk hero status, given a rough musical rendition by Thorncraft in the Royal Oak at Arlington:

> Collins is merry merry there;
> And we will be merry, merry here,
> And set the barns on fire,
> About their ears.

Collins's downfall followed theft accusations levelled against brother-in-law Gorringe, and the arrest of confederate William Pearson, who eventually cracked after repeated judicial interrogation. He, and Gorringe, saved themselves by giving evidence against Collins, who was arrested while driving through Lewes on 26 November 1831. Excited press speculation at the impending dissolution of the Alfriston gang extended to farmer Ade, who had Thorncraft arrested, but quickly lost his nerve when unable to expeditiously find a magistrate to commit, and Thorncraft was released. Collins, charged with corn theft and receiving, rather than the sheep stealing of legend, knew on his committal on 2 December that he faced transportation. On the 4th he conferred in Lewes jail with his attorney, and paid his mortgage by signing over the Market Cross to his father.[25] Collins subsequently handed over 'several thousand pounds' to his daughter, thus evading the sequestration to the crown of transportees' assets. Ironically, many of the propertied inhabitants of Alfriston, including Collins, had been summonsed for jury service at the same Assize at which he was indicted; in the event farmers from Hamsey and Newick – themselves the recent targets of Swing and serious sufferers from crime – deputised. Social tensions in the district increased in the days preceding the trial on 13 December. Sinister conversations were overheard in the beershops and at The George. On Sunday 11 December the dispute at Alfriston Chapel exploded into riot, and Brooker laid charges against two members who took the Revd Betts's side, but the sparse evidence does not reveal any relevance to the impending trial of Collins. That evening, concerted attempts to intimidate prosecution witnesses commenced, with arson attacks on Ade at Arlington and Brooker at Alfriston. Ade's three barns, full of corn, and two adjacent hay stacks were fired. 'Several well known suspicious characters' drinking at The George, and more from the 'various beer and pothouses in the neighbourhood, left *en masse*', some to 'render assistance', others including those responsible, Thorncraft and John Reeds to watch. At this moment an incendiary device exploded in Brooker's warehouse, only to be immediately extinguished by a passer-by, or 'the whole of the adjacent premises' would have ignited and spread to the 'very old . . . buildings in the town'. In the event the witnesses against Collins held fast; indeed, Brooker was so determined to give evidence, that he distinguished himself by stating that on the night central to one charge, 'I saw a cart under the trees, but cannot swear that it belonged to Collins'. This presumably contributed to Collins's acquittal on the receiving charge, together with Huggett tried for theft itself; Collins was convicted on the other charge, although his co-defendant, Robert Adams, was found not guilty. Collins was sentenced to seven-years' transportation, as was Lewis Awcock, convicted of robbing the itinerant jeweller.

Meanwhile the net closed on Thorncraft. The Bow Street detective sent down, discovered incendiary devices, including a 'scallop shell with . . . brimstone in it', at Thorncraft's lodgings, and it was also established that Thorncraft had tried to implicate a fellow employee, who had accused Thorncraft of thieving, in the arson attack. His accomplice, Reeds, quickly calculated that the preservation of his own life depended on a swift confession, and he went on in a 'cool, deliberate and unfeeling manner' to give the evidence to the March 1832 Assize which sealed Thorncraft's fate. After his conviction:

he stood unmoved during the passing of the sentence, and at its conclusion several of his companions advanced to shake hands with him.

Among them were most of the witnesses, including the wives of the proprietors of beershops patronised by him, the labourer subjected to his attempted incriminations, and other workmates, at least two of whom were from families like his own who had worshipped at Alfriston Chapel. Thorncraft 'assumed a ferocious appearance, and . . . shook . . . his fist at' Reeds. Thorncraft's religious upbringing was reflected when he told his aged parents that while he did not fear death, 'I fear some dread on meeting my God'; he refused to name any partners in crime, stoically refused twice to make the customary scaffold speech regretting his criminal career: instead, his 'composure and fortitude' sufficed to 'astonish the spectators'.

The removal of Collins, Thorncraft, and two others in 1831–2, dealt with but a minority of criminal associates. As one Alfriston resident, Ann Marchant, confided, the authorities had 'secured some but . . . there are still many left'. Henry Pagden's new vigilante patrols, comprising the more determined farmers, scored a few minor successes, although they were not responsible for the successful charges brought in 1835 against John and James Huggett for assault and robbery, sheep stealing, and animal maiming, for which they were transported. Too many of the old confederates remained active, including John Reeds, and the 'inveteracy for thieving' hardly abated. In the early 1830s the press was discouraged from reporting incendiarism, but one Lewes journalist who reported another Arlington blaze in the autumn of 1832, also claimed that the current situation mirrored that obtaining two years earlier during Swing.[26] Meanwhile, Charles Brooker who was also a recurrent victim of crime after Collins's transportation executed some extraordinary property deals. In May 1832 he purchased the Market Cross for £800 from Collins's father, raising £500 through mortgaging the building to Lewes butcher Waters. As Brooker soon claimed that Collins's nine-year-old son, also Stanton, was his tenant, this deal was clearly part of the plan to preserve Collins's Alfriston business intact.[27]

This tense situation in the district was aggravated further by the furore of the protracted Reform Bill crisis, and the subsequent politicisation campaign by working-class radicals in the countryside. Alfriston was one theatre where 'the poison of some popular political publications has been instill'd into' workers.[28] The passage of the radically utilitarian Poor Law Amendment Act, and the arrival of assistant commissioner Hawley to implement the legislation in the area in September 1834 brought this tension to fever pitch. Hawley ordered existing poor law authorities to soften up current claimants by modifying existing relief schemes on the new Act's principles, notably that no payments should be made to the able-bodied, until rigorous examination of every recipient's circumstances, and then only in return for work:

> The work itself should be digging, and it is quite immaterial whether or not it returns one farthing to the Parish purse as a lucrative speculation, it is from the System and not from the Profit that the parish will reap its remuneration and advantage. . . . By a strict adherence to this System you will find that you shortly get rid of some of your worst and most idle

characters and though a first essay may not . . . induce . . . all to find more desirable and more profitable employment elsewhere immediately, still it will have the effect of making them more provident in future, and the [harvest and ploughing] wages of the ensuing Autumn will be laid by, to avert the necessity of accepting Parish relief on the above terms the following Winter.

Hawley also insisted that existing workhouse inmates be subjected to rigorous discipline. A crop of summary convictions reveal that the magistracy supported parochial poor-law authorities in their various responses to Hawley, 'some trying gradual & minute alterations; some plungeing at once into bolder & harsher measures'. Those on the receiving end asserted that 'Government is not the Poor Man's Friend', as:

> a cruel & unjust law has been passed, that they are deprived of their rights, & that the magistrates are disgraced for having taken their parts against their Oppressors.[29]

The Act's support derived mainly from landowners and major farmers, including Pagden. The latter's support at Alfriston for Hawley's crusade stimulated an incendiary attack on his farm, and goods worth over £700 went up in flames. It caused prodigious alarms, press comment that 'the character of the English peasant is entirely changed', and proof of Hawley's contention that the village was 'notorious for the bad Character of its inhabitants'. John Reeds and another were arrested immediately, 'somewhat hastily . . . interrogated without . . . a magistrate', and released, while another suspect fled reputedly to America; rewards, and another Bow Street detective drew blanks, except an anonymous letter threatening Pagden's life. Miscellaneous protest, notably covert 'depredation and wanton outrage' continued throughout the 1834–5 winter.[30]

These events galvanised fierce opposition to Alfriston's – and Seaford's – incorporation into Hawley's proposed Eastbourne Poor Law Union; his insistence 'would destroy the harmony that would otherwise prevail' amongst agrarian capitalists in the other parishes. Hawley was undeterred, as his political calculations projected a pliant Board of Guardians, with existing premises in the former barracks used as a workhouse, ideal for the immediate classification of inmates on the new Act's principles, to quickly create a model Union in the South at Eastbourne.[31] Charles Brooker, horrified over the un-Christian separation of man and wife under the new regime, decided to fight it from within by election to the Board, which entailed standing against Pagden backed by 'a Combination of agriculturalists'. Brooker claimed that 'the Trade, or rather the Householders are for me', but he was supported by only one farmer, the dissenter Bodle, who shortly died. 'Death or Liberty' flags accompanied the election, which Brooker won, but on Pagden's instructions, the responsible parish officers, including farmer Dray, the owner of the barn where the anti-Brooker dissenters worshipped, ruled illegally that Brooker's property qualifications were inadequate, and formally returned Pagden. Brooker was personally rebuffed by Hawley, who nevertheless privately informed the Poor Law Commission that Brooker had been 'ousted . . . unfairly'.[32]

Brooker fought on, 'harangued the populace in the Public Highways', and appealed for support from 'the Working People', thereby generating their 'hostility to their Employers', who responded by a printed spoof royal proclamation against 'persons assembling together'. In April 1835 Brooker arrived at the inaugural meeting of the Board of Guardians, but was refused admission. His return to Alfriston was 'met by a considerable concourse . . . with banners and mottoes', and a band. He orchestrated a petition from 'the labourers of Alfriston', took it personally to Somerset House, where he was denied an audience by Edwin Chadwick. Further covert protest erupted, especially malicious damage to the properties of those 'Farmers and Tradesmen' joining Pagden in a boycott of Brooker's and his son-in-law's businesses. Hawley argued for Pagden's maintenance in office, as a new election would galvanise 'renewed excitement destructive of all parochial government'. Chadwick penned a masterfully tactful letter to announce the decision, pragmatically attributing electoral 'irregularities' to 'misapprehension' on the parts of the churchwardens and overseers: Mrs Marchant, the wife of one, whose devotion to 'a quiet social life' underpinned her long-term aversion to Alfriston, neatly portrayed relationships in the 'place; . . . a scene of discord and to be free from it I must remain for ever in my own little circle'.[33]

The Amendment Act's implementation caused a further furore; the election of two working-class delegates from every parish to lobby the new Board, was quickly subsumed by the emergent 'United Brothers of Industry', a farmworkers' trade union, formed to prise out wage increases to compensate for the abolition of allowances in-aid-of wages. Union recruitment forged ahead through rallies, which are difficult to demarcate from the repeated mass lobbyings of the Board; the 'machinations . . . of desperate Characters in . . . Alfriston' were central in both phenomena, and possibly to a riotous explosion of open protest in nearby Willingdon when the new relieving officer was ceremoniously carted out of the parish. Hawley seized on this incident to orchestrate show trials, which reflected traditional divisions, with farmers giving evidence for the prosecution, and tradesmen for the defence. The jail sentences were met with two Downland fires, and further incendiarism in September, when the huge crowd which convened revealed 'great apathy' to firefighting. The remainder of the year witnessed repeated 'wanton' slaughter of notably

Guardians' sheep, the carcasses ostentatiously left in the fields. Only Hawley's repeated attendance at Board meetings, combined with strategic deployment of army detachments, infiltrations of secret policemen, and the collapse of the 'United Brothers' after a lock-out, saw the belated introduction of workhouse classification. The house itself remained a centre for protest – from within. Regular revolts by youths, more by able-bodied men refusing to work and visiting their wives *en masse*, and the 'demolition' of 'three very strong cells', originally designed to incarcerate soldiers, eventually broke the governor, who took to heavy drinking. His replacement's arrival was greeted by an attempt to fire the house.[34]

Covert protest characterised the later 1830s and early 1840s. Nevertheless, the Eastbourne Board emerged as a cohesive and determined administration, and Brooker abandoned plans to fight Pagden electorally, in favour of a more ambitious political campaign. Through a series of press articles, pamphlets, and rallies, he attempted to imitate the northern Anti-Poor Law Movement, and eventually became a Chartist, twice standing unsuccessfully for the Brighton parliamentary constituency, shortly before his death in 1843. He made at least one rhetorical reference to earlier events:

> We have heard of the Alfriston gang, and no wonder that persons have been sent abroad for outrageous proceedings at Alfriston; pity, it seems, that a few more, as associates to accompany them, had not been shipped off from Alfriston.[35]

The Barcombe Gang

Barcombe, in the Ouse Valley three miles to the north of Lewes, comprised 'remarkably neat houses, but scarcely anything in the shape of trade', other than a corn and oil mill. The village experienced typical post-war demographic growth, rising from 753 inhabitants in 1821, to 1,028 in 1841. Several of the larger farmers, including Nathaniel Guy, also cultivated land in adjacent parishes, and Lewes butchers, among them Benjamin Morris, rented or owned pastoral land in Barcombe. Amongst the wealthiest residents was the rector, Robert Allen, possessed of the living annually worth £719, and Captain Richardson JP, the largest landowner. Allen, like Morris, was a Swing target in 1830, and the rector claimed that several of the farmers, in cahoots with Richardson, directed a mass assembly of labourers to the rectory, who were appeased only by promises of tithe reductions. Acrimony between the two men continued for years, with Allen repeating and Richardson denying the allegations to the Tithe Commissioners in 1838. Pre-1834 poor rates were high, and administered by a tight, oligarchic vestry comprising the richest farmers in close consultation with Richardson; the rates 'would never have been collected' from the lesser contributors, but for the exertions of a full-time, professional assistant-overseer. The notorious Roundsman System was used, but only ephemerally to counter peak January lay-offs of farmworkers, whose deteriorating attitudes to their employers were attributed exclusively by Richardson to the influence of the new beershops, which he argued required much stricter control or 'there will not be an industrious man in the Parish'. Barcombe did not figure in the anti-new poor law riots of 1835, though neighbouring Ringmer witnessed a fierce protest, and the imprisonment of a core of leaders. In the later 1830s Barcombe vestry annually excused between twenty and forty of the smallest ratepayers, mostly labourers, from payment.[36] The high incidence of crime, including periodic 'wholesale robbery' especially of fowls and sheep, and perennial poaching, was attributed to the proximity of Lewes. The larger farmers subscribed to the Hamsey, Barcombe and Chailey Prosecuting Society, whose regular resort to rewards rarely resulted in criminal convictions.[37]

In 1839, in the words of a member, the 'Ringleader . . . for some years' of the Barcombe gang was thirty-three-year-old William Heasman, a 'smooth-faced light haired gawky countryman', domiciled with his wife Martha, four children under ten, and his aged mother, in the 'old workhouse premises', converted into a row of tenements. Heasman received old poor-law benefits prior to 1835, but under the new legislation was excused rate payments as his children were 'all young'. Heasman was one of several children; a brother was a farm foreman, and an unmarried sister was a yearly servant on village farms. Like many of his plebeian neighbours, Heasman kept a pig and fowls; he 'never had constant work', but did specific tasks on a casual basis for village farmers, and on occasion laboured for Lewes residents. In common with many farmworkers he migrated for the hop-picking season. Perhaps he was one of those locally identified to the Constabulary Commissioners as 'idle drunken fellows who could hardly live upon the wages they chose to earn and have recourse to other means'. Heasman certainly achieved notoriety among his class for 'getting his living by thieving', and he boasted that his livestock was raised on stolen corn, while his fuel came from raids on faggot and hop-pole stacks.[38] There is evidence that Barcombe farmworkers, like those elsewhere, were divided into 'roughs and respectables',[39] the latter rewarded for their honesty including the character who handed over a concealed hoard of three fowls to their owner, and received them back for his own consumption. One young labourer, Elphick, would not join Heasman for poaching, saying that 'my Father and Mother would be crazy if I ever did'.

Heasman particularly feared, on three counts, his next-door neighbour bar one, thirty-year-old James Towner. First, Towner was in Richardson's permanent employ. Secondly, Heasman knew that Towner saw 'him bring things home at different times', and was 'afraid . . . [he] should tell some of the Captain's Men'.[40] Thirdly, Heasman's attempts to protect himself by drawing Towner into the criminal fraternity were vehemently opposed by Towner's wife, because even the suspicion of wrong-doing could jeopardise her husband's job. Heasman intimidated those workers he believed might incriminate him:

> if he knew any one saying anything against him or trying to hurt him he would . . . have his revenge . . . in any kind of way by poisoning their Hog if they had one or destroying their Bees.[41]

A combination of sympathy, temptation and intimidation, served Heasman well between 1835 and 1839. Towner – and Elphick – were eventually drawn in; George Tapp, employed by the Revd Allen, was clearly intimidated. The village shoemaker concealed vital information about shoes mended by him, and worn by a Heasman associate, from constable Austin in pursuit of the robbers of a Ringmer barn. Big farmer Knight's employees 'did not make much answer' to questions about the discovery of stolen sheep skins. One labourer said it all with the admission that:

> I never told . . . my Master nor a Peace Officer nor to any one which might have led to detection, but I spoke of it amongst my fellow workmen.

Heasman's known criminal associates were principally drawn from his working neighbours. Thirty-six-year-old John Jenner, a self-employed carpenter, commonly worked 'Trug making . . . Fence making', but like so many craftsmen in the depressed post-war years was reduced to 'Farming' labour on occasion. William Miles (21) and George Day (22) were both principally, though neither permanently employed at the Mills. The remainder, Richard Funnel (45), Joseph Markwick (35) and Elphick (24) were all agricultural day-labourers. Jenner and Markwick were family men; Funnel and Towner had five and six children respectively, and were invariably excused poor-rate payments.[42] Only George Ware, a higler of Buxted, and later of Lewes, was not a local man.

The catalogue of this asociation's exploits, once Heasman 'confess[ed] . . . to all I can recollect', was extensive; the absence of corroborative evidence restricted criminal charges to the asterisked items only on the following list:

*23 April 1836: Hamsey: theft of two sheep from farmer Nathaniel Guy; Heasman and Funnel.

*30 November 1837: Barcombe: theft of one sheep from Benjamin Morris; Heasman and Funnel.

*27 May 1838: Barcombe: theft of two sheep from farmer James Brook; Heasman and Funnel.

*11 August 1838: Wellingham: theft of two sheep from farmer John Rickman; Heasman, Jenner and Funnel.

*3 September 1838: Barcombe: theft of partridges, beehives and onions from farmer Richard Knight; Heasman and Jenner.

*14 September 1838: Fletching: theft of three sheep from farmer Charles Cave; Heasman, Jenner and Markwick.

*8 November 1838: Chailey: theft of four lambs from farmer Charles Carey, part of flock depastured for Lewes auctioneer, Richard Verrall; Heasman and Jenner.

*7 December 1838: Barcombe: theft of three sheep from the 'Common Field', occupied by farmer Lashmar, who farmed Great Henver Street Farm, Hamsey, though domiciled in Lewes; Heasman and Jenner.

*20 January 1839: Hamsey: theft of twenty-one chickens from Morris's labourer, who kept them on commission for Barcombe farmer, Henry Guy; Heasman and Miles.

9 February 1839: Barcombe: theft of 60lbs. pork, 40lbs. butter, from forcibly-entered dairy of N. Guy; Heasman and Jenner.

*19 February 1839: Ringmer: theft of a sack of oats from farmer Water's barn, and wheat from Clayhill Farm, owned and farmed directly by Henry Blackman JP; Heasman and Miles.

April/early May 1839: Barcombe: theft of three sheep from Richardson; Heasman, Jenner and Markwick.

*10 June 1839: Newick: theft of one sheep and a lamb, from farmer John Ellis; Heasman and Day.

*21 July 1839: Barcombe: theft of three hens and eight turkeys from farm of Brighton banker, George Wigney; Heasman, Day and Elphick.

August 1839: Chailey: theft of two 'sacks . . . of Wheat Ears' from farmer Carey's ripening crop; Heasman and Towner.

August 1839: Barcombe: theft of one chicken and six chicks from N. Guy; Heasman and Towner.

Early September 1839: Barcombe: theft of twelve chickens from farmer John Waters, and five geese from Knight; Heasman and Ware.

*12 September 1839: Hamsey: theft of one sheep from Waters: Heasman and Day.

Late September 1839: Isted: theft of ten geese from Mr Atree; Heasman and Ware.

3 October 1839: Hamsey: theft of eleven geese from blacksmith and occupier of Covell's Farm, Samuel Smith; Heasman and Day.

*6 October 1839: Barcombe: theft of six fowls from farmer Thomas Foster; Heasman and Day.

11 October 1839: Barcombe: theft of three sheep belonging to Morris, but depastured on Allen's glebe; Heasman and Towner.

Heasman, who poached game and fish, and stole fuel and grain on his own, took one and occasionally two of his associates on these raids. Although his criminal activities were regular and extensive, and his notoriety thoroughly earned, at times he was directly motivated by poverty; there is a suggestive chronological coincidence between the apparent start of his criminal career, and the first winter of the New Poor Law, which was particularly severe on the casually employed. One November (1838) when demand for labour customarily plummeted, Heasman 'came' to Jenner 'and said he was starving' as he had no work; desperation on this occasion clearly stimulated determination, for having failed to entrap the first target of sheep, 'Heasman said he must have something he would rob a hen roost'; they ended up at Chailey and unusually took four 'rubbishy things' from a flock of lambs. Heasman also exploited his neighbours' poverty. In February 1839 Miles 'said he had got no work' and 'he didn't know what he should do'; Heasman recommended that 'we get a little Wheat and . . . have it ground into Flour' and they raided two barns. In June 1839 Heasman and Day 'had nothing to do that day and we agreed to have a sheep'. On Saturday 5 October following, Heasman contacted Day 'told him I should like to have something for a pudding . . . for tomorrow', and with Day's concurrence in securing a decent Sunday dinner, fowls were stolen. Towner's poverty drove him to join Heasman in 1839, a year of inflated living costs; unable to afford his customary breast of lamb, Towner was reduced to boiling bones for fat for suet 'cakes . . . for the Children which was cheaper than Bread and Cheese and Meat'. His crisis broke when he 'must kill my Pig' although 'it was doing well . . . for I could not keep it longer'. But unemployment, financial difficulties and hunger, were not invaried stimuli; Jenner 'had work' when he went after sheep, and succumbed to Heasman's stated preference for Jenner as he 'had been before'.

The participants invariably divided the booty, though status clearly mattered, with younger and less experienced partners receiving smaller portions. Mutton and lamb were partially eaten fresh, and the remainder salted, and concealed outside homes, including meat hidden in a rick thatch and taken 'a bit at a time when we wanted'. Stolen beasts were always eaten, and never sold, and skins abandoned; the sale of fells was commonly the source of rustlers' detection.[43] Getting stolen wheat ground caused problems when it was 'missed' and 'enquiries made', and had to be concealed until the heat died down. Heasman fenced some poultry through Barcombe butcher Coppard, and also disposed of booty through the notorious beershop, brothel and lodging house, kept by Traft at Lewes.[44] Heasman spent the odd day at Traft's establishment, tippling with the serving girls, and on one occasion when Heasman arrived with eleven partridges, Traft despatched the one-legged Smith, who hung about the beershop executing such commissions, to licensed dealer Oliver. He made an offer, and tangential evidence suggests he was supplied by several poachers and fowl-thieves.[45] Samuel Simmons who 'sold fish and poultry' was another 'likely man' to purchase stolen articles, and representative of those at the bottom of market-town entrepreneurial hierarchies, whose insecure base was reflected in his residence in Hailsham workhouse a year later. Higler Ware was similarly placed; on one occasion he 'must have some . . . Geese or Chickens . . . soon for he had got no Money' to finance legitimate deals. Ware encouraged Heasman to become a regular supplier, initially in January 1839 'when Fowls sold so dear'. But Ware never paid 'the full price as he knew how we came by them', and Heasman also supplied him on credit. Although Ware went on some raids himself, his heavy drinking worried Heasman, who preferred simply to supply those in need of Dutch courage.

Heasman was resourceful and careful. Targets were usually identified beforehand, and friends often supplied intelligence in the comfort of the Royal Oak at Barcombe, where some raids were planned. Further intelligence derived from Heasman's sister, including that of her employer's recent slaughter of a hog, which could be 'got out pretty easy', and Jenner came too despite acknowledgement that this constituted 'House Robbing'.[46] Heasman refused to operate in wet weather to avoid the chance of detection through footprints, the recurrent fate of thieves in the countryside. The record is full of Heasman's caution, typified by his killing and disposal of a day-old chick, which he intended to raise with his own fowls, when he noticed its deformed claw. He was furious with Towner's theft of feeding dishes which enhanced the possibility of detection. Heasman drank moderately, if at all before setting out, and enforced the same on his partners. He operated in a restricted district with which he was thoroughly familiar, and his furthest – and temporary – fence lived eight miles away, which in the main minimised distances to be traversed with stolen goods. Moreover, only one known victim was targeted for reasons other than pure theft. Heasman noted that farmer 'Knight and I are not very good friends', which derived from being sacked, and vengeance motivated Heasman's planned robbery of the partridges Knight shot on the first day of the 1838 season. When a mere eleven birds were found in the farmer's safe, Heasman 'said it would not satisfy him', so he took a beehive and two bushels of 'pretty good onions'. Heasman's abstinence from 'protest theft' was probably contrived to minimise suspicion.

On 15 October 1839 the victim of fowl thieves obtained a warrant to search Heasman's house; no fowls were discovered, but forty pounds of mutton temporarily there – which Heasman admitted 'looks bad' – were.

He decided to pre-emptively incriminate his partners, correctly anticipating that either Jenner or Towner might turn informer to save themselves, and in the event they were encouraged to think they might become Queen's Evidence by the wily Henry Blackman, who spent days interrogating these men and achieved confessions from all three. Heasman's crew had not simply and extensively thieved from local farmers and two landed gentlemen and magistrates; the fraternity had targetted the properties of important members of the urban bourgeoisie, including Brighton banker Wigney, butcher and meat merchant Morris, and wealthy auctioneer Verrall, both of Lewes. In addition, Heasman had supplied urban criminals, including the notorious Traft, against whom charges were also brought. Heasman's evidence permitted five charges against Jenner, four apiece against Day and Funnel, two against Miles, and one each against Towner and Elphick, and the net was closing on Ware, who decamped, only to be arrested in 1840. Their convictions would dissolve a major criminal association comprising primary thieves and active fences. The Grand Jury came under pressure from the Sessions's chairman to indict, despite evidential flaws. Although Heasman, described by the press as a 'rustic Jonathan Wild',

> gave his evidence on each trial in a quiet and unconcerned manner, as if he had been the most innocent person in the world, describing the details of each robbery with perfect coolness and without the least hesitation,

the prosecution partially collapsed. The first trial, of Miles for theft, brought a rider to the guilty verdict that he had 'been drawn . . . by an older offender'. The second case against Miles was dropped. The prosecution's resort to the evidence of Heasman's wife against Funnel, was rejected by the court, and two other charges against him dropped; a joint charge with Jenner was 'abandoned' during the trial. Other prosecutions were also abandoned while in process, and additional charges withdrawn. Traft too was acquitted. Jenner's, and Towner's confessions served, to secure their conviction, and respective ten and fifteen year transportation sentences. Miles escaped with a year's hard labour. If Heasman's performance evinced 'a possibility of contrition in his mind', he did not return to Barcombe, though the acquitted Funnel and Markwick were both subsequently listed as excused ratepayers.[47]

The Battle Gang

Farmworker Jack Wood, and bricklayer George Stunt, were the dominant members of a gang active in the Battle area in the later 1830s, before it was broken up in 1840. Jack, married to Phoebe, and the father of several children, received poor relief in the early thirties, and had been acquitted of arson at the December 1833 Assize.[48] Stunt, unlike his confederates, was domiciled at Hastings with his wife and stepson. He probably came from Hawkhurst, and narrowly evaded conviction for breaking into a windmill in 1837. Ironically, one of his subsequent partners in crime, thirty-one-year-old journeyman butcher James Jenner, was at that time a part-time paid 'helper to a constable', and involved in Stunt's arrest. Jenner moved to Battle, where the other gang members – farmworkers William Foord and James Marchant, both thirty – lived. Jack Wood's notoriety derived in part from suspicion that he was an arsonist; Stunt's 'character . . . was tolerably well known' at Battle, customers at the Half Moon on one occasion 'kept on chaffing him about various robberies', including burglary at a church. Jack's arrest in December 1839, his conviction and fifteen-year transportation term imposed in March 1840, triggered a chain of events, which included Stunt's arrest, and confession, followed by his turning Queen's Evidence against his confederates.[49]

Stunt's truncated catalogue of criminality started with a raid on a potato stack with labourer Thomas Langley in November 1838; in the following March they were joined by Horace Metcalf in chicken stealing. Six days later, Stunt conspired with James Marchant, then lodging with fellow labourer Timothy Potter – who had given evidence against Wood for arson[50] – to leave the front door open to facilitate access to bacon which Potter had smoking up his chimney. Marchant would 'go in and blunder about as if I was drunk as I have done before'. Stunt implemented the plan, but escaped detection only through hiding the bacon in a 'Brick Kiln', from whence it was lifted by unknown parties, 'sack and all'. This petty criminal profile changed once Marchant and Stunt teamed up with Jack Wood, as reflected in their first known job, namely the burglary of a farm bailiff's house on Stunt's old stomping ground at Hawkhurst. The haul comprised a shotgun, cloaks and other clothing, a writing desk, violin, tea-caddy, nine items of marked silver-ware, and three bottles of spirits.[51] The loot was taken to Wood's house. Marchant presented the tea-caddy to a girl-friend, and Stunt sold the violin to a Hastings 'broker' through his ten-year-old stepson, who was instructed to say that 'his father sent him as he wanted to buy victuals and had no work'. The disposal of the silver and the gun required greater exertions; the trio went to Brighton, with which they were familiar,[52] selling the cloaks at a Lewes 'Secondhand Shop' en route;[53] Marchant pawned the gun for the unrealistically low sum of fifteen shillings, leaving the ticket with a local villain, a common ploy with experienced thieves. A woman pawned the remaining clothes for Stunt, while Wood arranged for 'a man to carry' the silver to London, but refused to reveal the carrier's name to Stunt.

On 4 December 1839, Stunt, Wood and Jenner teamed up to burgle a shopkeeper at adjacent Whatlington; the loot comprised '3 bladders of lard', eight cheeses, 'a quantity of mens . . . and boys ready made Jackets', trousers, various women's gowns, shawls and petticoats, and several pairs of sheets. Although Stunt and Jenner decided against wearing the jackets which they selected for themselves, Wood who was becoming flushed with success, openly wore his, correctly calculating that precise identification of such mass-produced articles was impossible. On the following Saturday, these three, now joined by William Foord, got so drunk that they were refused further service, and once Stunt revealingly argued that 'we were not going to rob the Man . . . the money belongs to the [Turnpike] Commissioners', cavalierly implemented their plan to rob the keeper of the Tavoli Tollgate. Disguised with masks, they stole a horse to lure the keeper from his house, but a melee developed, because they had not reconnoitred and were unaware that a gamekeeper was also staying at the gatehouse. Although the four-man gang escaped, and made their separate ways home, Wood had been identified despite his hood, and press reports confidently and correctly anticipated his arrest. The Battle Petty Sessions swallowed members' 'astonishment' at Wood's insistence on an Assize trial, rather than commitment to the imminent Quarter Sessions, where he feared that 'local prejudice', privately communicated by local magistrates on the score of 'character' to the Chairman, would engineer a stiffer sentence.[54]

If this arrest stunned the partners, the resultant dilemma dictated further recourse to crime to realise the cash 'to employ a Counsellor for Jack Wood'. Two raids were planned, one after sheep, the other for flour, which could be sold. Both expeditions succeeded on 2 and 3 March, but the stress clearly showed, with Foord having to be pressurised to go for the sheep, and Stunt keeping out of the way while the flour was distributed among plebeian neighbours and Phoebe baked mutton pies for Jack to eat in Lewes Jail. When Stunt sent his stepson to fetch more flour for his use, his wife acknowledged the risk by beating the lad for going; little Thomas passed Jenner's message 'that the Philistines were about' to his stepfather, whose predicament was aggravated by the simultaneous news that William Cobbett's barrister son John, briefed for Wood's defence, had lost the case, whereupon a fifteen-year transportation sentence was imposed. Stunt's subsequent conduct suggests concern that Wood might seek a reprieve through impeaching his confederates; when taunted over Wood's sentence in an angry exchange in the Half Moon, Stunt blurted out that 'he would speak the truth', and gave some details; he was arrested, and once his ploy that 'he might have told . . . any lies he pleased' in the pub, failed to convince the examining justices in a five-hour marathon hearing, he finally confessed to the eight offences enumerated above. Only Foord among the main members escaped conviction on at least one charge, and Jenner, Marchant, and Metcalf, all received seven-year-transportation sentences. Two minor associates were acquitted on indictment for theft, as were Phoebe Wood and two others on receiving charges, and thus compromised journalistic confidence that 'a gang of the most desperate characters in the neighbourhood' had been annihilated.[55]

Clarke of Brighton and Wicks of Lewes

Frederick Clarke, a twenty-five-year-old hairdresser, ran a 'much frequented' lodging house in Thomas Street, part of a well-known Brighton rookery, with Martha Lemon who posed as his wife. Among their criminal associates were shoemaker Charles Wicks (33) of Lewes, his girlfriend, a prostitute, Ann Peters, originally from Chichester, Ned Moore, an elusive character possibly based in Southwark, and his mistress, Mary Baker, who came from Keymer, seven miles from Brighton where her mother lived. The latter couple were travelling hawkers, dealing in lace and ribbons. Another character, who was never named, was an accomplished thief, and like Moore, used 'picklock keys'. In mid-December 1839 they targetted a Lewes beershop, run by an elderly couple, who were rumoured to keep considerable sums of money in their private quarters over the bar. Lemon and Clarke, and Moore and Baker, put up separately overnight in Lewes, the latter couple staying at Traft's notorious establishment, meeting up together with Wicks in the morning, the day of 'the great cattle show' when the town was packed with 'many strangers'. Later that afternoon Wicks and Clarke reconnoitred the target beershop, and returned in the evening, feigned inebriation, 'and said that they had been to all the Houses in the Town but could find no company to suit them because they were . . . drunk'. Heavy drinking was followed by rumbustious singing, painter Howell, a temporary lodger, 'never heard a man sing louder or have a stronger voice'; 'singing and making a dreadful noise' in the landlady's parlance, whose husband was 'pressed . . . to sing' as well. Clarke popped outside occasionally, saying 'that the Beer was strange to him . . . and ran through him very quick', but in fact opening up the landlord's private quarters, and then ensuring that his confederates – Moore and the un-named man – had finished the job. Twenty-one pounds in money, 35s. worth of silver and other cutlery, and ten silk neckties, were stolen, together with lodger Howell's 'box' containing clothes, £2 10s. and 'a Gold Brooch with "Mary" engraved on the back of it'. The total value of the haul was calculated at £27 10s.[56]

These goods were immediately despatched to Clarke's at Brighton in a pre-arranged fly. The unknown man slipped off with £10 in cash, leaving the three men, and two ladies to regroup, and share the remaining booty. They used a device, common among thieves, of making cash payments to compensate for unequal divisions of the property. After a night in Brighton, Clarke and Wicks headed independently for Portsmouth, Wicks leaving Peters at Chichester, while Lemon stayed to manage the lodging house. Although the robbery was discovered within the hour, detection came not from close pursuit, but through the liaisons of different police forces, spiced with sheer luck. Two days later, Wicks went to the Chichester draper's shop of Robert Pascoe, who was also chief of the city police. Pascoe thought Wicks's demeanour strange, and 'instructed my son to watch him', but suspicion ended once Wicks spent £1 12s. on a 'Mackintosh' and left. Three hours later Pascoe received information – including descriptions of some of the suspected parties – from the Brighton police. Pascoe went to the coaching inn, and arrested Wicks who was waiting for the Portsmouth stage. Wicks failed to secrete the neckties he was carrying, and after a night in the custody of the Brighton police, was returned to Lewes where he confessed to the interrogating magistrate, though he disclaimed knowing Moore's surname or the identity of the unnamed man. The Portsmouth police arrested Clarke on 16 December, but not his two companions, presumably Moore and the other character, because their descriptions were unavailable.

On 18 December the Brighton police raided Clarke's premises, and went to Baker's mother's place at Keymer on the 19th; on Christmas Eve, Traft's establishment was searched, and he, his wife and employees, subjected to prolonged magisterial interrogation. Suspected stolen property was found on all three premises, but none of it from the beershop robbery. 500 yards of ribbon, 100 yards of edging lace, and ten shawls, were identified as part of a haul, valued at £50, taken during a burglary of 'General Shopkeeper' Arnold of Bolney, twelve miles from Lewes on 3 December 1839.[57] Although the 'shop marks' had been removed, the evidence sustained the prosecution of Lemon for receiving, Clarke for receiving and the beershop robbery, and Wicks – who failed in his attempt to turn Queen's evidence – for robbery. Clarke was acquitted of robbery, but not on the receiving charge to which the gold broach was central. He and Wicks were transported for ten years, and Lemon spent six months in Lewes Jail. Moore and the un-named man were never apprehended, and Traft escaped yet again; he could not be held responsible for the contents of parcels entrusted to his care by occasional lodgers.

The Guildford Connection

Excellent evidence of the relationships between itinerant and principally unskilled workers, nomadic hawkers and general dealers, and criminal gangs, derive from those responsible for an extensive number of burglaries, primarily in Sussex and rural Surrey in 1850–1, and almost certainly before. Two components of this loose, indeed amorphous association, were tried for major crimes, namely four for the burglary and murder of the Revd Hollest at his Frimley vicarage, Surrey, on 28 September 1850, and seven for the burglary at the Misses Farncombe's mansion near Uckfield on 1 January 1851.[58] The evidence proves the involvement of those named in the following list of crimes:

4 June 1850: Kirdford, Sussex: burglary, with violence, at Mrs Harriett Stoner's 'small grocer's shop'; theft of £11 10s. in cash: John Isaacs, Samuel and Levi Harwood, James Jones, John Smith, James Hamilton.

4 July 1850: Cuckfield, Sussex: burglary of John Penfold's farmhouse; theft of a watch and a gun: James Hamilton, Edward Isaacs, William Brooks.

16 July 1850: Hayward's Heath, Sussex: burglary of Mrs Kennard's public house; theft of two gold and three silver watches, plate, clothing, and a gun: James Hamilton, William Brooks, John and Edward Isaacs.

28 August 1850: Portslade, near Brighton: burglary of general dealer Baker's premises: theft of clothing and cloth: committed by unknown confederates, but James and Sarah Edwards among the receivers.

20 September 1850: Arlington, Sussex: burglary with violence, at vicarage of Revd Vidal; theft of cash, three watches, plate, and silver cutlery, valued at over £40: Hiram Smith,[59] Levi Harwood,[60] and at least one more man.

28 September 1850: Frimley, Surrey: burglary at vicarage and murder of Revd Hollest; theft of twenty-one guineas in cash, several watches, two snuff boxes, bloodstone brooch, silver pencil case and ornamental knife: Levi and Samuel Harwood, James Jones, Hiram Smith.

30 November 1850: Frensham Common, near Farnham, Surrey: shoemaker Charles Marshall, lured from his house by traveller asking directions, and knocked unconscious; sister assaulted: theft of silver watch, 'old sovereigns', two pistols, two pairs of trousers, and other unspecified items: William Brooks and seven unknown others; receivers included the Edwards, Elizabeth Oliver, James Gulliver.

Early December 1850: Maresfield, Sussex: burglary of Knight's workshop: theft of various tools, subsequently used for breaking and entering, found in possession of two of the Uckfield burglars, William Hillyer and Thomas Morgan.

12 December 1850: Chailey, Sussex: burglary of the Six Bells, proprietor Mrs Hurst; theft of watch, spoons and other items: William Brooks and unknown others.

31 December 1850: Holtye Common, Hartfield, Sussex: burglary of the White Hart, proprietor Mr Kenward; theft of a bundle of calico, sheeting, and a 'considerable number of silver spoons': James Hamilton, John and James Smith, Thomas Morgan, William Hillyer.

1 January 1851: Uckfield, Sussex: burglary of elderly Farncombe sisters' mansion: theft of £20 in gold, one £10 and seventeen £5 banknotes, some silver money, forty-five items of silver cutlery, silver watch chain, pepper box, several brooches, two mourning rings, gold chain, two gold seals, and a diamond ring, alone valued at £70: William Brooks, James Hamilton, John and James Smith, Thomas Morgan, William Hillyer, Joseph Carter.

Some details are known about these criminals. Richard Trower, who adopted the alias of Hiram Smith, by which he will be known here, was born at Merton in 1826; his father, foreman at a paper mill, was transported in 1830 for thieving from his employer, and his three children were brought up on their mother's earnings as a laundress. Hiram worked with her until 1844 when he became a potboy at Wandsworth, which he abandoned after eight months and 'joined a gang of tramping hawkers'. He was described as a hawker on his arrest for robbery from a person in the vicinity of Gravesend in November 1849, only to be acquitted at the Kent Assize in March 1850. Arrested shortly afterwards with one of the Isaacs on suspicion of housebreaking, and the still unsolved highway robbery and murder of the Brighton brewer Griffith in February 1849, which attracted an offer of a pardon for an approving accomplice and a £300 reward for information, both men were released for lack of evidence.[61] Several of Smith's criminal associates lived in Guildford, a notorious centre for criminals active in the adjacent unpoliced and wild countryside, which embraced 'a great quantity of waste land';[62] they included Levi Harwood, who lodged with girlfriend Mary Ann Croucher at the Swan beershop, a decidedly shady establishment.[63] Harwood had been imprisoned as a youth in 1842 for burglary at Guildford.[64] The other two of this core, 'called the Guildford men', by associates elsewhere, were Levi's cousin, Samuel (25) and James Jones. Jones had had a narrow escape earlier in 1850, when he successfully claimed that he had bought articles, proved to be stolen, in his possession, though Levi's close mate, George Brisk, was transported for this offence in March. Samuel Harwood and Jones lived at The Wheatsheaf; Benjamin Downes, who helped run this pub, 'did not know that they work for anyone', though both were 'out at night at times'. The Wheatsheaf, at which several labourers lodged, the Rose and Crown, the Malthouse Tap – a beershop run by Jones's brother-in-law – together with the Swan, were all subject to regular surveillance by the town's small police force headed by Superintendent Hollington.[65]

Itinerant criminals commonly contacted this Guildford core to act with them. John Isaacs (25), a hawker, 'had no regular residence, but lives in a travelling waggon', recruited both Harwoods and Jones for the Kirdford burglary in June 1850. In the following month, Isaacs took valuables stolen at Hayward's Heath to Levi Harwood, who used his superior knowledge of London fences to dispose of them. Isaac's brother, Edward, was an occasional criminal partner. James – 'Butcher' – Hamilton, aged twenty-nine, dealt in horses and 'travelled about the country selling brooms', while his wife and small daughter resided in a house on a 'remote part of Woking Common', 'the heart of a notorious resort for Gypsies, vagabonds and other indifferent persons', where 'scarcely three days elapse . . . without the Commission of . . . greater or less depredations'.[66] Hamilton first met John Isaacs at Farnham Fair, where they traded a stolen donkey. Three more associates, William Hillyer (23), Joseph Carter, and Thomas Morgan (30), also had 'huts' on Woking Common. William Brooks was another nomadic hawker, who lived in a tent with thirty-year-old spinster, Elizabeth Oliver. Brooks's uncle, bricklayer James and aunt Sarah Edwards, both aged fifty, were domiciled in a cottage in an obscure part of Crowborough Common, which was also used as a depot for stolen goods by Brooks. His sister, Eliza Howis, currently lived with James Gulliver, and periodically at the Edwards's; both traded in items stolen by Brooks, often with brothers John (25) and James Smith (18), both basket-makers, a common itinerant's trade. Indeed, only shoemaker Morgan had a skill, though most associates laboured occasionally. Carter worked on a school built at Uckfield in the spring of 1850. Hiram Smith sought labouring work at the 'new water works' erected at Kingston-on-Thames. Hamilton – who still went hop-picking – Hillyer and Carter, came from the Rotherfield district of Wealden Sussex, and had been employed as ploughboys by farmer Acheson.[67]

Most of the victims lived in relatively isolated locations, and were targeted on the basis of variously obtained intelligence. Carter identified the Farncombes' mansion while working nearby, and had known one of the servants for some years. The sisters lived on investment income, which – incredibly in one journalist's estimation – 'was usually transmitted by the carrier's', half yearly, though a delay in the despatch of the payment about the time of the robbery denied the gang an even larger haul of cash.[68] Hollest's Frimley vicarage was reconnoitred by Hiram Smith while peddling plates at the house four days before the robbery. Hollest's disinterest in the merchandise was followed by his refusal to give Hiram food or drink; Smith used the incident to strike up conversations with two men encountered in the street, complaining that his reverence 'was a tight fit' for not buying plates, 'and I also tried it on for a bit of chuck [food] . . . but it was no go: the bloody Parson . . . would not give me so much as a drop of small beer'. Ironically, one of these characters was builder and parish constable Macey, though as he was working, he had no mark of office. Through visual observations, and in these and other conversations, Smith learned that Hollest had four or five domestic servants, and that he kept the funds of the National School.[69]

Having identified a target, gang members normally travelled in pairs to a nearby rendezvous. All four concerned in one raid on an inn were encamped in Copthorne Common; they went in pairs the seven miles to 'the Ouse Valley Viaduct on the Brighton Railway', and then together at night walked the mile and a half to Hayward's Heath along the permanent way. Greater planning accompanied other exploits. John Isaacs and Hamilton identified the Kirdford shop, went to Guildford to apprise the others, liaised at Godalming, split into two groups for the twelve-mile hike to Balls Cross, just a mile from the shop. Hamilton, Hillyer, the Smith brothers, and Brooks, spent Christmas 1850 at Woking discussing possible targets, and then met up with others, including Carter and John Isaacs, at Brooks's tent, pitched near Edenbridge in Kent on 30 December, prior to the proposed raid on Downlands at Uckfield. By then Hamilton had additionally identified the White Hart at Hartfield, but only the Smiths, Morgan and Hillyer, went on this job on 31 December. They returned to Brooks's tent, shared the food with those present, but not the other booty. On the following night the entire gang raided Downlands. Chief Justice Campbell, who tried these men, expressed some astonishment at their capacity for 'Meeting together in four different counties', and a West Sussex magistrate advanced the burglars' organisational prowess as revealed by 'the system of communication adopted by tramps', as a powerful argument for reform of his unprofessionally policed county.

On arrival in the target's vicinity, an advance party reconnoitred, before a final decision to break-in. Look-outs were invariably posted; the raiding party discarded shoes and top clothes, donning old garments which were usually destroyed afterwards. Premises were often entered dexterously. At Kirdford one of the Harwoods 'bored a hole in the shutter with a centre bit', melted the lead in the exposed window with a candle, and removed a 'whole frame of glass'. Entry into the Frimley vicarage proved more complicated; the woodwork holding iron bars across a scullery window was cut away, and the bars removed: the next obstacle, a locked door to the kitchen, was bored through in two places with Levi Harwood's 'worm', permitting 'a person with a crooked instrument to pull back the bolt on the opposite side'. Some of the burglars were 'very small men' and two were 'scarcely five feet high'.[70]

Having effected entry, the burglars silently amassed booty from items found on the ground floor. Intelligence rarely extended to the precise location of money, which was commonly kept with other valuables in bedrooms; fear of burglars was the reason for shopkeeper Stoner concealing her takings under her pillow. Many householders, especially those in remote parts, kept loaded firearms at the ready. Captain Marples JP, domiciled in rural Surrey, observed that:

> his house had been armed for a long time, and he never went to bed without having a six-barrelled revolving pistol under his pillows.

Among those 'always' keeping loaded guns at their bedsides were shoe-maker Marshall of Frensham Common, and butler Wood at the Uckfield mansion. The need to interrogate victims over the whereabouts of money and valuables and to terrorise them, dictated the use of masks and arms. The Harwoods used pistols, loaded with marbles, and gang members not carrying guns, carried alternative weapons, swords, crowbars and jemmies. Victims, or their servants, regularly resisted; Mrs Stoner was dragged about by her hair until 'nearly fainting' before she revealed the hiding place. The Revd Vidal was assailed in his sleep, said his cash was in a desk, and handed over the key accompanied by an impromptu lecture on the hereafter; the burglars:

> dragged him to his study, where they took upwards of £20 in gold and silver. The man with the sword drew it across his [Vidal's] throat, and threatened to use it if he made a noise.

He was then locked in his bedroom during his housekeeper's interrogation; she too 'courageously offered them the Bible'. At Downlands Wood was disarmed while trying to use his gun.[71] At Frimley, the Revd Hollest leapt out of bed, and was shot while attempting to seize the poker; he pursued the burglars, fired a shotgun at them as they fled across the lawn, and collapsed. The police faced armed men in pursuit of these criminals.

Despite their panic, the four attackers rigidly adhered to their practice of dividing into pairs when leaving the scene; one pair returned to Guildford, the other went directly to London with the booty. The seven Uckfield raiders split into three groups, and met up eight miles away on Crowborough Common. Some of their booty was divided, with bargaining and compensatory cash exchanges, but valuables, including plates with identifiable crests, and some, but not all, banknotes, required elaborate disposal, and John Isaacs took such items to Guildford immediately for courier despatch 'by the early train' to London. Final settlement was made after these goods were sold to fences, though this created a fertile forum for distrust and argument, and for unequal sharings, in part legitimised by individual status and the running of additional risks in getting goods to fences. Elizabeth Oliver, Brooks's cohabitee, was arrested in Tunbridge Wells; a bag, hidden in her skirts, contained watches and seals, and sixteen guineas, the proceeds of fencing. One of the watches, according to a watchmaker, had been subjected to 'a process technically called "christening" . . . the plate had been turned upside down, and the name and number obliterated'. But less valuable items of loot were also identifiable, and many gang members concealed shares in remote places, for later recovery. When Brooks's uncle's cottage was searched, the police discovered 'a large quantity of the most heterogeneous description . . . jackets, trousers, shawls, silk and cotton handkerchiefs, calicoes, pillow cases. . .'; 'cart loads' were removed.

The Hollest murder and the Uckfield robbery, together with the impressive list of unsolved crimes, generated criticism when they took place within the jurisdiction of professional police forces, and castigation of the situation – notably in rural Surrey – where the only professional forces, were the tiny borough establishments. Frimley, 'at the centre of the hop country' with '40 or 50 straggling houses', was one of ninety-three Surrey parishes policed under the ancient system of elected amateur constables. The positive role of the current incumbent, Macey, was restricted to evidence of his fortuitous encounter with Smith during the latter's begging encounter with Hollest. Although first on the scene, Macey was too overwhelmed even to take charge of the housebreaking implements strewn about the scene, or to search the gardens.[72] Immediately intelligence reached Justice Austin of the Godalming borough police committee, he ordered the head policeman, Inspector Biddlecombe, to the scene ten miles outside his jurisdiction, on the following morning (28 September); he was soon joined by Detective Kendall of the Metropolitan Police, who went on Home Office orders, though in the event his expertise was limited to co-ordinating tangential enquiries. The vigilant Guildford borough police made the key breakthrough, with the arrest of three of the four responsible at their lodgings on 29 September on the grounds that they were 'all absent from home' on the night of the 27th. The police's success was compromised by the necessity to hold them overnight in the single cell available, before solitary confinement was achieved through dispersal to police custody at Farnham and Godalming. The fourth man, Samuel Harwood, was also shortly arrested in

Guildford, in possession of the sole stolen item recovered, a Georgian penny token.[73]

Immediate offers of a £150 reward for the arrest of the murderer, and a pardon for the evidence of any accomplice who had not fired the fatal shot, paradoxically both hindered and facilitated the creation of a strong prosecution case. It created 'jealousy' between the Guildford and Godalming forces. Inspector Biddlecombe had established how the burglars broke in, discovered the footmarks of two sets of naked feet, and detected where one burglar had fallen heavily on a gravel path. Biddlecombe also established that a servant girl had seen the gang loitering in the village about midnight, and could identify Jones and Hiram Smith. The Guildford police found dried blood between Levi Harwood's toes, and established circumstantial evidence of various sitings of gang members by townsfolk over the period 25–29 September, including Jones's purchase of an ounce of gunpowder, and Smith's enquiry over the prices at a gunsmith's. Bloodstained stockings, and some cloth identical to that used for the two 'green baize masks', discovered near the vicarage, comprised the remaining evidence; this was not the stuff for murder convictions, and as the press admitted, a confession was desperately needed.[74]

During the time of the repeatedly adjourned inquest hearings, Smith coldly analysed his predicament; his mother, who had supplied the sixteen pounds to pay for his successful defence seven months earlier at the Kent assizes, refused further funds, and Smith feared that he would be undefended on a murder charge, committed in fact by Levi Harwood. On 10 October, Superintendent Hollington of the Guildford police, exploited the fact that the prisoners could no longer liaise, and engineered rumours of a 'split' between the suspects, and with these percolating 'a complete disclosure' was confidently predicted. On the 13th Smith said that 'it behoves every man to take care of himself', closely studied the terms of the pardon outlined in the handbills, and despite the studied refusal of either his jailer or Hollington to confirm that the pardon would be 'acted upon', decided that he was eligible. The publicity accompanying his confession released a further flood of rumours that he had also admitted to 'several other murders and burglaries in different parts of the country', including the killing of Brighton brewer Griffith. Although the latter claim made periodic appearances in the press, it was categorically denied by the Guildford police in October 1850. If Smith had admitted to Griffith's murder, he would have been tried, thereby nullifying his strategy over the Frimley killing. Moreover if he had even admitted complicity in another murder committed during another robbery, his evidence against his Frimley partners might be fatally compromised in jurors' estimations. It was for precisely these reasons that lawyers defending the Harwoods and Jones hammered away over the Griffith case, but they failed to elicit anything other than a denial from Smith under intense cross-examination. Smith's evidence was crucial to the conviction of Levi Harwood and Jones, but Samuel Harwood evaded conviction with these two on 15 April 1851, principally because he was not in the room when the fatal shot was fired. Levi Harwood reserved admitting that he fired the gun until the morning of his execution. On cousin Samuel's acquittal, he was re-arrested, and charged with the Kirdford shop burglary in June 1850.[75]

The evidence for this charge derived directly from the detection of the Uckfield burglars. At daybreak on 2 January 1851, butler Wood contacted P.C. Relf of the professional East Sussex county force. Relf, accompanied by his son, spent an inordinate time investigating the mansion. Eventually, details were circulated to the Metropolitan Police, and all forces in Kent, Surrey, Sussex and Hampshire; they reached the Guildford police on the 4th. By then a major breakthrough had been fortuitously made. James Hamilton, John and James Smith, with their part of the booty including banknotes, calicoes and an umbrella, spent much of 2 January regaling themselves at the Rose and Crown at Groombridge, twelve miles across the Kent border from Uckfield. Arguments developed when Hamilton initially resisted the Smiths's insistence that he conceal the umbrella and calico in a nearby wood. The landlady sent for the local amateur constable Piddleden; he kept the pub under surveillance for three hours, during which a further row developed when John Smith picked up a sovereign and refused to return it to Hamilton. Piddleden appeared on the scene, and incredibly Hamilton had John arrested. A crowd gathered, and somebody informed Piddleden of the hidden package, and he arrested the other two. Although this district was under the permissory 1842 Parish Constables Act, whereby a professional supervised all the village police-men, Piddleden failed to inform his superior, and hurriedly took his three prisoners the three miles to Tunbridge Wells, as that borough force had cell accommodation. The borough police had heard of events at Uckfield, recognised that three prime suspects had come their way, and at this juncture completely seized the initiative, despite the fact that these men had committed no crime in their jurisdiction. Hamilton, who rapidly decided to approve, confirmed the police's suspicions.[76]

When the Guildford police received details of the burglary, they went to the notorious Swan, where they encountered, and after a struggle, arrested Hillyer and Morgan, armed with a pistol and a knife respectively; the former managed to 'swallow something', presumably a banknote, and 'nearly choked'; a search revealed that he was penniless but in possession of a good quality jacket. Morgan had a marked towel, and a decent cloak, all items on the list of stolen goods. Superintendent Morton, had established the Guildford connection from Hamilton's confession at Tunbridge Wells, and Morton arrived at Guildford to find these two suspects in custody. Morton secured the help of the Guildford police to assist with the arrest of Carter at his Woking Common residence. Only Brooks and John Isaacs remained at large, and between 5 and 10 January Morton, 'scoured . . . Surrey, Sussex, Berkshire, Hampshire, Wiltshire and Oxfordshire', after leads, but returned to Tunbridge for the committal hearings on the 11th. Meanwhile his colleague, Superintendent Dadson, had followed up Hamilton's information that goods had been concealed on Crowborough Common, and from this location traced footprints to the Edwards's house, and without informing the East Sussex police, discovered the store of articles stolen by Brooks. Elizabeth Oliver was not present, but she was detected among the huge crowd hoping to catch a glimpse of the prisoners being taken to court. The Tunbridge police seized on her possession of goods stolen at Hartfield, also in Sussex, to investigate that burglary too. Dadson and Morton then renewed their hunt for Brooks who had been sighted at beerhouses at Bagshot and on the Surrey–Hampshire border, and subsequently in the notorious countryside between Woking and Chertsey. As the net closed, the Tunbridge men secured the services of other officers; heavily armed and 'disguised as gypsies' they 'made a minute examination of the district. Lodges, barns, stables, piggeries underwent the closest inspection', and Brooks was surprised, asleep under straw in a barn, and handcuffed before he had chance to use his knives. Only John Isaacs remained at large, his description circulated to police forces nationwide.[77]

On 17 January the Tunbridge Wells Bench committed Brooks and the five principals to Lewes Jail for the Uckfield break-in. All seven, including approver Hamilton, set out – heavily ironed – in the Tunbridge police's open 'cart', guarded by a strongly-armed detachment of the chagrined East Sussex force. The gang tried to engineer incidents by frightening passing horses, and a superb chance presented itself when:

> seeing a gang of Irish labourers approaching and calculating . . . on their sympathy, [Brooks] raised his heavily manacled hands and aimed a blow at Dadson, knocking off his hat . . . at the same time he called upon his fellow prisoners to leap . . . Hillyer instantly responded . . . by dashing his handcuffs against the side of the vehicle . . . to snap them but failing that . . . attempted to throw himself on the road.

Police threats to shoot the first man to move kept the Irish at bay, leaving Brooks to make a final, forlorn bid for freedom, to the crowd milling outside Lewes prison.[78]

At the Sussex Assize on 12 March 1851, Hamilton's evidence sufficed to convict all six for the Uckfield job; Edward Isaacs was found guilty of the Hayward's Heath burglary. A miscellany of additional charges against various men were dropped once all were sentenced to life transportation. Receivers Oliver, Gulliver and Howis, were transported for fourteen years, while Brooks's uncle Edwards was sentenced to the mitigated penalty of two years' imprisonment, after a solid character reference from his periodic employer over thirty years. Hamilton, who claimed to be penniless and 'in considerable peril', was retained in police custody, 'until his services can be dispensed with'.

They were soon in demand. The arrests of his partners permitted John Isaacs to invest the proceeds of goods fenced by him in London, in a new travelling van. He moved to Somerset, another county which had resisted implementation of the 1839 Rural Constabulary Act, to live at Frome, policed by two paid and seven amateur policemen, all of whom were reputedly too terrified to confront the substantial criminal element in the town, some of whom were 'connected with gangs in Bath, Bristol, Bradford and Trowbridge'. Isaacs was allegedly 'organising another gang' when arrested in undisclosed circumstances, on 11 April 1851, and handed over to the Tunbridge police, together with items of jewellery stolen at Uckfield. Dadson and Morton, while collecting Isaacs, also investigated his new van, discovered over forty miles away, but the jewellery found in it, was not on any police list of stolen property. Isaacs was committed, after three 'densely crowded hearings' with 'gypsies forming a large part of the auditory', by Horsham Petty Sessions. By the time of his and Hiram Smith's trial for the Kirdford shop burglary in August 1851, all their partners in the Frimley and Uckfield robberies had been 'executed or transported'; these remaining two were also convicted principally on Hamilton's testimony, and sentenced to life transportation.[79] One final dramatic incident ensued. In October 1851, John Isaacs, while awaiting transportation in Lewes Jail, dexterously fashioned a key from wood, cotton and tin, accomplished the 'extraordinary' feat of opening his cell door, and made a dash for freedom when the gates were opened to admit warders on the morning shift. He was seized in the High Street and ordered into leg-irons for the remainder of his stay. An enquiry revealed that the cell doors could be unlocked – but only from the outside – 'by a bit of wire'.[80]

Most southern towns contained poorer districts crammed with impoverished inhabitants, among which were criminal elements, including itinerants and vagrants, putting up overnight or for lengthier stays, in varieties of cheap lodgings. Gangs, often comprising ephemeral associations of less-skilled criminals were commonly formed to prey on targets in the adjacent countryside, notably in districts without a professional police force in the mid-nineteenth century. At times, usually during the winter months of peak under- and unemployment, criminal activity achieved a crescendo, virtually terrorising affluent residents. At the end of 1852 for example, villains based in Frome committed 'numerous felonies and depredations' in Nunney, Cloford and Marston Biggott, including two actual and one attempted burglaries, three barn break-ins, a big fowl theft and a highway robbery, in the space of three weeks.[81] During the same winter the unpoliced area of rural West Sussex near Brighton, suffered a spate of burglaries. The 'mansions' of prosperous members of the Brighton bourgeoise, and parsonages, formed the principal targets, but several lesser establishments, including commercial premises, were also burgled. Some of the bigger houses were repeated targets; the Revd Wheeler's was entered thrice, the banker Hall's twice, and Buckingham House, owned by Henry Colville Bridger, also thrice. Entries were invariably gained through obvious weak spots, notably dairy windows, with elementary tools, including knives and on one occasion, an 'iron bed screw'. This apparent lack of sophisticated equipment, possibly explains the numbers of abandoned break-ins, by would-be burglars not in the same league as the Guildford connection, with operations restricted to the theft of clothing and food found on ground floor rooms only. Most items were consumed, sold through the second-hand market, or pawned.[82]

Conclusions

Much of this evidence compromises or challenges both a range of analyses of social crime and popular protest, and even more assumptions about these topics. Indeed the very notion of gangs, requires qualification. Much organised crime was committed by a complex series of changing partnerships, with up to seven or eight people at times, as at Downlands and Farnham Common; some of these people had specific skills, especially over breaking and entering, which appear to have put their services at a premium among often widespread and numerous, but loose and shifting criminal associations. The Guildford connection contained men whose expertise at house-breaking derived from their minuscule size and dexterity · with implements. If some characters, including Heasman, were demonstrably major initiators, a series of ephemeral but precise circumstances governed the choice of partner for particular enterprises. Poverty was an important ingredient, though its force as stimuli varied. Unemployment, impecuniousness, and indeed hunger, repeatedly figured in Barcombe events. Some farmworkers were permanently employed, but like Thorncraft at Arlington, thieved to supplement their income, or like Towner at Barcombe, adopted criminal strategies originally to get through a crisis. There is a suggestive chronological coincidence between the apparent start of Heasman's criminal career and the implementation of the Poor Law Amendment Act. Three members of the Guildford connection came from one highly impoverished Wealden district, where

farmers discriminated against younger unmarried labourers for employment, and the timing of this three's virtual abandonment of farmwork and
resort to itinerant criminality occurred at about the age of eighteen.
Itinerants and vagrants were the perennial organisers of joint criminal
expeditions, including raids into the hinterlands of towns. Some of this
crime was committed by people simultaneously engaged in miscellaneous
petty trading, and hawking provided a cover both for the gleaning of
intelligence of targets, and for the disposal of certain stolen goods, notably
items of clothing, but also wholesale volumes of textiles burgled from
village shopkeepers. Contemporaries accurately identified a close relationship between itinerancy, hawking and crime, as revealed by several
of the gangs studied here.

But organised criminality was neither the sole prerogative of impoverished farmworkers, nor itinerants and vagrants working the marginal and
black market economies. Skilled men including carpenter Jenner and
bricklayer Stunt, were representative of rural artisans who were victims of
the post-war depression, and the latter's explanation that unemployment
drove him to sell articles, including a stolen violin, was unquestioned. To
the several artisans encountered above, we may add a twenty-two-year-old
mason, employed by a criminal association active at Chiddingly in
1818–19, to make a breach in the roof of a building, and after the robbery
hired to repair it by the unsuspecting owner.[83] Many petty dealers,
especially those who dealt in perishable farm goods, and organised the
supply from country to town, had perilously insecure financial bases, and
are found as thieves, in their own right, in partnership with others, and as
important disposers of stolen goods, as revealed by the details from Lewes.
There is some evidence that pre-1834 demographic growth was in part
absorbed by men, unable to secure farmwork, getting a foothold in rural
craft industries[84] and the petty entrepreneurial ladders; under the old poor
law, both categories received some aid from public funds.[85] The reformed
social security system ended such assistance, while the prospect of the
workhouse simultaneously increased the pressures to somehow contrive a
living, which led to a marked expansion of the numbers of small-time
dealers. Dealing partly in stolen goods could make the difference between
success and failure.[86] There are examples of criminal gangs including men
from the ranks of the hard-pressed small farmers, like Stevens of
Chobham, the son of one, whose share of extensive thieving was partly fed
to his horse, ownership of which he was determined to preserve.[87]

Attree of West Firle was not the only smith who equipped himself with
the keys to the premises of neighbours. Master blacksmith Langridge of
Hayes, Kent, gave wet clay to labouring associates to take the impressions
of keys, and they subsequently used the fashioned article to gain entries to
steal foodstuffs, chickens 'times out of Number', iron for Langridge's forge,

and also silver plate.[88] The theft of such valuables, like Attree's encouragement of repeated raids on Ellman's wine-cellars, suggests though it does not prove, that these characters were hardly exclusively motivated by poverty. Want certainly did not motivate Collins at Alfriston, nor his brother-in-law the miller. Collins entertained socio-economic aspirations, and while his engagement in smuggling was seen as a legitimate exercise by some – but not all – of his affluent neighbours, his orchestration of numerous robberies to further inflate his income was universally condemned by the propertied inhabitants of Alfriston and adjacent parishes.

In their justly famous study of Captain Swing, Professors Hobsbawm and Rudé, project a picture of essentially innocent but deprived farmworkers driven to revolt by the duration of intolerable living standards and experiences.[89] In fact, a proportion of Swing activists had criminal records,[90] and as revealed here, other Swing protesters, including William Pearson of Alfriston, and Jack Wood of Battle, were members of subsequent criminal organisations. Alfriston particularly had a long history of the use of incendiarism as popular protest, yet some arson – and other forms of covert protest – was also the product of intimidatory strategies deployed against victims and potential prosecution witnesses. The puritanical Brooker suffered intimidation on both counts, while Thorncraft – convicted of theft while a youth – intimidated his own long-term employer with thinly-veiled arson threats, and stole with virtual impunity. The permutations of social crime and popular protest experienced at Alfriston, derive from juxtapositions of variously motivated incendiarism and other forms of covert attacks on property, smuggling, working-class trade unionism and politicisation, and Brooker's campaign against the New Poor Law, further intermixed with long-term religious differences and the struggles between ratepayers with opposing interests. Alfriston's experiences may have been unusual owing to their intensity and complexity, but less-rich variants are found elsewhere. Barcombe's subjection to Swing, was followed by Heasman's career, and he used terrorist tactics to prevent suspect proletarians from informing, though his targets contained just one known example of selection for purposes of personal revenge, to which one detects at least a tinge of 'popularity' over the issue of sackings. Parallels include fraternities which troubled Brenchley, Kent, and Chobham, Surrey, in the later 1840s; the former adopted incendiarism to cover house-breaking expeditions, because as members had 'steady work they would not be suspected'. The village farmers repeatedly targeted by the latter, responded by funding the employment of a policeman: his activities compromised the gang, which reacted with anonymous letters threatening animal maiming and arson, 'if you don't due away with the Pleace'. The subscribers' steadfastness was rocked by seven fires in the space of a week.[91]

Yet some criminal associations reveal moralistic undertones. The Battle gang discussed the fact that the cash in the tollgate keeper's possession was not his, but the anonymous Turnpike Commissioners. Robert Hurd, one of the notorious Frome gangsters:

> boasted . . . of some of his exploits at races, fairs etc, and . . . that he had made up his mind never to murder, rape, or to rob a poor man, but . . . he considered it no harm whatever to rob any one who had plenty.[92]

There is no direct evidence that the Guildford connection was conditioned by such sentiments, and if their robbery of the Farnham Common shoemaker might suggest that they were not, these were ambitious criminals determined to steal very valuable items wherever possible, and this was reflected in their commonly targeting the very wealthy. Their hauls were often substantial, and at times they were flushed with cash. While they partially reflect Rudé's recent categorisation of the 'acquisitive criminal',[93] adopting illegal means to a higher standard of consumption, there is no evidence that they aspired to change their life styles, as symbolised by John Isaac's investment of part of the proceeds of robbery in a new caravan. The proceeds from crime at least permitted some of the more successful to cut something of a dash, exemplified by Charles Wicks who 'dressed in a rather swellish style'.

Gangs operative in the rural South in fact represent dimensions of an amorphous criminal network, with something of a metropolitan focus. Isaacs, the closest we have encountered here to a genuinely professional criminal, used London fences extensively. But this was not the sole prerogative of the more spectacular fraternities. The Battle gang was capable of arranging to have traceable valuables disposed of through London, and the associates of Clarke, who moved effortlessly from Brighton to Lewes, prior to lying low in Portsmouth, also included those with metropolitan connections. Provincial interconnections are exemplified by the trial of men convicted of wheat and hay thefts at Lympne and Sandwich in 1835, which revealed that they were part of 'a gang of thieves' who 'forwarded the goods stolen' in East Kent 'by boat to Brighton for disposal, and vice versa'.[94] Certain public houses, many beershops, and a multitude of lodging houses, were centres in these networks. In the later 1830s, the Royal Commission on Police was informed that Brighton:

> contained numerous lodging houses, the keepers of which furnish matches, songs, laces, and many other petty articles, which are hawked about as an excuse for vagrancy . . . and it gives them opportunities . . . of greater consequence, observing the fastenings and other circumstances that may lead to robbery . . . the principal robberies . . . have

been concocted in vagrant lodging houses, and rendered effectual through the agencies of the keepers . . . intelligence is given and received by clients.[95]

Clarke was the keeper of such an establishment in Brighton, and he knew Traft of the Lewes beer and lodging house intimately. The most rustic of our gangs, namely those at Barcombe and West Firle, disposed of some stolen goods through such agencies, whereby items stolen in these villages ended up, for example, in Lewes-baked pies, and on the slab of a licensed game dealer. Other urban traders, especially pawnbrokers and second-hand clothes dealers, were additional components; even town millers, or their employees, clandestinely processed stolen grain, and one journeyman at Brighton, hawked such flour round the beershops on Sundays.[96]

West Firle also proves that organised criminality was not the exclusive preserve of villains domiciled in the 'open' villages of contemporary legend, but extended to 'closed' parishes too. Criminal gangs, however, do confirm another contemporary claim, that they – and the beershops and other establishments patronised by them – were the agencies for 'progressive crime', whereby youths graduated from lesser to more serious crime. At Barcombe, the teenager who originally refused to accompany Heasman on poaching forays, later joined him for illegal fishing, and graduated subsequently to sheep-stealing.

But gangs had one fundamental weakness. It will have been noted that the convictions of gangsters we have encountered, virtually invariably derived from confessions. As a trial judge said of two sheep-stealers convicted on the evidence of a third at the Kent Assize in 1832:

members gave strength, and encouraged . . . crime, yet they also increased danger; for whenever the hour of difficulty arose . . . some were willing to sacrifice comrades . . . to extract themselves.

Hopes were entertained that publicity accruing to approvers would convince gangsters 'what slender ties men are bound together in crime', and arrested villains were pressurised 'to keep their guts in' and not 'snitch'.[97] While every case here conforms to the dangers identified above, the historical evidence itself principally comes from the depositions of witnesses, including approvers, and the press reports of criminal acts and trials. Such sources rarely permit the historian to assess the performance of undetected – or at least unprosecuted – criminal associators. Police officers often lamented their inability to collate evidence adequate to prosecution, at least for serious, as opposed to the petty crime, they were convinced gangsters were guilty of.[98]

Historians of policing customarily attribute increased support for compulsory statutory intervention to create professional forces to the industrial and political disorders of the 1830s and 1840s.[99] Yet the Chartist threat stemmed primarily from its metropolitan, Midland, Northern, South Walian and industrial Scottish epicentres, which were also the principal theatres of violent industrial disputes. In some senses the activities of criminal gangs performed a parallel function for Southern opinions on the police issue. Organised crime repeatedly exposed the deficiencies of the police, from which even the professional forces established under the Rural Constabulary Acts of 1839–40 were not immune. In 1845 for example, Chief Constable Mackay of East Sussex was compelled to defend his force from stringent criticism over their lack of liaison with the Brighton police, which facilitated the escape of a gang of burglars. Ironically, their eventual capture was achieved by Inspector Biddlecombe of Godalming who pursued them for five days, covering four hundred miles, during which he was 'scarcely out of the saddle, and . . . knocked up four horses'.[100] Equally crucially, organised crime, also generated acute public fears, symbolised by press debates over 'security . . . measures' to be taken by rural residents, which concluded that 'country ladies would not be the worse for knowing how to load and discharge a gun'. Although the Hollest murder was almost in a class of its own, it was in the context of the perceived 'fearful . . . increase . . . of burglaries and highway robberies'.[101] The Surrey Bench responded very quickly; a sub-committee recommended the implementation of the Rural Constabulary Act within two months of Hollest's death, emphasising that 'the efficiency of a Rural Police depends principally upon a vigilant attention to the movements of suspicious characters, and to their place of resort'. At the full Quarter Sessions in December 1850, a relatively huge number of magistrates – thirty-nine – gave their uniquely unanimous vote for the Act's immediate implementation, and their detailed proposal was accepted by the Home Office within two days.[102] The Kent Sessions also speedily insisted that all Petty Sessional divisions adopted the 1842 Parish Constables Act, while in East Sussex Mackay used the Arlington robbery, the Hollest murder, and the fact that 'people were really in constant fear', to wrest agreement to augment his force from an unusually united County Bench.[103] In January 1853, shortly after his arrival at the Home Office, Palmerston retorted to complaints of high levels of criminality from Devon, by suggesting the implementation of the 1839 Act, adding that 'this was not done in Surrey until the Frimley murder frightened the ratepayers and I suppose that the Devon farmers are waiting for some similar event'.[104] The scale of organised crime, and the apparent impunity of gangsters in unprofessionally policed districts, formed part of the evidence given to the 1852–3 parliamentary select committee to prove that amateur 'parish constables are not of the slightest use'. After a burglary at Frome, two parish constables cautiously tailed one suspect brazenly carrying a roll of stolen cloth, 'and although he was by himself they passed him' by, because 'he was such a desperate fellow'. Similar evidence was woven into the litany of police reformers, and was an important ingredient in their triumph with the 1856 passage of the County and Borough Police Act, which finally extended professional policing nationwide.[105]

Notes

1   R.A.E. Wells, 'The development of the English rural proletariat and social protest 1700– 1850'; *idem*, 'Social conflict and protest in the English countryside in the early nineteenth century; a rejoinder', *Journal of Peasant Studies*, 6, (1979), pp. 122–5; 8, (1981), pp. 516–24.

2   E.J. Hobsbawm and G. Rudé, *Captain Swing*, (1973 edition), *passim*.

3   W. Apfel and P. Dunkley, 'English rural society and the New Poor Law; Bedfordshire 1834–47', *Social History*, 10, (1985).

4   R. Wells, 'Resistance to the New Poor Law in the rural South', in M. Chase, (ed.), *The New Poor Law*, (University of Leeds, 1985), esp. pp. 43–5; *idem*, 'Social protest, class, conflict and consciousness in the rural South-east, 1700–1880', in M. Reed and R. Wells, (eds.), *Class, Conflict and Protest in the English Countryside 1700–1880*, (1990).

5   D. Foster, *The Rural Constabulary Act 1839*, (1982), *passim*; C. Emsley, *Policing and Its Context 1750–1870*, (1983), pp. 70–3; L. Radzinowicz, *A History of English Criminal Law and Its Administration from 1750*, 5 vols. (1948–85), IV, pp. 263–70. However, Edwin Chadwick's customary manipulation of local evidence, probably led the 1836–9 Royal Commission on Police to exaggerate the deficiencies of the unreformed police, as suggested by R. Storch's contribution to D. Hay and F. Snyder, (eds.), *Policing and Prosecution in Britain 1750–1850; Essays in the Social History of Criminal Law*, (Oxford, 1989). I am indebted to Professor Storch for permitting me to consult an early version of his essay.

6   J.A. Sharpe, *Crime in early Modern England*, (1986); C. Emsley, *Crime and Society in England 1750–1900*, (1987); J. Stevenson, *Popular Disturbances in England 1700–1870*, (1979).

7   J. Rule, 'Social crime in the rural south in the eighteenth and early nineteenth centuries', *Southern History*, I, (1979). Cf. R.W. Bushaway, *By Rite, Custom, Ceremony and Community in England 1700– 1880*, (1982), esp. chs. 5 and 6.

8   Wells, 'The development . . .'; E.P. Thompson, 'The crime of anonymity', in D. Hay, P. Linebaugh and Thompson, (eds.), *Albion's Fatal Tree*, (1975); J. Archer, 'The Wells–Charlesworth debate; a personal comment on arson in Norfolk and Suffolk', *Journal of Peasant Studies*, 9, (1982); *idem*, '"A fiendish outrage?": a study of animal maiming in East Anglia: 1830–1870', *Agricultural History Review*, 33, (1985); A.J. Peacock, 'Village radicalism in East Anglia, 1800–1850', in J.P.D. Dunbabin, (ed.), *Rural Discontent in Nineteenth-Century Britain*, (1974).

9   C. Steedman, *Policing the Victorian Community*, (1984), esp. pp. 25–6; Emsley, loc. cit., ch. 6.

10   *Sussex Weekly Advertiser*, 11 Jan., 14 and 21 Mar., 8 Aug. and 10 Oct. 1796.

11   *Reading Mercury*, 24 Sept. 1810. Cf. *Sussex Advertiser*, 13 Dec. 1824.

12   B(ritish) P(arliamentary) P(apers), 'Poor Law Report', (1834), Appendix B, Q(uestion). 128, reply of John Ellman. For a less than incisive study of the first John Ellman, see S.P. Farrant, 'John Ellman of Glynde', *Agricultural History Review*, 26, (1978).

13   Henry Kenward was arrested for stealing nineteen fowls from Ellman in 1814; *Sussex Weekly Advertiser*, 31 Jan. 1814. I am indebted to Shirley Chase for permitting me to read her unpublished paper on nineteenth-century criminality at West Firle.

14   Evidence of the West Firle gangs' activities derives principally from Horsecraft's voluminous confession, T. Howard's account of a lengthy conversation with Attree, and the interrogations of receivers Worsall and Tinsley, all Aug.–Sept. 1815, E(ast) S(ussex) C(ounty) R(ecord) O(ffice), QR/E745, plus arrest and trial details, *Sussex Weekly Advertiser*, 21 Aug. and 23 Oct. 1815.

15   BPP., loc. cit., Appendix A, pp. 501–2, 522.

16   There are two parish histories. F.A. Pagden, *History of Alfriston*, (1908 edn.), studiously eschews the author's family's role in early nineteenth-century events. A.C. Piper, *Alfriston, the Story of a Sussex Village*, (1970), is heavily dependent on the earlier work, and suggests that with the withdrawal of the heavy army presence at the end of the war in 1815, the place 'gradually settled down to become the quiet and peaceful village we know today . . . and there is little of historical interest to record after this date', p. 23. Piper reiterates Pagden's factual errors, which derive in part from oral sources and from T. Geering, *Our Parish*, (1884). In this account I have used family reconstitution methods, but the well-known difficulties of this approach, mean that I cannot be certain of the complete accuracy of all the personal relationships mentioned here. Sources used for these in the first three paragraphs, except where indicated, comprise: Alfriston; Anglican parish registers, Par. 230/1/2/1; 230/1/3/1; 230/1/5/1: vestry minutes, 1628– 1825, AMS. 5567: Congregationalist Church minutes, NC. 19/1/1: Land Tax records, 1780–1832, LT/Alfriston: Deeds, Market Cross, AMS. 5581/57/1–10. Chiddingly; Anglican parish registers, Par. 292/1/1/3; 292/1/2/1; 292/1/3/1: vestry minutes, Par. 291/12/1: Land Tax records, 1780–1832, LT/ Chiddingly: annotated copy of 1821, 1841 and 1851 censuses, Par. 292/37/1. Ade family; uncatalogued deposit, D.304. All in ESCRO. Alfriston Congregationalist Church registers, 1804–37. P(ublic) R(ecord) O(ffice), Registrar General, 4/2218.

17   *Sussex Advertiser*, 17 Feb. 1874.

18   I. Thomas JP, Willingdon, to Edwin Chadwick, 20 Sept. 1834; Hawley, and Brooker, to the P(oor) L(aw) C(ommission), 9 Feb. and 1 Apr. 1834, PRO. M(inistry of) H(ealth), 12/12854.

19   *Brighton Gazette*, 1 Dec. 1832. King and Fell, to J. Hitchens, and to E.J. Curteis, 10 and 15 (with enclosures) May 1822; 'Union Prosecuting Society' handbill, and Day to Duncannon, 8 and 26 Nov. 1834, PRO. H(ome) O(ffice), 64/1, ff. 205–8; 64/4, ff. 206–8. Pagden's deposition, 11 Feb. 1824; Thorncraft, summary conviction, 6 Sept. 1826, ESCRO. QR/E789, 799, *Sussex Advertiser*, 17 Jan. 1830.

20   Wells, 'The development . . .', pp. 128–31; idem, 'a rejoinder . . .', p. 527. *Sussex Weekly Advertiser*, 7 Apr. 1806, 1 and 22 Apr. 1822, 12 and 26 Oct. 1829. BPP., loc. cit., Ardingly answer to Q. 53, rural queries. Depositions against John Bonds, 8 Oct.

1813, ESCRO. QR/E737. Letters to Lewes solicitors King and Fell, from Curteis, and Hitchens, 5 nd 10 May; Searle's deposition, 1 Apr. 1822, PRO. HO. 64/1, ff. 205–8.

21 This listing of limited participation nevertheless exposes further deficiencies in the tabulation of incidents in Hobsbawm and Rudé, op. cit., appendix III. *Sussex Advertiser*, 22 and 29 Nov. 1830. *Hastings and Cinque Ports Iris*, 4 Dec. 1830. Indictments, Sussex Winter Assize, 1830, PRO. Assi(zes), 35/270/5.

22 *Sussex Weekly Advertiser*, 17 Apr. and 26 June 1815, 12 Dec. 1825, 23 and 30 Jan., 6, 20 and 27 Feb., and 6 Mar. 1826.

23 Depositions against S. Saunders, and Lewes Jail calendar, Aug. and Oct. 1831, ESCRO. QR/E809.

24 This and the following paragraph are based principally on reports in the *Sussex Advertiser*, esp. 1 Aug., 17 Oct., 7 and 28 Nov., 5 and 19 Dec. 1831, 16 Jan., 13 Feb., 6 Mar. and 7 Apr. 1832, trial reports of Collins, and Thorncraft, *Brighton Gazette*, 1, 15, 22 and 29 Dec. 1831, 22 and 29 Mar. 1832. Indictments, Collins, Huggett, Awcock, Thorncraft, jury lists and jail calendar, PRO. Assi. 35/271/5; 35/272/5. *Maidstone Gazette*, 30 Aug. 1831. Reward handbill, enclosed by the Earl of Plymouth's solicitors, to Melbourne, 11 and 17 Dec. 1831, PRO. HO. 64/2, ff. 502–5.

25 Deed, 2 Dec. 1831, ESCRO. AMS. 5681/57/5.

26 For non-reportage of arson see below. *Sussex Advertiser*, 16 Jan., 13 Feb. and 5 Mar. 1832. *Brighton Gazette*, 29 Nov. and 13 Dec. 1832. N. Barwell to the Home Office, 27 Nov. 1832, PRO. HO. 64/3, ff. 215–16. Indictment of Huggetts, PRO. Assi.35/276/5. Charles Wille, diary entry, 2 Nov. 1834; Mrs Marchant to S. Peskett, 8 Jan. 1832 and 26 Nov. 1834, ESCRO. AMS. 5569/28; 5574/4/5, 8.

27 Deeds, 1832, ESCRO. AMS. 5681/57/7–9. Brooker to the PLC., 1 Apr. 1835, PRO. MH. 12/12854.

28 Thomas to Chadwick, 25 Sept. 1834, PRO. MH. 12/12854. For a broader context, see R. Wells, 'Rural rebels in Southern England in the 1830s', in C. Emsley and J. Walvin, (eds.), *Artisans, Peasants and Proletarians 1760–1860*, (1985), pp. 140–3.

29 Thomas to Chadwick, 25 Sept. 1834; John Storr to the PLC, 28 Apr; Hawley to the Willingdon overseers, and the PLC, 7 and 9 Feb. 1835, PRO. MH. 12/12854. Summary convictions, 1834–5, ESCRO. QR/E826–7.

30 *Brighton Gazette*, 6, 20 and 27 Nov. 1834. Clerk, Hailsham Bench, enclosing reward bill, and Revd Day, to the Home Office, 8 and 26 Nov. 1834, PRO. HO. 64/4, ff. 188–9, 206–8. Wille diary entry, 2 Nov. 1834, ESCRO. AMS. 5569/28. Hawley, and Alfriston parish officers, to the PLC, 9 Feb. and 11 Apr. 1835, PRO. MH. 12/12854.

31 Lady Burlington's steward to Hawley, 10 Feb., and Hawley to the PLC, 9 Feb.; Hawley to Nicholls, 15 Feb. and 19 Mar. 1835, PRO. MH. 12/12854; 32/38.

32 Brooker, 17 and 19 Mar., 1 Apr. and no date, and Hawley, 11 Apr., to the PLC; Hawley to Nicholls, 12 Apr. 1835, PRO. MH. 12/12854; 32/38. *Brighton Patriot*, 7 Apr. 1835, and 31 July and 7 Aug. 1838.

33 Letters to the PLC from, Brooker, 17, 19, 20 and 24 Mar., 1 Apr. and no date, Hawley, 15 and 19 Mar., and 11 Apr., churchwardens and overseers, and draft reply, 15 and 24 Apr. 1835, PRO. MH. 12/12854. *Brighton Patriot*, 31 July 1838. Marchant to Peskett, 26 Sept. 1834, ESCRO. AMS. 5574/4/8.

34 Hawley to the PLC, 27 and 29 (twice) Apr., 1 May, 18 Oct., 28 Nov. and 26 Dec. (with enclosures), and to Nicholls, 12 Apr., 10 and 14 May; Clerk, Eastbourne Union, to the PLC, 28 Sept. 3 Oct. and 24 Dec; Storr to the PLC, 10 and 28 Apr;

Inspector Clarke to Col. Rowan, Commissioner of the Metropolitan Police, 29 Apr. 1835, PRO. MH. 12/12854; 32/38. Earl of Chichester, to Lord John Russell, 15 July, and F.H. Gell to the Home Office, 20 May 1835, PRO. HO. 52/27, ff. 217–18; 64/5, ff. 72–3. Ellman to the Duke of Richmond. 13 May and 16 Sept. 1835, W(est) SCRO, Goodwood Mss. 1573, 1578. *Brighton Patriot*, 14, 21 and 28 Apr., 5 and 19 May, 14 July and 29 Nov.1835. *Sussex Advertiser*, 18 May 1835 and 1 Feb. 1836. For the broader picture, see Wells, 'Resistance . . .', pp. 24–9.

35 *Ibid. Brighton Patriot*, 31 July 1838. Alfriston Chapel minutes, ESCRO. NC. 19/1/1.

36 Piggott's, *Sussex Directory*, (1845), p. 597. Revd Allen to Melbourne, 15 Feb. 1831, PRO. HO. 52/15, ff. 11–12. *Brighton Guardian*, 21 Nov. 1838. *BPP.*, loc. cit., Appendix B, Barcombe replies to Q's 28, 32–7. Wells, 'Resistance . . .', p. 22. Barcombe vestry minutes, 1837–57, ESCRO, Par. 235/12/1. *Brighton Herald*, 20 Nov. and 18 Dec. 1830.

37 *Sussex Advertiser*, 29 Aug. 1831. *Brighton Guardian*, 16 Mar. 1836.

38 Barcombe vestry minutes, 1 Feb. and 18 Nov. 1838, and 25 Apr. 1839, ESCRO. Par. 235/12/1. Chailey Union return to the Constabulary Commissioners, 1837, PRO. HO. 73/8, pt. i. Examination of Joseph Markwick, 1 Nov. 1839, ESCRO. QR/E865.

39 A. Howkins, *Poor Labouring Men: Rural Radicalism in Norfolk 1870–1923*, (1985), pp. 32–5. Wells, 'Rejoinder . . .', pp. 526–8.

40 Towner claimed that 'Heasman has always been against me because I worked for . . . Richardson'.

41 The evidence for the Barcombe gang principally comprises the fourteen confessional statements made by Heasman, further confessions by associates Towner and Jenner, and the statements of victims and witnesses, made Oct. and Nov. 1839, ESCRO. QR/E865; QCV/2/E31, and press accounts of the arrest and trials, esp. *Brighton Gazette*, 4 Nov. and 2 Dec. 1839. Detailed references are given only to other sources.

42 Vestry minutes, ESCRO. Par. 235/12/1.

43 For examples of such detections see R.A.E. Wells, 'Sheep rustling in Yorkshire in the age of the industrial and agricultural revolutions', *Northern History*, XX, (1984), p. 141.

44 Traft also 'sometimes worked for his Father', a barge-owner on the Ouse; his claim that his dealings with Heasman amounted solely to the exchange of beer for a puppy, was a lie. The beershop was a frequent target for police and judicial enquiries, including the activities of the Clarke gang, examined below, and in 1843 Lewes Town Commissioner Wille recorded, 'attended the magistrates respecting "Traffs" being a Bawdy house'; diary entry, 21 Feb., ESCRO. AMS. 5569/30.

45 Oliver gave an unconvincing account to the investigating magistrate, and was virtually forced to give evidence against Traft, with the unusually high surety of £30 being exacted as a recognizance to prosecute.

46 Jenner possibly tried to interest Heasman in burglary; Jenner could identify targets and reconnoitre house lay-outs while 'working'. Under fierce cross-examination, Heasman admitted that he had 'broken open houses', but the sole detail relates to Guy's dairy.

47 Barcombe vestry minutes, 1840–5, ESCRO. Par. 235/12/1.

48 Wood's indictment for firing farmer and overseer James Patching's corn stack, PRO. Assi. 35/273/5. Trial report, *Brighton Gazette*, 19 Dec. 1833. At least one altercation had occurred between the two when Wood refused to walk the six miles daily to designated parish employment on the roads, 'saying that to walk that distance was enough for a day's work': Patching capitulated with a straightforward cash relief payment.

49 Much of this evidence derives from Stunt's seventeen-page confession, in which he
    repeatedly refused to admit participation 'in more robberies', and the depositions of
    victims and witnesses, ESCRO. QR/E869. Committal and trial reports, *Brighton
    Gazette*, 8 Mar., 15 Apr., and 25 May 1840. Further references are restricted to
    additional sources.
50 Wood's indictment, loc. cit.
51 Lavendar the bailiff's failure to mention the spirits suggests that they were smuggled.
52 Stunt later mentioned several streets, and he patronised The Globe, a centre for
    organised labour and Chartists in the town. *Sussex Advertiser*, 29 July 1839. *Brighton
    Gazette*, 15 Apr. 1841.
53 Despite their being 'numbered and stamped with the Maker's name'.
54 'Those who have much experience in Quarter Sessions practice will not participate in
    the astonishment because they know that every prisoner who is arraigned at the county
    Bench labours under some local prejudice and the disadvantage of less intelligent juries
    than . . . at the Assizes; and if found guilty, the punishment awarded by the judge is
    free from prejudice on the score of character'. *Brighton Guardian*, 11 and 18 Dec. 1839.
    Brighton Gazette, 23 Mar. 1840.
55 *Brighton Guardian*, 15 Apr. 1840.
56 The main sources for the Clarke gang comprise Wicks's confessions, 13 Dec. 1839 and
    7 Feb. 1840, depositions of victims and witnesses, including police officers Solomon
    and Pasco, 13–28 Dec. 1839, ESCRO. QR/E867.
57 Arnold deposed, three weeks after the event, and subsequent to Clarke and Wicks's
    arrests, that a 'great quantity of my goods was missing. Several boxes which contained
    Lace, Lace Edgings, Men's Silk Neckerchiefs and pocket Hankerchiefs, Lace Inser-
    tions, a large quantity of plain, black, white, and coloured satin and Sarcenet Ribbons,
    some fancy satin and Lutestring and Guaze Ribbons. Ten or Twelve Shawls . . . also a
    quantity of women's Silk, Muslin and other Hankerchiefs . . . several . . . lengths of
    Persian, some . . . plain . . . others coloured and embossed. Six or seven pieces . . . of
    White Satin Jean . . . several figured waist Ribbons several Muslin Collars, and also
    various other articles', plus fifteen shillings in cash.
58 The *Brighton Gazette*, July 1850 to Aug. 1851 is a major source for accounts of
    individual crimes, incidents in the developing detection process, committal hearings,
    and the major trials at the Assizes for Surrey, for Mar., and Sussex, Mar. and Aug.
    1851. Detailed references are given for other sources, but only exceptionally to specific
    issues of the *Gazette* across this period.
59 An alias; see below. p. 161.
60 *The Times*, 22 and 31 Oct. 1850.
61 *Ibid.*, 19 Oct. 1850, 1 and 26 Apr. 1851. *Maidstone Gazette*, 26 Apr. 1850,
    Indictment, PRO. Assi. 35/290/5. For the Griffith murder see, *Brighton Gazette*, 8 and
    15 Feb. 1849. I am grateful to my step-son, Zach Hewlett, for searching press files on
    the Griffith case.
62 See esp. the speech of the Revd Carnagie JP, at the West Sussex Sessions debate
    respecting the implementation of 13 Vic. cap. 20 superintending constables act in
    each division, *Brighton Gazette*, 13 Apr. 1851. Guildford Board of Guardians, return to
    Constabulary Commissioners, 1837, PRO. HO. 73/5. The condition 'of several
    parishes may be deemed unfavourable for the development of industrious habits and for
    the apprehension of offenders'.

63 Run by Hannah and William Seabrook; Hannah 'misunderstood, or chose not to answer the very leading questions . . . put to her' by the Bench at the committal hearing of her lodger who 'shook his head' at her 'in a menacing manner'. At the police's suggestion, Hannah agreed to dictate and sign a deposition rather than deliver her evidence in open court. *Windsor and Eton Express*, 19 Oct. 1850. *Berkshire Chronicle*, 2 Nov. 1850.

64 *The Times*, 26 Apr. 1851.

65 Downes's deposition, 12 Oct. 1850, PRO. Assi. 36/6.

66 Woking, return to the Constabulary Commission, 1837, PRO. HO. 73/5. *The Times*, 13 Jan. and 24 Apr. 1851.

67 *Mark Lane Express*, 10 Nov. 1851. Superintendent Hollington's deposition, 29 Oct. 1850, PRO. Assi. 36/6.

68 *Maidstone and South Eastern Gazette*, 7 Jan. 1851.

69 Smith's confession, 13 Oct.; evidence of Macey, roadworker Hockley, and schoolmistress Bulpin, at inquest Oct. 1850, PRO. Assi. 36/6.

70 Evidence of Biddlecombe at Hollest inquest; Smith's confession, PRO. Assi. 36/6. *Windsor and Eton Express*, 5 Oct. 1850.

71 *Rochester Gazette*, 1 Oct. 1850. *Windsor and Eton Express*, 19 Oct. 1850. *Berkshire Chronicle*, 7 Dec. 1850. *Maidstone and South Eastern Gazette*, 7 Jan. 1851.

72 Macey's evidence at inquest, 22 Oct. 1850, PRO. Assi. 36/6.

73 The coin 'could pass for money altho' it would not be taken at some of the shops'; it had been the topic of a brief conversation following its receipt as a National School payment by Mrs Hollest: her husband 'observed that George the Third had not had much respect paid to his memory'. Evidence of Mrs Hollest, Kendall, Biddlecombe, and Hollington, at inquest, 8 to 18 Oct. 1850, PRO. Assi. 36/6. *Windsor and Eton Express*, 5 and 19 Oct. 1850. *Berkshire Chronicle*, 5 Oct. 1850.

74 *The Times*, 3 Oct. 1850. *Windsor and Eton Express*, 5 and 19 Oct. 1850. Inquest evidence, and depositions of Biddlecombe, Hollington, Sergeant High, servant Mary Gouldstone, gamekeeper Everett, gunsmith Adsett, shoemaker Cobbett, butcher Colebrook, bricklayer Perry, shop assistant Weston, W. Penny, and Swan landlady Seabrook, PRO. Assi. 36/6.

75 Evidence of Hollington and Keeve, adjourned inquest, 22 Oct. 1851, PRO. Assi. 36/6. *Berkshire Gazette*, 2 Nov. 1850. *The Times*, 1, 2, 8 and 16 April 1851. *Brighton Gazette*, 17 Apr. 1851.

76 *Maidstone and South Eastern Gazette*, 7, 14 and 21 Jan. 1851.

77 *Ibid.*, 14 Jan. 1851. The Tunbridge police continued to recover stolen property during the next three months from a variety of locations, including Crowborough and Guildford. *Maidstone Gazette*, 4 Mar. 1851.

78 *Ibid.*, 28 Jan. 1851.

79 *The Times*, 19 Apr. 1851. *Maidstone Gazette*, 8 and 22 Apr. 1851. Frome Petty Sessions, return to Constabulary Commissioners, 1836, PRO. HO. 73/5. *Keene's Bath Journal*, 11 Nov. 1851. Evidence of Alfred Hughes, ex-Surrey County Constabulary, subsequently Chief Constable of City of Bath Police, BPP., 'First Report of the Select Committee on Police in England, Scotland and Wales', 603, (1852–3), vol. xxvi, Qs. 1292–5.

80 *Brighton Gazette*, 16 Oct. 1851.

81 Clerk, Frome Petty Sessions, to the Home Office, 6 Dec. 1852, with enclosed depositions, PRO. HO. 45/4085. These incidents seem to have been studiously

ignored by the Bath press which served Frome, namely *Keene's Bath Journal*, and the *Bath Chronicle*.

82 *Brighton Gazette*, Dec. 1852 to Mar. 1853. It was reported that 'it is not a little singular that the property stolen' in nearly twenty burglaries, 'has been of very small value, the total losses . . . under £50'.

83 *Sussex Weekly Advertiser*, 5 and 12 July 1819.

84 E.A. Wrigley, 'Men on the land and men in the countryside: employment in agriculture in early nineteenth-century England', in L. Bonfield, R.M. Smith and K. Wrightson, (eds.), *The World We have Gained*, (1986).

85 Among the thousands of examples was the £5 paid by Frant parish to Thomas Page 'towards assisting him in the Business as Butcher'; vestry minute, 2 May 1831, ESCRO. Par. 344/12/1/3.

86 Wells, in Reed and Wells, (eds.), loc. cit.

87 *Maidstone Gazette*, 16 and 30 Jan. 1849.

88 Confession of John Williams, Maidstone Jail, 6 Apr. 1829, and unsigned 'Remarks', PRO. HO. 52/8, ff. 109–10; see also *Kent Herald*, 11 Mar. 1847, for the case of another 'very extensive gang' which specialised in corn robberies using 'skeleton keys', based at Langley, and principally concerned in supplying the black market at Rochester.

89 Hobsbawm and Rudé, op. cit., *passim*.

90 Wells, loc. cit.

91 *Maidstone Gazette*, 16, 23 and 30 Jan., and 20 Mar. 1849.

92 *Bath Chronicle*, 22 Apr. 1852.

93 G. Rudé, *Criminal and Victim: Crime and Society in Early Nineteenth Century England*, (Oxford, 1985), esp. pp. 78–9.

94 *Kent Chronicle*, 9 June 1835.

95 *Sussex Advertiser*, 29 Apr. 1839.

96 *Brighton Gazette*, 4 Nov. 1841.

97 *Ibid.*, 4 Mar. 1841 and 24 Mar. 1842. *Maidstone Gazette*, 7 Aug. 1832.

98 *BPP.*, loc. cit.

99 Radzinowicz, op. cit., IV, ch. 6, pt. v, 'The challenge of disorder'.

100 *Brighton Gazette*, 16 Jan., 6 Feb., 13 and 20 Mar., and 10 Apr. 1845.

101 *Maidstone Gazette*, 22 Oct. 1850.

102 *Report of the Committee of Justices . . . for Extending the Protection of a Police Force*, (1850), enclosed by Surrey Clerk of the Peace, together with magistrates' petition, to Sir George Grey, and reply, 2 and 4 Dec. 1850, PRO. HO. 45/3308.

103 *The Times*, 15 Oct. 1850. *Maidstone Gazette*, 22 Oct. 1850.

104 Cited by C. Emsley, *Policing and its Context 1750– 1870* (1983), p. 79.

105 *BPP.*, loc. cit., Qs. 1293–5.

8

'The Scum of Bath': the Victorian Poor

G. Davis

Bath College of Higher Education

Bath is widely regarded as living off the faded memory of a glorious past, a place ideally suited for maiden aunts living in respectable retirement. More serious comment is invariably connected with the work of Professor R.S. Neale, father of the 5-class model and author of the substantial work, *Bath 1680–1850 A Social History or A Valley of Pleasure, yet a sink of iniquity.*[1] This essay, however, is concerned with a lesser known aspect of the city and attempts to set Bath and the work of Professor Neale in the context of recent research into Victorian Bath and its most notorious slum district,[2] and includes comparative comment on the urban poor and on working class districts in nineteenth-century cities.

Almost everyone is familiar with the heyday of Georgian Bath: Richard 'Beau' Nash, Master of Ceremonies and self-styled 'King of Bath'; John Wood, father and son, who designed many of the great architectural masterpieces; and Ralph Allen who built Prior Park as a showpiece to advertise the qualities of Bath stone from his Combe Down quarries and made it a centre for writers and artists of the period. The city of Bath became the premier resort of fashion in the country, attracting everyone of note at some time or other, ostensibly for the cure but as often in dubious pursuit of gambling, vice or political intrigue.[3] This 'Georgian Summer', as one authority has described it, lasted for only two generations.[4] Bath went into a slow social decline sometime after the death of Nash in 1761. Curiously, it was a victim of its own success in attracting so many people and investment in speculative building on a massive scale. The city doubled in population and size in the last 20 years of the eighteenth century, becoming too popular and crowded for the taste of the fashionable company.[5] At the same time rival attractions appeared among seaside resorts and the smaller spa towns. Brighton blossomed under the eccentric patronage of the Prince Regent and Cheltenham and Leamington developed a following for specialist cures. Certainly by the early nineteenth century, Bath was no longer the exclusive attraction of the highest social quality. This social decline has coloured much that historians have written on Bath in the nineteenth century in a kind of mournful lament over an assumed fall from grace.[6]

The exception is R.S. Neale. He has exposed the polite, guide-book view of Bath as being created in the eighteenth century by the triumvirate of Nash, Allen and the Woods, as a kind of benevolent paternalism at work. Instead he offers a powerful analysis of investment in the building of Bath, representing an estimated capital input of the order of £3 million, or to provide a period perspective, the equivalent of the entire capital investment in the British cotton industry. Neale specifically identifies two capitalist entrepreneurs – the Duke of Chandos and William Johnstone – as the key examples of the way Georgian Bath was built. Chandos was at the centre of a web of international credit in the early eighteenth century. He made separate princely fortunes out of the lucrative post of Paymaster-General during the War of Spanish Succession and from speculation during the infamous South Sea Bubble affair. His involvement in the building of Bath through the employment of John Wood the Elder was largely unsuccessful but he remains an outstanding example of how outside money was invested in property speculation in the city. Johnstone, who changed his name to Pulteney on marrying into the family, was responsible for the building of the famous Pulteney Bridge in 1774 which began the process of developing a landed estate into a Georgian new town on the eastern side of the city.[7]

Neale's work points to a fundamental change in the city's economy. He argues that Bath became too large to be a mere resort sustained by a short season of fashionable visitors. From the late eighteenth century, it was becoming a residential city for the genteel classes and had recruited thousands of workers into its expanding building and craft industries. By the early 1800s, Bath was an important market town for agricultural produce from the surrounding counties and was the market for coal from the Somerset coalfield centred on Radstock. It was becoming a regional shopping centre in high quality goods and was expanding its commerce and industry. Building, brewing, engineering, cabinet and carriage-making, printing and the cloth industry – all featured prominently in providing employment in the city. Neale's survey of employment in Bath's industries and his study of working class movements in the first half of the nineteenth century justify the claim that he 'discovered' the working classes of Bath.[8] In any other city such a claim might appear incredible but in Bath the working classes have been so discreetly camouflaged into becoming mere appendages of the genteel classes that it is akin to discovering new territory.

The 'genteel image of Victorian Bath' was created as a response to national trends – moral earnestness, philanthropy and temperance – but also to meet a perceived local need, that is to replace the custom of the departed fashionable company.[9] Bath sought a new market for trade and created a new image to secure it. The city modified the traditional appeal of the waters, gambling and sex, and the attraction of rubbing shoulders with the great. The new package brought a more indirect association with the famous as the Victorians created the notion of eighteenth-century Bath in terms of commercial appeal. The idea was to encourage people to visit Bath to see where famous people had stayed or to live in and enjoy the elegant surroundings, the refined setting, the mild winters, but also to take advantage of cheap lodging, food and coal, and one of the lowest levels of rates in the country. Respectability and economy were powerful inducements. Above all else, however, was the escape from vulgar industrialisation and a chance to enjoy a nostalgic return to good manners and polite society. It appealed particularly to elderly people living on fixed incomes. This account of 1844 sets the appropriate mood of refinement:

> The visitant is well aware that Bath is not a city of trade. No manufactures worthy of notice is carried on within its limits, nor is it the resort of commerce . . . Of all places in the Kingdom, Bath is best fitted for the retirement of individuals with independent incomes, whether small or large. For those past the meridian in life, its quietness, beautiful neighbourhood, and warmth of climate particularly recommend it.[10]

And again this comment of the mid-nineteenth century echoes the same sentiment:

> The tone of a city can generally be ascertained from the character of its shops: in Milsom Street we see at once Bath is entirely a place of 'genteel' resort and independent residents.[11]

Without fully recognising the creation of the 'genteel image', Neale saw through the contemporary pretence that industry and commerce had no real place in Victorian Bath. He did, however, share with contemporary writers[12] the belief that there were many 'mere' dependents of the genteel classes – shop assistants, domestic servants and others providing services to the wealthy such as laundresses and dressmakers – who might more legitimately be regarded as belonging to the working classes. The mass of the labouring poor, he grandly dismisses as 'the lumpen proletariat'.[13] Their chief offence being a lack of political and class consciousness. Neale's heroes, of course, were the artisan class whom he identifies as the principal support for J.A. Roebuck, the radical MP for Bath in the period 1832 to 1847, and who also formed the backbone of Chartist activity in the city.

Neale's analysis of occupational distribution and the voting behaviour of artisans in St. James's parish in the south of Bath form the crucial elements in the famous 5-class model, incorporating concepts of deference or class independence alongside socio-economic categories of class differentiation. [14] The model proposes a dynamic element in the 'middling class', straddling horizontal class barriers to include movement from lower professionals, petty tradesmen and the artisan class. All this reflects what Neale found in the radical politics of early Victorian Bath, effectively an alliance between individuals and sections of the middle and working classes united in a common set of grievances against powerful propertied interests in the city and in the country at large. The 5-class model has attracted some ridicule on the grounds that the city of Bath, on which it is based, was hardly representative of a developing industrial society. The simple association of the north with industry and the south with agriculture remains a cherished belief. Moreover, people who know little of Bath are easily misled by the genteel image of the city which persists today in the commercial marketing of the city to appeal to modern tourists.

In truth, Neale has had too little credit for establishing that Bath had a substantial industrial base. Also with a large working-class electorate, forming a quarter of those eligible to vote after 1832 which was rather more significant than in many medium-sized industrial towns like Rochdale or Oldham, a Bath-based model is by no means preposterous and should properly be considered alongside those drawn from other towns. [15] Certainly, to equate the working class with those who worked in factories, as Wadsworth appears to suggest in a study of leisure in Bath, so eliminating the working classes in the city, is to be seduced by Bath's carefully fostered respectability. [16]

However, one criticism which can be made of Neale is over the 'middling' class which he identifies in a particular phase of radical politics. In moving away from a 3-class to a 5-class model, Neale remains wedded to a horizontal class view of the social structure. In fact, the practice of parliamentary and extra-parliamentary politics, Neale observed in Bath, exhibits a pattern of shifting class alliances and vertical interest groups when taken over a longer period. [17] There was a constant movement over time and a re-grouping dependent on the issues in question. This pattern of shifting alliances more accurately describes not only the heady agitation of the Reform era but is precisely repeated in the municipal politics of the 1860s in Bath. [18] This suggests that the 5-class model is time-bound and city-bound and therefore of limited value in terms of comprehensive application.

A further criticism of Neale would be that his obvious disillusionment over the defeat of Roebuck in 1847, and the demise of the Chartists in Bath, has coloured his view of Victorian Bath itself. Rather like Roebuck, he takes his leave of Bath somewhat ungraciously and gives it up as unworthy of his further attention:

So they closed ranks, the wealthy and respectable Victorian occupiers of the upper town. Protected against the taint of trade and manual labour by the skirts of 10,000 domestic servants and against the sight and touch of those who laboured in the lower town by the space around them and their basement railings, they closed ranks to block the political aspirations of the tradesmen and artisans, shoemakers, and the others of the labouring population. They were able to do so because middling-class Radicalism had spawned a working class politics that threatened middling-class interests as well as upper class hegemony. . . . And as time passed the city became a place where neither the occupants of Bath chairs, nor the labourers who felt themselves privileged to pull and push them, challenged the economic and political structures which determined their social relationships. Bath was a valley of pleasure still, and for the poor, a sink of iniquity.[19]

In fact, it is quite mistaken to believe that the wealthy and propertied classes in the upper part of the town closed ranks to restrict the aspirations of the trading and labouring population of the city. As a minority sectional interest they were in no position to do so. The predominant ruling Liberal group on the Town Council were the commercial middle class, supported by working class traders and artisans centred on the lower part of the town. The upper-town gentry and liberal professions were, for the most part, the out group within the ruling classes of the city. Upper class hegemony, however much it appealed to Neale, was not a reality in Victorian Bath. When the wealthy ratepayers of Lansdown became sufficiently roused in defence of their interest, as in the water supply question in the 1860s, they had to appeal to the working classes and have recourse to central Government pressure to oppose the policy of the Liberal Town Council. Moreover, commercial middle class interests relied on working class support to retain their political domination of the council.[20] It is possible to agree with Neale that the labouring poor suffered by exclusion from the franchise but the condition of the poor remained an important issue and the working classes a vital element in municipal politics. Neale's picture of the docile Bath chairman at the end of the nineteenth century more aptly represents Bath's 'genteel image' than the commercial and industrial city it became in the Victorian period. An engineer, cabinet maker, printer or railway worker offer more representative figures of the working classes in Bath.[21] Both in imagery and in terms of class analysis, Neale's view is altogether too static and simplistic. More pertinently, in terms of the subject of this essay, he demonstrates an elitist attitude to the poor, the 'scum of Bath'.

It has not been sufficiently understood that Bath as a fashionable resort in the eighteenth century, and as a genteel, residential city in the

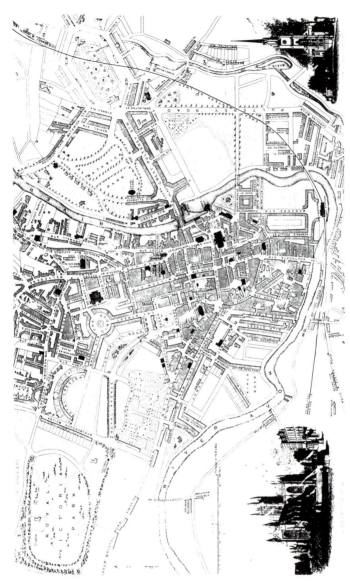

The City of Bath in the mid-nineteenth century

nineteenth century, attracted a host of undesirable elements – beggars, tramps (an estimated 20,000 a year in the 1840s),[22] thieves, pickpockets and prostitutes. The Bath beggars were legendary. The nursery rhyme, 'Hark, hark the dogs do bark, the beggars are coming to town', is a description of Bath beggars dated about 1790.[23] Since medieval times, Bath had drawn to it the sick, the lame and the poor in search of miracle cures from the waters and alms from its many charities. The Georgian heyday of Bath as a fashionable resort was something of an aberration, a brief interlude in a long association with the needs of common people. When it was fashionable to pen a few lines in celebration of a visit to Bath, the beggars were a subject of common complaint:

> I always have heard that the provident mayor
> Had a terrific rod to make beggars beware;
> But I find to my cost, they infest ev'ry street –
> First a boy with one eye, – then a man without feet,
> Who cleverly stumps upon two pattern rings, –
> One bellows, one whimpers, one snuffles, one sings;
> From Holloway's garrets and cellars they swarm;
> But I'll pause, – on this subject I'm growing too warm.[24]

Holloway was a rough district, just outside the southern boundary of the city and beyond the jurisdiction of the city's magistrates. By 1830 it was no longer the principal lodging-house district of Bath. This honour was assumed by the Avon Street district, the plague spot of Victorian Bath, a classic slum, criminal quarter, red-light district, and centre of epidemic disease. It acquired national notoriety, with its inclusion in Edwin Chadwick's monumental work on the sanitary condition of the labouring poor, published in 1842. The local information was supplied by the chaplain to the Bath Union, the Revd Whitwell Elwin:

An epidemic small-pox raged at the end of the year 1837, and carried off upwards of 300 persons; yet of all this number I do not think there was a single gentleman, and not above two or three tradesmen. The residences of the labouring classes were pretty equally visited, disease showing here and there a predilection for particular spots, and settling with full virulence in Avon-Street and its offsets. I went through the registers from the commencement, and observed that, whatever contagious or epidemic diseases prevailed – fever, small-pox, influenza – this was the scene of its principal ravages; and it is the very place of which every person acquainted with Bath would have predicted this result. Everything vile and offensive is congregated there. All *the scum of Bath* – its low prostitutes, its thieves, its beggars – are piled up in the dens rather than houses of which the street consists. Its population is the most disproportioned to the accommodation of any I have ever heard; and to aggravate the mischief, the refuse is commonly thrown under the staircase; and water more scarce than in any quarter of the town. It would hardly be an hyperbole to say that there is less water consumed than beer; and altogether it would be more difficult to exaggerate the description of this dreadful spot than to convey an adequate notion to those who have never seen it.[25]

Clearly the moving force behind such a description was moral indignation. There was a complete ignorance of the origins of epidemic disease and a powerful misunderstanding of the cultural values inherent in a slum community. To the outsider, it was uniformly abhorrent but in a sense too, perhaps, a shade comforting. The Lord knew instinctively where to smite down the ungodly. To those who looked down from their villa residences on the city slopes, it was assuring to be safe in the knowledge that they deservedly enjoyed the Almighty's approval.

Surprisingly, Neale takes Elwin's view at face value and employs it to write off the people of Avon Street as the 'lumpen-proletariat'.[26] They share common ground in righteous condemnation. Neale refers to the evidence of riot and disorder as indicating a savage people hell-bent on self-destruction. Suicide was rife and the people of Avon Street appeared to knock each other about as a popular pastime.[27] Contemporary newspaper accounts created the impression of a no-go area:

MON – AN AVON STREET RIOT

Richard Barrett, an Irishman, was charged with being drunk and disorderly in Avon St., on Saturday night.

It appeared that a crowd of people were assembled before the door of the Fountain public-house, in consequence of some outrage committed by the prisoner, while he was at a window, upstairs, threatening the mob outside. Presently afterwards some woman connected with him, hurled a lump of coal upon their heads. Some of the crowd, in retaliation, smashed the window, when the prisoner rushed out of the house, furiously wielding a poker, and followed the people down the street, attempting to strike indiscriminately, as he proceeded. Patrick Sweeney, a labourer, with a head bandaged from recent injuries, stated that, as he was standing at the door of the Fountain, about half past nine o'clock on Saturday night he heard the cry of 'Murder' and went to the prisoner's house, a little further down the street, from which the cry issued. He had not been there but a few minutes, when the prisoner took up a fender and struck him on the head inflicting several wounds, from the bleeding of which he fell to the ground insensible. He attributed the assault as an old grudge of the prisoner against him. . . .[28]

This incident took place in the 1850s when Avon Street played host to an Irish colony whose presence attracted adverse publicity.[29] Yet complaints about disorder and vice continued at least through to the end of the century, long after the Irish had departed. In the 1880s, the newly-appointed Rector of St. James's parish, the Revd W. Jay Bolton, found to his horror that in St. James's Court, within a few yards of his parish church was a nest of brothels, with upwards of 60 prostitutes operating from the 20 houses in the court and immediate neighbourhood, encouraging each other in drunkenness, debauchery and profanity:

> By day, even on Sundays, and within a stone's throw of St. James's Church, dissolute women, half-dressed, would stand in groups, soliciting passers-by. At night, riots, fighting and piano playing disturbed the whole neighbourhood. Respectable people were ashamed to live in or pass through such a district.[30]

These are the perspectives of upright citizens who as outsiders seized on the worst examples they could find to condemn both the labouring poor as a class as well as certain of the districts they inhabited. Every sizeable city had such a district[31] where, by common consent, the police, if they ever penetrated such places, were always to be seen in pairs. There is a great mass of surviving evidence in Royal Commission reports, sanitary reports, the annual reports of Chief Constables and in the multitude of pamphlets and tracts, penned by clergymen and temperance reformers, that unite in a chorus of condemnation of Victorian slum districts and their poor inhabitants.[32] To the educated outsider, the condition of the poor was explained by their own moral fecklessness.[33] This not only brought reassurance to the God-fearing middle classes but also absolved them from responsibility for the plight of the poor. A blend of enlightened self-interest and religious conscience persuaded some to support charity for the 'deserving poor'[34] and made many sensitive to horror stories about the primitive savagery that lurked in 'darkest England'.[35] In the political debate, the urban poor were not only excluded from the franchise but were the victims of partisan rhetoric as each camp dealt in highly emotive imagery. Reformers, anxious to implement municipal schemes for slum clearance and sanitary provision, dealt in lurid descriptions of squalor to justify the need for action before the moral fibre of the decent working class was undermined.[36] Anti-reformers, wishing to avoid increases in expenditure seen as imposing 'crippling' burdens on the rates and on business enterprise, argued that the slumdwellers had themselves created the conditions of the slums. They were the damned beyond all hope and certainly beyond the influence of municipal schemes which could not be expected to change human nature. Both political ideologies exaggerated the condition of the worst slums and their inhabitants into a universal plight. The Victorian urban slum, like the modern concern over the inner cities, represented an attitude of mind as much as a physical condition.

Research on the Avon Street district of Victorian Bath began as an exploration of the sensationalist reporting in the press and of the numerous references in all the sanitary reports and in the debates in the Council Chamber. A critical study of these sources allied to a detailed analysis of the census enumerators books slowly compelled a different view to take shape. The condition of Avon Street was not uniformly awful, despite the constant vilification of local councillors, clergymen and officials. What emerged was a contrast between image and reality. The reputation of the slum district took on a life of its own.[37] Neale has shown the Avon Street district was already experiencing a process of social descent in the 1760s, only 30 years after building of the street began with fashionable lodging-houses designed by the Bristol architect, John Strahan.[38] With further building in the late eighteenth century, Avon Street had become the home for the large influx of building workers required for the physical expansion of Bath. Literary references to the 'nymphs of Avon Street' confirm an early reputation as the 'red-light' district of Bath.[39] By the 1820s, Avon Street hit the headlines as a criminal quarter and in the new mood of moral earnestness in Bath, the presence of brothels in the street excited rigorous disapproval.[40] In the 1830s, Avon Street took over from Holloway as the principal common lodging-house centre in the city and in response to increasing problems from the presence of itinerant tramps, a Refuge for the Destitute was established there. In the 1830s and 1840s, Avon Street again attracted adverse publicity as the centre of cholera and typhoid epidemics.[41] Throughout the second half of the century, even when notable improvements were effected – overcrowding greatly reduced, mortality rates lowered and educational provision developed – the compounded reputation of Avon Street lived on.[42]

The reputation which historically had its roots in real conditions continued to reflect the condition and behaviour of perhaps a mere tenth of the population resident in the street. It was the case that every week saw some people from Avon Street before the magistrates bench for petty misdemeanors but the great majority aspired to be hard-working, respectable folk who sent their children to school, showed a concern for their neighbours and shared a strong community spirit.[43]

Of necessity, the surviving perspectives of insiders are few and far between but they do contrast with the condemnation of outside officials.

Indeed, resentment and hostility to the condemnation of outsiders is very evident as the following examples reveal:

Letter from Ratepayer of St. James's

Sir,

I was much startled and began to rub my eyes on reading in one of the newspapers the remarks at the Council Meeting by Mr. Alderman Bright, with reference to the proposed improvement in Avon Street. Surely this tribune of the people, as he prides himself on being, must have sadly forgotten the character he assumes when he exclaimed "Fancy respectable people making the transit of Avon Street", and then following this up by insinuating that the residents of Avon Street are a set of thieves, for this it amounts to, inasmuch as he says he would not have advised two lady friends to walk up Avon Street with parcels in their hands at seven o'clock in the evening. I should tell Mr. Bright that there are residents in Avon Street as honest and much to be trusted as there are in Southgate Street or other parts of the city. [Mr. Bright kept a chemist's shop in Southgate Street.] Mr. Bright need not be afraid that they wish to thrust themselves between the wind and his nobility.[44]

In similar vein, a letter written in 1887 complained about the description given by a Mr Howard J. Goldsmid of one of Avon Street's lodging houses. Goldsmid, the author of a book on the lodging houses of London had in the tradition of late Victorian investigative journalism disguised himself as a tramp, spent the night in an Avon Street lodging house and exposed what he saw in the local press.[45] The incident caused a considerable storm not least among the residents of Avon Street. Mr George Gould, of 3 Avon Street, was one of a number who complained about Goldsmid's article:

I have lived in the street for a number of years and know no such place in any respect either as regards the people he came in contact with or the description of any lodging-house in this street. It is a sad thing that people should go about the country in false colours doing all the harm they can to honest, hard-working people under the cloak of religion.[46]

These authors of letters to the editor of the *Bath Chronicle*, publicans, shopkeepers and lodging-house keepers, all regarded themselves as respectable working class citizens. They frankly resented the imputations of dishonesty and disorderly conduct with which they had been publicly branded. There is, moreover, a clear sense of hostility to the kind of

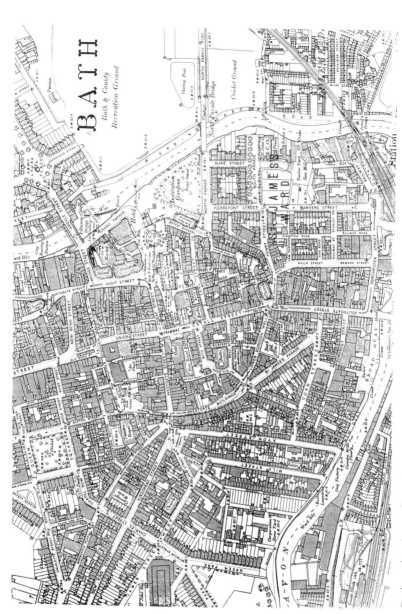

Bath – the Avon Street area

elected councillors who posed as friends of the working classes at election time but were quick to disassociate themselves from working class districts, once safely returned to the more elevated platform of the council chamber. The clergy, who were in the forefront of those passing moral judgement on the slum districts, were identified as enemies of the working class. It was no secret that the Revd F.M. Caulfield had invited Goldsmid into the city with a view to exposing the condition of Avon Street. In the face of such attacks from outside, even to the extent of infiltrators sent into the slums as 'spies', there was a well developed sense of working class solidarity in these letters.

This sense of common identity and alienation from other parts of the city is further demonstrated in a report on a presentation made to a local hero who had saved many people from drowning in the river:

> Presentation to Mr. J. Linsley, currier, New Quay, at the Public Baths and Laundries, Milk Street, of a silver medal, in commemoration of 13 persons having been saved from drowning in the past seven years. The Bath Humane Society in 1872 presented him with a handsomely bound volume of the 'Pictorial Gallery of Art', but he has not, despite his laudable efforts in life-saving, received the society's medal. So a fund was instituted to provide him with one. Subscriptions were confined to the Quay, Avon Street, and Milk Street. Some other persons living in a wealthier neighbourhood offered to contribute, but their offers were declined, as it was wished that the gift should emanate exclusively from the poor of the neighbourhood bordering on the river.[47]

This action reflects the view that the Humane Society's medal was earlier denied to Mr Linsley on grounds of social discrimination because he lived in the slum district.

For people who grew up in the district in the early part of this century, Avon Street was by no means regarded as the worst part of it. To Bill Cottle, a street newspaper seller, crippled at birth, Avon Street was the rich quarter where the 'aristocrats' lived – lodging-house keepers, publicans and tradesmen – many of whom owned their own premises and lived as petty capitalists in a slum community.[48] To Louie Stride, 'this part of the city was a real hive of industry and commerce on a small scale . . . [a] working class district, and it was 'working' in every sense of the word, there was no dole or poor relief, or at least only in exceptional cases i.e. cripples or bad illness, and even then people were too proud to let anyone know and the relieving officers, as they were known, would come nosing round, so it was seldom anyone didn't work'.[49] Louie Stride experienced all the poorest districts of Edwardian Bath doing a 'moonlight flit' with her mother and all their belongings on top of a rented handcart. In moving from Corn Street in the Avon Street district to the Dolemeads, she found 'this area was a completely different type to the last one, this was [a] real slum . . . There were some houses quite uninhabitable, in fact some were just rubble, then one or two good ones, and across the road the same'.[50]

Historically, it is interesting that Avon Street received all the public attention but was not the worst part of the district while other districts, like the Dolemeads and some of the courts in the Walcot Street area, were in a worse condition. Why, therefore, did Avon Street remain notorious in Bath? Firstly, the reputation was rooted in historical experience in the late eighteenth and early nineteenth centuries. Certain associations with its criminal condition, the presence of prostitutes and tramps, and specific incidents of epidemic disease, became fixed in the public mind. Secondly, its physical location behind the main commercial streets as a cul-de-sac bordered by the river, made it a place people read about but rarely visited. Its very separateness encouraged the perpetuation of myths. Thirdly, it gave a physical expression to conflicting Victorian beliefs about the condition of the poor. Avon Street, like Brixton, Toxteth, Handsworth and St Paul's today, became a symbol in political debate. Fourthly, Avon Street served as a focus of attention for repeated investigations by city officials and private individuals and numerous proposals for improvement and charitable endeavour. This was because it formed part of the marginal Kingsmead ward and was crucial in the political struggle for control of the Town Council between the Liberals and Conservatives. Ironically, the chimney sweeps and traders of Avon Street offset the influence of wealthy residents of the Royal Crescent and Circus in Kingsmead ward.

Finally, there is an interesting connection between the genteel image of Bath and the notorious reputation of the Avon Street district. The protracted discussion of a proposed street improvement scheme creating a link between the city's two railway stations points to the way municipal policy and the needs of the people were subservient to preserving the good name of the city. The Master of St John's Hospital, a charity which owned extensive property in Avon Street, lamented the lack of progress:

When a road was proposed to connect the Great Western and the Midland Stations in 1867, one councillor said "he had no sympathy at all with Mr. Jolly's scheme, as it would have the eminent advantage of landing visitors from Liverpool, America, and the Colonies, [from] which the new line was to bring them, in Avon Street and the adjacent locality . . ." It would be entirely changed if a good street was opposed under the idea that if persons passing through Bath saw only its back streets, it would be prejudicial to its renown as a fashionable resort.[51]

Notes

1   R.S. Neale, *Class and Ideology in the Nineteenth Century*, (1972); R.S. Neale, 'The Industries of the City of Bath in the first half of the Nineteenth Century', *Somerset Archaeological and Natural History Society*, vol. 108, 1963–4; R.S. Neale, 'The Standard of Living 1780–1844 – A Regional and Class Study', *Economic History Review*, vol. 19, 1966; R.S. Neale, *Bath 1680–1850: A Social History or A Valley of Pleasure, yet a sink of iniquity*, (1981).

2   G.P. Davis, 'Image and Reality in a Victorian Provincial City: A working class area of Bath', unpub. PhD thesis, University of Bath, 1981.

3   Graham Davis, 'Entertainments in Georgian Bath; Gambling and Vice, in *Bath History*, vol. 1, (Gloucester, 1986), pp. 1–26.

4   D. Gadd, *Georgian Summer*, Bradford-on-Avon, 1972.

5   The population of the city of Bath was an estimated 3,000 in 1700 and had risen to 33,000 by 1801, when Bath was the tenth largest city in England.

6   See D. Jeremy, 'The Social Decline of Bath', in *History Today*, vol. XXIII, 1967; V.J. Kite, 'Libraries in Bath 1618–1964', unpub. thesis submitted for fellowship of the Library Associationm 1966, p. 76.

7   See Neale, *Bath 1680–1850*, Chapters 5 & 7, pp. 116–70, 226–63.

8   R.S. Neale, 'Economic Conditions and Working Class Movements in the City of Bath, 1800–1850', unpub. MA thesis, University of Bristol, 1962.

9   Davis, thesis, chapter 1, 'Image and Reality in Victorian Bath', pp. 37–113.

10   S. Gibbs, *The Bath Visitant*, (Bath, 1844).

11   ——, *Bath Miscellanies*, (Bath, c. 1850), p. 14.

12   Warner, *The History of Bath*, (1801).

13   Neale, *Bath 1680–1850*, pp. 217, 271.

14   Neale, *Class and Ideology*, pp. 29–34.

15   M. Drake, *An Introduction to Historical Psephology*, (Milton Keynes, 1974).

16   P.M. Wadsworth, 'Leisure in Nineteenth Century Bath', unpub. MA thesis, University of Kent, 1977.

17   G. Best, *Mid-Victorian Britain 1851–1875*, (1971), pp. 250–305; D. Smith, *Conflict and Compromise: Class Formation in English Society 1830–1914*, (Cambridge, 1982).

18   Davis, thesis, chapter 8, The Politics of Improvement, pp. 503–92.

19   Neale, *Bath 1680–1850*, pp. 377–80.

20   Davis, thesis, p. 607; see also D. Fraser, *Urban Politics in Victorian England*, (Leicester, 1975).

21   Davis, thesis, pp. 78–91.

22   Sir Henry de la Beche, *Report on the Sanatary Conditions of the City of Bath*, Health of Towns Commission, (1845).

23   *The Beggars of Bath*, Grosse's Glossary, (1790).

24   Fussleton Letters, Letter VIII, from Sir Hector Stormer to Admiral Tornado, *Bath Pamphlets*, vol. 40.

25   E. Chadwick, *The Sanitary Condition of the Labouring Population of Great Britain*, (ed.) M.W. Flinn, (Edinburgh, 1965), pp. 235–6.

26   Neale, *Bath 1680–1850*, pp. 287–94.

27   *Ibid.*, p. 93.

28   *Bath Chronicle*, 22 January 1852.

29 Davis, thesis, pp. 352–6.

30 Revd W.J. Bolton, *St. James's Court: A narrative of events*, Bath Tracts, 1884.

31 R. Samuel, 'Comers and Goers', in H.J. Dyos and M. Wolff, *The Victorian City*, vol. 1, pp. 123–60.

32 See H.J. Dyos, 'The Slums of Victorian London', *Exploring the Urban Past: Essays in urban history*, (Cambridge, 1982), pp. 129– 53.

33 J.P. Kay, *The moral and physical condition of the working classes employed in the cotton manufacture in Manchester*, (Manchester, 1832).

34 Lord Ashley, MP for Bath, addressing the inaugural meeting of the Baths and Laundries Society, at the Assembly Rooms, Bath, *Bath Chronicle*, 27 January 1848.

35 P. Keating, *Into Unknown England 1866–1913: Selections from the Social Explorers*, (Glasgow, 1976).

36 A. Mearns, *A Bitter Cry of Outcast London*, (1883).

37 Davis, thesis, chapter 2, The Reputation of the Avon Street District, pp. 114–63.

38 Neale, *Bath 1680–1850*, pp. 216–17.

39 Graham Davis, 'Entertainments in Georgian Bath', pp. 1–26.

40 *Bath and Cheltenham Gazette*, 20 November 1821.

41 R. Mainwaring, *Narrative of the Progress of an epidemic disease which appeared in Bath in the Autumn of 1832*, (Bath, 1833); Chadwick, pp. 235–6; *Registrar-General's Report on Cholera in England, 1848–9*, 1849, p. 257.

42 Davis, thesis, chapter 2, pp. 114–63.

43 The evidence of Bath Coroners' Inquests, 3 vols., 1798–1835, the census enumerators books, Avon Street 1851 and 1871, Walcot Parish, Bath and letters to the *Bath Chronicle* from Avon Street residents support these conclusions.

44 *Bath Chronicle*, 20 October 1881.

45 For the story of the Avon Street lodging-house scandal, see Davis, thesis, pp. 475–97.

46 *Bath Daily Chronicle*, 25 January 1887; see also *Bath Daily Chronicle*, 26 January 1887.

47 *Bath Chronicle*, 19 December 1878.

48 Bill Cottle, interviewed in 1980, lived in Corn Street, Bath, in the early years of the century.

49 Louie Stride, *Memoirs of a Street Urchin*, (ed.) Graham Davis (Bath, 1985), p. 20.

50 *Ibid.*, p. 27.

51 *Bath Charities*, vol. 1 St John the Baptist Notes, Items 81–2, Letters of Master.

9

Master and Man: Farmers and Employees in Nineteeth-Century Gloucestershire

C. Miller

The relationship between employer and employee is nowhere so complex, confused, and apparently ill-documented as it is in farming in the nineteenth century. Yet in country areas it was the most commonplace of all working relationships; many farm workers were still hired at annual hiring fairs according to a time-honoured formula,[1] and hiring agreements were made there between farmers and farm workers. Such agreements, although usually verbal, were sometimes recorded. Source material *is* therefore available for study, if somewhat difficult to find, and analysis and interpretation of some of the available Gloucestershire records yields some fascinating detail and sheds much light upon working relationships within the nineteenth-century farming community in the county.[2]

In 1845 Engels lamented the passing of 'the patriarchal relation between master and man' in agriculture. Although the rural way of life which existed prior to the intensification of farming in the eighteenth and nineteenth centuries is almost invariably over-romanticized, there is some truth in Engels' claim that 'In the patriarchal time, the hands and their families lived on the farm, and their children grew up there, the farmers trying to find occupation on the spot for the oncoming generation; day labourers then were the exception, not the rule.'[3] The decline of the 'living-in' system (where all hired workers were boarded at the farmhouse) was indicative of a move away from a patriarchal type of relationship between farmer and farmworker and towards a purely contractual relationship. It is impossible to pinpoint exactly when hired men and their families, instead of living on the farmstead with the farmer and his family, were provided with a money wage and a cottage (the 'tied' cottage) which was often at some distance from the farmhouse. Possibly it was an increasing trend in the last half of the eighteenth century – it was certainly common practice by the mid-nineteenth century. The procedure was long drawn-out in southern England, spanning a century or so, and having its roots in the massive social and economic changes of those years. So far as the agricultural labour force was concerned the changes were bound up with the intensification of farming, massive population growth, the decline of rural industries, and the consequent growth of a surplus labour force in many parishes.

In Gloucestershire the living-in system did not die out completely, but by the mid-nineteenth century it was largely restricted to young unmarried men and boys and was more common on the smaller farms of the lower-lying pastoral clayland areas of the county than on the generally larger farms of the upland corn-growing areas. The contractual relationship which grew up between farmer and farmworker did not actually replace the living-in system but developed within the lifetime of the system and continued to evolve during and after its decline. Some nineteenth-century hiring contracts have survived and they tell us a great deal about the structure of the farm workforce, hours and conditions of work, wages and payments in kind, as well as labour relations.

Generally speaking, the nineteenth-century farm labour force could be divided into two categories:

1. **Hired workers** (including bailiffs). The men, boys, and women who worked with animals (shepherds, cowmen, oxmen, pigmen, carters, ploughmen, ploughboys, and dairymaids). These workers were usually hired by the farmer for the year at special hiring fairs held at Michaelmas or, in some areas, at Lady Day, so that he could guarantee the use of their services at the crucial times of year relative to each, i.e. lambing, calving, foaling, harvesting, preparation of the seed bed, and cheese-and butter-making. They fell into two sub-groups:

   a) *Farm servants*, who lived in, i.e. were boarded at the farmhouse or sometimes in lodgings at the farmer's expense. They were usually paid quarterly. In the eighteenth century they would have accounted for most of the hired workers on the farm, but their numbers dwindled rapidly during the Victorian era. The 1851 census shows 3,870 farm servants in Gloucestershire (2,263 men and 1,607 women), but by 1871 their numbers had fallen to 1,690 (1,298 men and 392 women). 1871 was the last year in which their numbers were recorded separately in the census, so no comparison is possible thereafter. Dairymaids usually fell into this category.

   b) *Weekly-paid workers*, men who were hired by the year but paid by the week or fortnight. They were usually supplied with a rent-free cottage by the farmer – a direct link with the old living-in system, in that the cottage was provided in lieu of board.

2. **Ordinary (day) labourers**. There were many sub-groups within this category, but basically they were the workers who performed all the work of the farm unconnected with animals. With the exception of a

few general farm servants, these men and women were hired informally by the day or week and their pay calculated by the day. They were employed only when the farmer needed them. This was the group of workers described by Engels as 'the exception and not the rule' in 'the patriarchal time',[4] but by 1851 they constituted by far the largest (and the lowest paid) sector of the farm labour force in southern England. In Gloucestershire ordinary labourers still accounted for 52 per cent of a much-reduced agricultural labour force in 1901.

Formal hiring usually took the form of a verbal contract. For senior farm workers (those who worked with animals) this took place at the hiring fair – the 'mop' in Gloucestershire. Mops were frequently combined with markets and pleasure fairs and by the early nineteenth century the local mop had become a traditional holiday for farm workers. Until the mid-nineteenth century they were often colourful and boisterous occasions where drunkenness was common, thus attracting a volume of disapproval commensurate with the growth of the temperance movement and the increasingly sombre tone of public morality in Victorian England, and well-intentioned attempts were made to substitute other forms of hiring. By the end of the century fairs which had retained their hiring function were few in number, although in a few cases the name of the fair has remained unchanged to the present day. At the mop the terms of employment were discussed between employer and potential employee, an agreement was reached, and the hiring shilling (a token that the worker had been engaged by the farmer) changed hands. In most cases this was all that the hiring agreement consisted of: a purely verbal agreement reached between farmer and worker, sealed by the symbolic exchange of money. But some farmers did keep records of the agreements in diaries, cash books or labour account books, outlining the conditions of employment and remuneration and sometimes giving a brief job description.

Examples of Gloucestershire Hiring Agreements, 1867–93

Shepherds
1. 1867
    Thomas Dunn agrees to serve as shepherd at 2s. above day men, 25s. for the eaning instead of his meals, 1s. 6d. for every score for shearing and beer. (Fairford, Gloucestershire)[5]
2. 1870
    Robert Little agrees to serve as shepherd for the year at 2s. per week more than the other men also his meals for five weeks in the lambing time. (Fairford, Gloucestershire)[6]

3. 1873
   J. Joynes Senr. shepherd 15s. 6d. per week £1 for ewe eaning Do. Shearing Do. Haymaking to have the same chance as other labourers in the harvest 1d. per Lamb when cut. 1s. hiring for one year. (Longborough, Gloucestershire)[7]
4. 1893
   G. Hyatt hired Daniel Nurden from Michaelmas 1893 to Michaelmas 1894 at 13s. per week, 7s. extra for haymaking and £1 extra for harvest and 2 bus. malt 1 for each 25s. for ewe eaning and 6d. for every lamb over number of ewes put to at cutting time 1s. 6d. per score for shearing. (Snowshill, Gloucestershire)[8]

Under-shepherd
1873
J. Green to have 6s. per week all the year round one bushel malt haymaking & Do. Harvest & 10s. if deserving at Michaelmas 1874 as under Shepherd &c. 1s. hiring. (Longborough, Gloucestershire)[9]

Carters
1. 1867
   Griffin agrees to serve as carter as before 2s. above daymen and 1s. for every wagon load of corn going out. (Fairford, Gloucestershire)[10]
2. 1870
   Thomas Evans agrees to serve as carter for the year 2s. per week more than the day men and one shilling for every day he goes out of the town with his team also his dinner. (Fairford, Gloucestershire)[11]
3. 1893 (Tom Parker)
   12s. per week from Michaelmas 1893 to Michaelmas 1894 2 bus. malt or money for haymaking. £1 extra for harvest month, 7s. extra for haymaking. (Snowshill, Gloucestershire)[12]

Ploughboys
1. 1869
   John Tombs agrees to serve to hold plough with the horse team milk the cows and do anything he may be required to do at 8s. to Lady Day and 8s. 6d. to Michaelmas. (Fairford, Gloucestershire)[13]
2. 1870
   George Hope agrees to serve as ploughboy for the year at 3s. 6d. per week and 5s. over at Michaelmas. (Fairford, Gloucestershire)[14]

These written agreements really amount to contracts of employment and they tell us a good deal about the position of the workers concerned within the farm labour hierarchy. Several of them show the strict wage differential maintained by employers between senior farm workers and ordinary labourers – in these cases the weekly wage is set at a specific level above the average weekly rate for day labourers, although for this differential stockmen would be expected to work a six-and-a-half- to seven-day week, as opposed to the day labourers' six-day week. The terms of employment reflect the importance of the various categories of workers to individual employers: men who worked with animals were vital at certain times of the year, such as lambing, calving and foaling and a large part of the farmer's capital investment rested in their hands. The hiring agreement guaranteed their availability throughout the year, especially where a Michaelmas bonus was involved, for the bonus was not paid until the completion of the year's hiring. Two of the agreements cited above illustrate this: J. Green (under-shepherd) and George Hope (ploughboy). The agreements relating to Manor Farm, Longborough are also interesting in that this meticulous farmer recorded even the payment of the one shilling hiring fee.

Agreements occasionally reflect how the stockman's skill was rewarded in the form of specific bonuses. For the year Michaelmas 1873 to Michaelmas 1874 shepherd Joynes was to receive a bonus of 1d. per lamb born 'when cut', that is, when the ram lambs were castrated and the lambs were counted. But in 1893, shepherd Nurden was to receive a bonus of 6d. for every lamb exceeding the number of ewes put to the ram, again to be calculated 'at cutting time'. Other stockmen received similar bonuses and, although these cannot be traced in the agreements quoted here, they can be seen in the pages of farm wage books and in other sources. Some horsekeepers or carters received bonuses for each live foal born,[15] and on some farms where oxen were used for ploughing and haulage oxmen received a bonus for breaking in young oxen to the yoke.[16] Cowmen reputedly received various forms of bonus: for calves reared, cattle fattened and sold,[17] and a share of the fee for service where bulls were kept,[18] but there are no examples of these in surviving Gloucestershire wage books.

Many hiring agreements reflect vestiges of the living-in system in the form of payments in kind. The shepherds' agreements cited above show that one of the most common payments was for the 'eaning' or lambing period. Traditionally this was made in the form of meals taken in the farmhouse at this time (see Robert Little's 1870 agreement), and as such it is in direct line of descent from the time when all farm servants were lodged at and took their meals there. But in some cases this payment in kind was commuted to cash, as in the agreement for Thomas Dunn (1867), J. Joynes (1873), and Daniel Nurden (1893). Payment in kind at lambing time seems, in fact, to have become comparatively rare by 1870. Payments in kind of bushels of malt for haymaking and harvest (J. Green 1873, Daniel Nurden 1893) probably reflect the beer ration traditionally given by the farmer to his workers during these thirsty labours – shepherd Dunn was still receiving beer at shearing time in 1867. But these payments were also commuted to cash, as in the case of J. Joynes Senr. (1873) and Tom Parker, the Snowshill carter, who was given the choice of malt or money in 1893. Additionally, these payments could also be construed as a form of bonus for stockmen who, because of their responsibilities to their animals, could not join in the more highly-paid harvest work. Thus, Daniel Nurden received a £1 bonus and a bushel of malt at harvest time in 1893. But shepherd Joynes, who had an under-shepherd to deputise for him, was allowed 'to have the same chance as other labourers in the harvest' instead of the £1 bonus he had received at shearing and haymaking. The eleven-man harvest contract for Manor Farm, Long-borough quoted below contains the name of Joseph Joynes and the sum stated in the contract is £7 per man – if Joseph Joynes was shepherd Joynes, then he was quite right to insist on his freedom of choice in this respect.

Carters also received payments whose origins derived from the living-in system. In 1867 Griffin received one shilling for every wagonload of corn taken off the farm. The meaning of this payment can be seen more clearly in Thomas Evans' 1870 agreement, when he received 'one shilling for every day he goes out of the town with his team also his dinner' – in other words, the payment represented out-of-pocket expenses for overnight stops.

Hiring agreements are therefore a mine of information concerning conditions and terms of employment for hired employees, wage differentials, bonuses, and payments in kind. They also contain a few fossilized remnants of the once universal living-in system, mirroring the transition from the 'patriarchal relation between master and man' in farming to the commercially-based relationship of the nineteenth century – the wage contract. The second tier of the farm labour force, the ordinary labourers or day men, made short-term contracts with the farmer, usually by the week, but the term 'day men' indicates that they were really employed by the day only, i.e. when there was work for them to do. The single exception regarding contracts for the ordinary labourer seems to have been the piecework contract. A man or group of men (or women) would undertake a specific piece of work such as harvesting, haymaking, or hoeing at a specified rate per acre or per worker. In the following example the rate was £7 per man for the whole harvest operation. The agreement was usually verbal but this farmer recorded everything, or so it seems:

This agreement was entered into this 1st day of August 1879, between Charles Shillam of Longboro' and John Scovell of Batsford, Charles

Shillam (on behalf of James Williams, John Newman, John Webb, Samuel Clark, Joseph Joynes, Charles Marshall, George Dabney, Joseph Coats, William Robins, George Tufley) agrees that he will on their behalf enter into this agreement to cut, carry, stack and pare the ricks of all the corn on the farm in the occupation of J. Scovell (excepting the vetches and peas which shall be done by the day) for the sum of seven pounds per man and 1/– hiring money.

Dated Augst 1st 1879

John Scovell (signature)
Charles Shillam (signature)[19]

In some instances the hiring agreement was put on a much more formal basis – a printed contract, signed and recorded at the hiring fair. The following example shows the form that these agreements took. It relates to Henry Whale, a boy or a youth who was almost certainly living-in, if his annual wage can be used as an indication of this.[20]

WOOTTON BASSETT HIRING FAIR

MINUTE OF CONTRACT OF HIRING, BETWEEN THE MASTER HIRING AND THE SERVANT HIRED, AND ON THE TERMS FOLLOWING.

Name of Master, George Worlock   *Residence*, Codrington, Gloucestershire
Name of Servant, Henry Whale   *Residence*, Cliffe Anstey
For what time hired – *For the term of* One year *from the* sixth
day of April 1855
WAGES at the sum of Four pounds
For what purpose Servant hired – *To serve as a* General Farm Servant

(signed)
George Worlock   *Master*

Henry Whale's   *Servant*
mark X

These printed contracts were presumably intended as an insurance for both parties, for things did sometimes go wrong – farmers sacked unsatisfactory workers they had hired, or hired workers, finding conditions not to their liking, ran away. At Winchcombe in Gloucestershire, three mops were held on consecutive weeks in October and the third and last was known as the 'Runaway Mop'. This mop was obviously intended as a final opportunity for workers who had already left employment and farmers who had lost or dismissed employees to better suit themselves.

Instances of hired workers running away from unsuitable or uncongenial work or hard masters were not uncommon. One such Gloucestershire instance was that of John Beard, who ran away from Puckpool Farm in the Severnside parish of Arlingham in November 1836. The runaway youth was apprehended by his master and taken before the local magistrate, John Sayer. The case seems subsequently to have been dropped by the farmer since there is no record of its having gone any further, but the draft deposition made before Sayer has survived:

> The deposition of John Carter of Puck-pool in the parish of Arlingham in the county of Gloucester taken on his oath before me, in the presence of John Beard, this November 7, 1836 – who saith –
>
> I hired John Beard to be my servant in husbandry at the Middle Gloucester Mop, last past; one Monday night, the 24th of October last he ran away and left my service without leave. I agreed to give him eight guineas for the twelvemonth.
>
>
> Sworn before me
> the day and year
> above written
>
>
> (signed) John Sayer
>
> John Beard, being asked what he had to say in his defence – said –
>
> I did not like attending two blind horses. I could not eat fat bacon.
>
> (signed) John Sayer.[21]

The usual fate of the worker when such a case came before Petty Sessions was a fine, with imprisonment as a penalty for non-payment. For instance, Miles Hampton of Pope's Hill was summoned by Mr John Morris of Newnham-on-Severn at Newnham Petty Sessions in June 1872 for neglecting to fulfil a contract as a farm worker (the precise type of work was not stated); Hampton was ordered to pay the sixteen shillings claimed by farmer Morris.[22] John Creed of Bagpath was ordered to pay a fine of ten shillings plus costs for a similar offence, but was sentenced to two weeks imprisonment in default.[23]

It would therefore seem that the hiring process and the hiring contract were one-sided agreements existing to ensure that the farmer had the services of key workers when he needed them, and defining the terms of those services. The employer retained the right to dismiss a hired worker for whatever reason, but the employee seems to have had little or no redress against such arbitrary dismissal. The formal hiring contract probably owed its being to the decline of the living-in system (where farm workers lived with the farmer and all their living expenses were found by the farmer) and the rise of the wage contract, whereby workers were physically separated from the farmer and his family and paid their own living expenses. Vestiges of the living-in system survived in the tied cottage which was frequently the perquisite of the stockman, and in the payments in kind embodied in many hiring contracts, although these were increasingly commuted to money payments in the second half of the nineteenth century. Hiring as a custom and the hiring agreement as a practice did not die out completely in Gloucestershire during the Victorian era, but the means by which workers were hired had largely changed by 1900. Labour supply and demand had virtually equalized during the 1870s and it had become common for workers simply to stay with a compatible employer rather than to move on each Michaelmas as a matter of course. When a farmer needed to replace a worker he found that a newspaper advertisement usually had the desired effect and so newspapers were increasingly used as a recruiting medium. By 1898 the hiring fair was almost redundant, and Gloucestershire was one of only four counties in England where 'a little hiring' still took place at only three fairs.[24]

The emergence of new types of economic and social relationships between farmer and worker confused and complicated their working relationship. The social boundaries of the old patriarchal system had been well defined, but no-one was sure where new definitions could or should be drawn. Consequently, labour relations in agriculture worsened throughout the nineteenth century, reaching their lowest ebb in 1872–6 with the formation of the National Agricultural Labourers' Union (NALU) and the strikes and lockouts of those years. Whilst Gloucestershire farm workers insisted on the one hand that they were 'overworked as well as being underpaid',[25] farmers on the other hand reacted with indignation because their workers demanded 'to be paid in money, and none in kind or kindness'.[26] The repercussions could still be felt in 1880 when one Gloucestershire farmer complained that the NALU had 'caused bad feeling between masters and men, and the men evidently do not try to do the work that they used to'.[27] The NALU sank without trace in Gloucestershire during the early 1890s, and the relations between farmers and farm workers reached a state of 'quasi compromise between the old order and the new', with the workers still striving for higher wages and greater freedom whilst clinging to the idea that their employers were under certain obligations not comprised in the pay. But of the farmers it was said that only a few, mainly those in a large way of business, strove to meet those obligations.[28]

Relationships at a personal level between farmers and farm workers were inextricably linked with their economic, social and working relationships. As John Chalmers Morton pointed out: 'The relationship between master and servant is mixed up in agriculture with much beside a mere bargain for the sale of services – with much that is personal.' It was, he said, a relationship which did not permit half-measures: 'If I had a single sentence to describe the relation of master and servant in the agricultural world, it would be to assert that nowhere is it better and nowhere is it worse . . . the two are never . . . indifferent to one another – they love, honour, and respect each other, or they distrust and hate.'[29] This ambivalent relationship may well have resulted from the gradual expulsion of the farm worker from the farmhouse and the consequent destruction of a symbiosis necessary and natural to farming and farm work. For agriculture, then as now, demands a real commitment from both farmer and worker, master and man; it can never be a job – it is a way of life.

Notes

1 Hiring fairs probably had their origin in the Statute of Labourers (1351), which ordered farm servants to appear in the market towns to be publicly hired. W. Hasbach, A History of the English Agricultural Labourer (second edn., 1968), p. 23.

2 All the hiring agreements referred to in this paper relate to the ancient county of Gloucestershire, i.e. the county prior to local government reorganisation in 1974.

3 Frederick Engels, The Condition of the Working Class in England (St Albans, 1974), p. 287.

4 Engels, Condition of the Working Class in England, p. 287.

5 G(loucestershire) C(ounty) R(ecord) O(ffice), D 1070/1/173 (Park Farm, Fairford).

6 G.C.R.O., D 1070/1/173.

7 G.C.R.O., D 4084 Box 29 (Manor Farm, Longborough).

8 G.C.R.O., D 2267/A8 (Snowshill Farm, Snowshill).

9 G.C.R.O., D 4084 Box 29.

10 G.C.R.O., D 1070/1/173.

11 G.C.R.O., D 1070/1/173.

12 G.C.R.O., D 1070/1/173.

13 G.C.R.O., D 1070/1/173.

14 G.C.R.O., D 1070/1/173.

15 G.C.R.O., D 2267/A8; George Chadband 1889, Tom Parker 1895.

16 G.C.R.O., D 2267/A8; James Standley 1879.

17 F.G. Heath, British Rural Life and Labour (1911), p. 30.

18 Royal Commission on Labour, The Agricultural Labourer P(arliamentary) P(apers) 1893–4, XXXV.493 (C. 6894–IV). Report by R.C. Richards on Cirencester and Monmouth Unions, p. 55.

19 G.C.R.O., D 4084 Box 29.

20 G.C.R.O., D 3979. The contract is printed as it appears, the roman type representing the hand-written sections.

21 G.C.R.O., D 2685/26.

22 Stroud Journal, 28 June 1872.

23 *Stroud Journal*, 28 June 1872.

24 *Report by Mr. Wilson Fox on the Wages and Earnings of Agricultural Labourers in the United Kingdom* P.P. 1900, lxxxii.557 (Cd. 346), p. 18.

25 *Gloucester Journal*, 10 Feb. 1872.

26 *Gloucester Journal*, 6 Apr. 1872.

27 *Royal Commission on the Depressed Condition of the Agricultural Interest* PP 1881, XVII.I (C. 3096), p. 178; evidence of H.S. Hayward, Frocester Court.

28 *Royal Commission on Labour, The Agricultural Labourer* PP 1893–4, XXXV.493 (C. 6894–IV). Report by R.C. Richards on Cirencester and Monmouth Unions, p. 20.

29 J.C. Morton, *Hand-Book of Farm Labour* (1868), pp. 91–2.

10

The Peasantry of Nineteenth-Century England: a Neglected Class?

M. Reed

Agricultural England in the nineteenth century presented a unique and amazing spectacle to the enquiring foreigner: it had no peasants.

He still kept the farm modestly, for he was anxious to be able to do without help except from Beatup. His young family were also an expense. For a few years more he must expect to have them rather heavily on his hands . . . then Albert and the twins would be able to do a little work, and gradually both the capacity and number of his labourers would increase, till at last perhaps he would be able to discharge Beatup, and Backfield alone fight Backfield's battle.[1]

It is a pervasive argument in the historiography of rural England that by the nineteenth century, large-scale capitalist farming was ubiquitous in the English countryside. As Eric Hobsbawm put it: 'England was a country of mainly large landlords, cultivated by tenant farmers, working the land with hired labourers'.[2] Such claims have occasionally been challenged, but with little impact. The challenges have either been ignored, or, if at all persuasive, dismissed as highlighting groups of people who were of very minor significance since they worked only a small proportion of the acreage, employed only a tiny portion of the workforce, or were only part-time farmers.[3] Such critiques have been easier to sustain, since the historians so criticised have themselves seen these groups as of little real importance within the countryside.[4] If this is really the case, then one might as well concentrate on 'the larger farmers, who occupied most of the land and employed most of the labourers', and pass over the rest.[5]

In this article I will suggest that such arguments are misplaced and impede our understanding of rural society. I will argue that the small farmer was far more widespread than is usually believed, and, with the small rural tradesperson, played an important economic and social role in the countryside. The work is still very much 'in progress' and draws largely on material from the southeast of England. Not all the hypotheses can yet be fully substantiated, and the article is as much about asking questions as formulating models. Finally an attempt to 'place' the group theoretically will be made, though once again this must be considered as an exercise in posing questions, rather than full-blooded assertion.

I

Historians are fond of comparing English agriculture with that of the continent, but the differences while very real, are usually exaggerated. Hobsbawm and Rudé point out that at mid-century about half of the 225,000 farms in Britain were between 100 and 300 acres in size, compared to in 1882, a mere 140,000 out of 5.7 million French 'exploitations' (2.5%).[6] This, though, is not comparing like with like. The French returns refer to all 'holdings' while the English census figures refer only to the holdings of those persons who returned themselves as 'farmers' in the 1851 census. If we look at the British agricultural returns, we find that in 1885 only 17.8% of all agricultural holdings in Great Britain were over 100 acres, while for England alone, the figure was 18.2%. The difference with France is marked, but it is greatly reduced. Over 80% of English agricultural holdings were smaller than 100 acres in extent, and over half were less than 20 acres. Only in Berkshire, Essex, Northamptonshire, Northumberland, Oxfordshire, Suffolk, and the East Riding of Yorkshire, were more than 25% of all holdings larger than 100 acres. For Norfolk, often taken as the quintessential county for large-scale capitalist farming, the figure is only 17.3%.[7] It becomes easy to see why one French observer of English agriculture in the mid-nineteenth century, was able to write that:

> . . . the agricultural prosperity of England is generally attributed to large farming; but . . . ideas on the subject are much exaggerated . . . No doubt there are very large farms, just as there are very large estates; but these form by no means the majority. There is a multitude of farms under the middle size, which would pass for such even in France; and the number of small tenants is infinitely greater than the number of small proprietors.[8]

Of course, the mere existence of many small farms means little on its own. Market gardening and similar forms of intensive agriculture, requiring a great deal of capital and considerable labour might have been widespread.[9] We are reminded by Peter McPhee that 'for the purposes of conceptualising agrarian social structure, the critical issue is not the size of the unit of production, but what is done with the land and by whom'.[10] In nineteenth-century England, historians have little doubt that the land was exploited by capitalist farmers with the use of hired labour. Hobsbawm believed that:

> families owing or occupying their own small plot of land, cultivating it substantially with the labour of their members, and indeed very often – perhaps mostly – still practising subsistence agriculture, even when they sold some of their produce in the market, supposing they had a surplus (were) . . . unimportant minorities

which, by the nineteenth century, were to be found only in parts of northern England, 'and local concentrations . . . here and there in other parts'.[11]

The evidence suggests otherwise. Since contemporaries themselves were somehow often convinced of the absence of these groups, official data seldom provide unambiguous information about them. Fortunately, the census of 1831 is an exception, though not without its own problems of reliability. Male agricultural occupiers over the age of twenty, were placed in two categories, those hiring labour and those not doing so. In England as a whole, 40% of all occupiers employed no labour. To be sure, they were most numerous in the north, but most counties had a substantial minority of family farmers. Only six counties, Berkshire, Buckinghamshire, Essex, Hertfordshire, Oxfordshire, and Suffolk, had fewer than 25% of occupiers of this kind. Norfolk, the classic capitalist farming county, had over one-third, while the south-eastern counties, Kent, Surrey and Sussex, had 33%, 28%, and 29.6% respectively. Furthermore, the data were published for each parish in the land allowing fairly precise location of these farmers. In the three south-eastern counties, it is clear that survival of family farming was widespread but localised. Such farmers formed a majority or large minority of occupiers in very many areas, especially in the High Weald of Kent and Sussex; the Weald Clay of these two counties and of Surrey; the North Downs, especially east of the Medway; parts of east Kent; north-west and south-west Surrey; and even some parts of the classic corn belt of Sussex, the Coastal Plain, in particular the extreme west and an area midway between Chichester and Arundel.[12]

Contemporary observers made clear on occasion, that subsistence farming survived quite vigorously. In 1836, James Hudson claimed that small wealden farmers 'raise their subsistence principally within themselves', and at mid-century, on the borders of Surrey and Hampshire, 'everyone lived on the produce of their farms and holdings, the only outside requirements being groceries, which for the most part came into store every quarter'.[13]

Reliance on family labour is also clear from sources other than the census. Appendix D of the Poor Law Report contains an enormous amount of material relating to the Labour Rate, which was extremely unwelcome amongst this group. W. Ledger of Ulcombe in Kent, married with nine children, said 'my farm (of 10 acres) was not large enough to employ them; for that reason I hired a parcel of land, about 31 acres . . . to employ them upon. To get a livelihood, myself and wife and children all work upon the land, that are able'. In Binsted, Surrey, Thomas Hawkins did 'the work on my small farm solely with myself and family'. In Sussex, L.D. Smith of Henfield stated that 'I am a householder, and occupy a small grass farm, and only employ a labourer occasionally. . . .'[14] Similar cases are to be found throughout the century. In 1867, in the Hailsham district of east Sussex, 'the smaller holdings (were) worked entirely within the family . . .', while in 1889, the Revd E. Littleton described a High Wealden farmer who '. . . has not anybody in his employ except a carter boy; he himself and his son with his wife and daughter do the whole of it. . . .' He went on to state that there were 'a great many' farmers of this kind in the area. The farmer described had 'three horses and five cows, and he grows a miscellaneous lot of things; he has hops, oats, wheat, root crops'. Describing the Heathfield poultry farms of the 1880s, Henry Rew observed that the smaller farms worked by the family produced 'the most noteworthy results . . . probably by reason of the constant personal supervision which they can give'.[15]

The census of 1851 at first sight runs counter to this argument, suggesting a significant decline in family farms since 1831 in the south and east of the country. In England as a whole the proportion was almost precisely the same as 20 years earlier, 40.6%.[16] In the north and west, and the west midlands, the proportion of farmers not employing labour remained constant or even increased, but it declined considerably in those counties south and east of a line from the Wash to the River Exe. The consistency of this change cannot be lightly dismissed, but it may be unwise to read too much into it. A sample of every fifth 'farmer' in the manuscript enumerators' schedules for Kent, Surrey, and Sussex, suggests that the published figures for hired labour need cautious interpretation. Farmers were notoriously inconsistent in their responses to the census questions, often including their family amongst the labour employed, despite being expressly asked not to do so.[17] The census sample suggests that hired labour was at most, only a supplement to that of the family on very many farms in the south-east. It is possible to suggest that this is the case on most holdings smaller than 100 acres on most soils, though on the heavy soils of the Weald Clay, 80 acres might be more accurate, and on the light sandy soils of the High Weald and the western Weald, 120 acres. This accords remarkably well with Herman Levy's observation that family labour was usual on farms smaller than 100 acres at the end of the century, and with Ian Carter's work in north-east Scotland.[18]

Since the census only asked those persons returning themselves as 'farmers' to give details of land held, it gives virtually no information about landholding by people in other occupations, thereby seriously understating the numbers of occupiers of land. This is especially true at the lower end of the unit size scale where dual or multiple occupations were most common. The agricultural returns of later in the century suggest that occupiers of agricultural land were probably twice as many as the number of persons calling themselves 'farmers' would indicate. There is no reason to think that the total number of holdings increased significantly during the era of 'high farming' from about 1850 to the 1870s, so that the statistics of 1875 probably give a reasonable indication of the situation in 1851. At the earlier date the number of 'farmers' occupying holdings smaller than 50 acres, was only 21% of the number of such holdings in 1875 in the three south-eastern counties, and those 'farmers' with farms between 50 and 99.9 acres in 1851 held only 62% of the number returned in 1875.[19]

Some of these holdings were doubtless held by wealthy businessmen, clergy and similar groups, but most were held by rural tradespeople. It has been claimed that 'nearly all tradesmen also followed some form of agriculture either as a major or subordinate source of income',[20] which suggests that to differentiate too much between tradespeople and small farmers is hazardous. Most rural tradespeople probably relied mainly on family labour. The 1851 census allows us to demonstrate this at the regional level. In some trades 'more than one half' of all masters in the south-east region as a whole (including the towns) made no return. Of masters who did, 26.3% employed no labour, while another 22.1% employed only one person.[21] The half who made no return, were more likely not to hire labour then those who did.

Arthur Brook of Henfield in Sussex, protesting at the labour rate in 1832, wrote 'I am a carpenter in a small way, but do it all myself, not wanting a man. I have also about five acres of meadowland. . . .' At Ifield in the same county, William Davey stated 'I use about six acres of meadow land, in connexion with a small trade as grocer, & c. which together do not fully employ my own hands'.[22] At mid-century in Lodsworth in the western Weald, dual occupations were common. Henry Tribe was a blacksmith farming 50 acres, and James Child was a grocer and draper with 66 acres of ground. William Hills, also a blacksmith, held 4 acres at South Heath in the parish, and John Baigent, with $1\frac{1}{2}$ acres, was a tailor, while William Wakeford was a carpenter who cultivated nearly 3 acres. Of the nineteen tradespeople in Kelly's directory of 1852, all but four occupied more than 1 acre of ground.[23]

Lower in the social scale perhaps, was the labourer with land, or perhaps we should say the family farmer who augmented his or her income with wage labour. Raphael Samuel rightly insists that 'the whole question of proletarian land-holding in the countryside cries out for investigation. . . .'[24] In the south-east they still survived throughout the nineteenth century. In the 1870s Henry Evershed described such people and their holdings at the Dicker in east Sussex. 'There is a number of small farmers entrenched on a remarkable spot in the Weald of Sussex where they still hold their own, secure at present, on a poor soil which few people covet. . . . Any person . . . desirous of seeing a farm labourer with land, should come down here before it is too late. . . .' He described 'the system, the small plot and cow-keeping of old England' which kept the family occupied, and provided, for one family at least, weekly sales of butter amounting to 28s.[25]

Despite Evershed's conviction that such a system was very unusual, similar kinds of small scale agriculturalists survived all over the country. So strong was the obsession of nineteenth-century commentators with improved farming and large scale agriculture, that when they found different systems, usually where they lived, they were sure that they were seeing something unusual, and historians have tended to take their observations at face value. In fact they were wrong. Small farming and farmer-labourers survived in many places. Often they relied on common land, as well as their main holdings. Samuel points out that 'heaths and commons did not disappear from the countryside with the advent of enclosure, though their size was drastically curtailed'.[26] In the south-east they were still quite widespread. Richard Heath noted in 1872 that:

> It is still almost true that a man may ride from Ascot Heath in Berkshire, across Surrey to Bexley Heath in Sussex a distance of thirty miles, and hardly leave common land the whole way.[27]

Ashdown Forest in east Sussex, was a similar area. The foresters, dubbed 'the Sussex crofters',[28] survived by cutting peat, litter, wood and so on from the forest. They dug stone and turned out sheep, cattle and horses, as well as other livestock throughout the century.[29] In the New Forest as well, similar groups were to be found. One historian concluded to his surprise, that a *peasantry* still survived here, though here alone, in the 1870s and later,[30] yet the groups he describes were no different to those similar groups of Ashdown or of west Surrey.

But the areas referred to were only the most extensive areas of common and waste. Smaller areas survived in very many localities of the south-east. The Dicker referred to above was one, but most Wealden parishes had some common, nor was it entirely absent from the coastal plain of Sussex. In the Kentish chartlands in the 1870s it was said that 'the chart is common land, and public property, so far as pasturing, fuel-cutting, and the other servitudes are concerned'. The inhabitants 'have the pigs they either feed on the refuse of their vegetables or turn out to grub and forage for themselves . . . and they may keep half-a-dozen sheep or a cow which take the free run of the common'.[31] Often, in addition to 'official' common land, there was land for which no right of common existed, but which was nevertheless used as such. Gosdens Heath in Lodsworth was an example: it was enclosed in 1836 but continued to be used as common throughout the century.[32]

Small-scale agriculturalists also gained access to the land through sub-letting. Precision is impossible but the sources create an impression that it was widespread. In Lodsworth, William Knight seems to have occupied several fields as a sub-tenant in 1810, while thirty-eight years later, the local squire, Hasler Hollist, complained repeatedly to Thomas Puttock, a miller, 'I am informed that you have ceased to occupy personally my little meadow at Lodgebridge, and that in fact you have underlet it. . . .'[33]

Odd scraps of land and field corners were utilised by the small occupier, who frequently planted them with crops often potatoes. This was common in the early nineteenth century, as the crop returns of 1801 make clear. In Lodsworth, in the 1830s a sawyer and small farmer, Phillip Rapson, had several small sections of other people's fields planted with potatoes and carrots.[34] The practice of 'winter keeping' similarly had the effect of enhancing the small farmer's access to land, since it permitted ownership of larger numbers of livestock than the holding would otherwise have been able to support. Phillip Rapson in Lodsworth, and John Payne in nearby Kirdford – neither of whom had more than five acres of land at any time – regularly placed their stock out to their neighbours for the winter when their own holdings could not support them.[35]

It seems clear that beneath the simplicities of historiographical orthodoxy, there lies a complex situation whereby small farmers, tradespeople, even labourers, were able to sustain agricultural undertakings, greater and more diverse than would seem possible at first sight. To be sure, few survived solely in this way, agriculture usually being only one aspect of their work. This fact has been used to justify their exclusion from the discussion of English farming and rural social relations. Farming is seen as only an adjunct to their trade or craft activities, or to their work as labourers.[36] In reality it demonstrates that occupational divisions were not clear cut.[37] We are seldom justified in making them so, nor should we be too hasty in categorising some forms of income as 'secondary'. A blacksmith with land is not necessarily a blacksmith first and a farmer second, nor is a labourer with land necessarily a labourer first. Instead, we should see the whole range of activities engaged in by these groups as of equal importance, though for each *individual* the various undertakings may well have had varying and different degrees of importance.

None of this however, negates the conclusion of many historians, that these groups are unimportant. No matter how numerous they were, it *is* clear that they worked only a small percentage of the acreage – though a larger portion than is often claimed – and they did only employ a tiny proportion of the workforce. Thus they can still be categorised as forming merely 'an undergrowth of economically marginal cottager-labourers, or other small independents or semi-independents. . . .'[38] It will be argued in sections III and IV of this article, that on the contrary, they *were* important, being neither economically nor socially marginal. But first a brief look at the household of the family producer is called for.

II

The second quotation at the head of this article describes how Reuban Backfield, the central figure of Sheila Kaye-Smith's book *Sussex Gorse*, anxiously waited for his children to grow up so that they could work his land and enable him to dispense with hired labour. References to the household of such groups in southern England are few and this section can only touch on the subject tentatively. Despite the comparative wealth of studies of the family in rural France, a historian has recently written that 'we do not know a great deal about the nature of relationships within the rural household.'[39] How much more true is this of England. Such work as there is has scarcely looked at relationships, nor has it attempted to situate the family and household within the context of the social formation, being content with a purely descriptive approach to the problem.[40]

It has been said that we do not know whether the agricultural labourer was 'man, woman or child'.[41] This is even more true of the people who are the subjects of this paper. The census of 1851 shows that only 6.5% of 'farmers' and 'graziers' in the south-east were women, and this was probably more or less true of those 'farmers' who only used family labour. But this is not the point. For the family producer, the whole family produced. Reuban Backfield could hardly wait for his children to grow and contribute to the production process, so that he could sack his labourer. Research is needed to find out how the use of hired labour fluctuated with the family life cycle. We have already seen[42] that extra land would be rented if possible to employ a growing family, and no doubt it would be given up as the family grew up and left home.

For Backfield, his wife, Naomi, was merely a producer of sons, and was excused farm work to enable her to concentrate on child-bearing and rearing. Before the birth of her second child, she expressed to her husband a wish that it be a girl since they did not want two boys, to which Reuban retorted:

Two boys! – not want two boys! – Why, we want ten boys! if I cud have twenty, I shudn't grumble. . . . I aun't talking nonsense, I'm talking sound sense. How am I to run the farm wudout boys? I want boys to help me work all that land.[43]

This was probably not general though. Women, while no doubt expected to produce future labourers, also worked in the enterprise, as did the children. When, in Lark Rise, 'old Sally' was a child in the early nineteenth century, 'everybody worked; the father and mother from daybreak to dark. Sally's job was to mind the cow and drive the geese to the best grass patches'.[44] Women's work seems to have been fairly clearly defined, and entailed responsibility for the house and for jobs that were done in the house, or in the immediate environs like the farmyard. At Mayfield in east Sussex, the dairy work amongst the numerous cowkeepers at mid-century, 'was almost exclusively done by females'.[45] Poultry were kept on most Sussex holdings, and were always the responsibility of the woman. Henry Evershed had no doubt that the women ensured that 'the small-plot people make profit of their poultry'. He described a farm where the woman looking after the poultry 'had sixty-three "little ones" coming on nicely'.[46] Probably the women in the small farming household had tasks very like those of a female indoor servant at a farm in Wadhurst in the High Weald of Sussex during the 1830s:

> I'd churning twice a week, and cheesing twice a week, and brewing twice a week, beside washing and baking; and six cows to milk every night and morning, and sometimes a dozen pigs to feed. There were four men lived in the house, and I'd all the bilin' to do – the cabbage and the peas and pork for their dinners – besides all the beds to make . . .[47]

If we know little about division of labour in this type of household, we know less about authority and decision making. Reuban Backfield is portrayed in *Sussex Gorse*, as a tyrannical autocrat, but we have as yet, no way of knowing if he was remotely typical, though Henry Rew observed that on the small farms of the High Weald during the 1880s, 'unfortunately the fact that the wife and children can well look after the poultry sometimes enables an idle husband to "sweat" them and live on their exertions'.[48]

In short, our ignorance is almost total regarding the household structure[49] of the nineteenth-century small farmers and tradespeople. What is clear is that the family as a whole was the production unit as well as the consumption unit. The implications of this will be discussed later.

III

The groups under discussion were, in very many parts of England, a numerical majority of the farming community – if we exclude the labourers – and although they only worked a small part of the acreage, we should perhaps heed E.P. Thompson's point in the different though related discussion of copyhold tenure:

> We should remember that there are two different totals to be counted: the acres and the farmers. . . . The point is important, since the economic historian may find clues to expanding agrarian process lie in the 'free' sector, while the social historian may find the psychological horizons and expectations of the majority of the farming community lie still within the customary sector.[50]

Similarly we may find that in the nineteenth century, 'the psychological horizons and expectations of the majority of the farming community' lie still within the family sector. Such a discussion must await another occasion, but what will, I hope, be demonstrated here is that these groups played a significant economic and social role within the English countryside.

It was almost certainly these small farmers who were the despair of the improvers' propagandists during the nineteenth century, by their reluctance or refusal to adopt 'improved' methods. William Marshall echoed complaints from all over the country, when he observed that Wealden farmers were 'as poor, weak, and spiritless as their lands', while half a century later, James Caird found them 'unskilful and prejudiced in their methods of cultivation'. It was doubtless these people that led a visiting Frenchman to comment in the 1840s, that 'in passing through the Weald, one might fancy they were in one of our second-rate provinces'. As late as the 1920s, the Wealden agriculturalist reminded another foreign observer strongly of continental peasant farming.[51]

As has been pointed out, we know little about the actual production process amongst these groups, but exchange is sometimes visible. A common feature of exchange, at least prior to the 1850s, is that the market figures less prominently than among capitalist farmers, being circumvented to some extent by the widespread recourse to credit and barter. Sometimes producers would refuse to sell on the open market. A slightly bemused William Stevenson commented on this practice among Surrey farmers 'who have so little of the impartial spirit of commerce, that they prefer selling their grain to an old customer at a lower price, to deserting him and accepting a higher offer from one with whom they have not been in the habit of dealing'.[52]

This was doubtless not simply altruism. The economy of these groups was based to a very great extent on the exchange of goods – barter – and the provision of credit. Cash featured in their economy primarily in their relations with larger or distant neighbours, or simply as an accounting device. It would seem that goods were exchanged throughout the year, and only periodically was a settlement made. This 'settling-up touch' has been described by Thea Vigne and Alun Howkins in nineteenth-century Oxfordshire.[53] John Payne of Kirdford in the Sussex Weald, conducted much of his business in this way. On 14 February 1825, he noted:

> Mrs Cobby and I settled all Accounts Up to Christmas 1822 and she left to Pay a Bill for 1823 and 1824 and I owed Her out of them Bills for old Iron and Oats and Pease to said amount £7 3s. (£7.15).[54]

The balance owed after 'settling' might be paid in cash at once, or more likely over a period, or most likely of all, be carried over to form part of the ensuing year's account.

Similarly, for Phillip Rapson of Lodsworth, barter and credit were normal. Henry Ede's dealings with him provide an example. In the autumn of 1837, Ede owed Rapson 14s. 6d. (72.5p). He then bought from the latter, two buckets, a washtub, and a pork tub, for which credit was given. He then worked for Rapson for thirteen days at 1s. 8d. (8p) a day, reducing his debt to 7s. (35p), which remained outstanding for a year when Ede bought another bucket on credit for 2s. 3d. (11p). This was followed by his doing a little work for Rapson, wheeling dung and opening a ditch, for which he was credited. He bought two pigs from Rapson for 17s. 6d. (87.5p) leaving a final debt of 19s. 3d. (96p). No cash changed hands in all this time, though it began to now, but it was mid-summer of 1840 before the debt was cleared.

Cash was often absent in rent transactions. William Leggatt rented a cottage from Rapson – his father-in-law – for years. He paid cash occasionally but usually provided labour or goods. As well as his cottage, Leggatt received from Rapson, over a five-year period, a pig, cider, apple trees, faggots, peas, ten bushels of swedes, a bedstead, and loans in cash. In addition, Rapson made seventy-two gallons of cider from Leggatt's own apples, for which he made a labour charge of 6s. (30p). He also paid Leggatt's taxes and rates. These items were debited to Leggatt along with his rent. The account was reduced by cash payment occasionally, paid in small amounts, but mainly by casual work or by supplying garden produce. Leggatt frequently did sawing jobs for Rapson who was a sawyer by trade. He also dug potatoes, cut grass, or with his family did the sawyer's haying. From his garden he supplied apples for Rapson's cider making.[55]

These features bring the production and circulation spheres into a tangled unity that can only be separated theoretically. Rapson entered into similar arrangements with persons who apparently never worked for him. Henry Boxall rented a cottage during the late 1830s, and again from 1841. He was usually several months behind with his rent, and only managed that by paying with apples for Rapson's cider making or, as in November 1838, by giving his pig to his landlord, thereby having 65s. (£3.25) deducted from his bill, amounting to six and a half months rent. Neither did a poor apple harvest leave him entirely at his landlord's mercy. In 1838, faced with such a harvest, he was allowed 10s. (50p) credit 'on account of no apples'.

The poor received a considerable part of this subsistence from small farmers and tradespeople. Both Rapson and Payne were cottage landlords and stockbreeders, providing young pigs for cottagers and labourers. Payne provided flour and malt for their baking and brewing, while Rapson provided cider, apple trees, buckets, pork tubs, dung for their gardens, and items such as soap and candles. Both men, but especially Payne, loaned cash in hard times. On 17 April 1830, he lent 'old Dame Hill' 5s. (25p) to be repaid 'when they sold their piggs'. Interest is never mentioned in the records though this does not mean it was not charged. The bills for these goods and services were paid in cash on occasion, more often by work or by the provision of other goods or services. Garden produce, fattened pigs, dung were just a few of the items used to pay debts. In 1826, Rapson was given thirteen geese by his son Anthony in lieu of rent.

These groups themselves depended on credit and barter to keep their own heads above water. Rapson mortgaged his copyhold premises in Lodsworth on several occasions between 1813 and 1851. In October 1836, he mortgaged one of his cottages to Charles Muggeridge, a shoemaker of nearby Byworth, for £40 at 5% per annum interest. By the end of 1837 he owed £6 in interest and repayment on the principle. Only £1 18s. 3d. (£1.91) was paid in cash, the balance being cleared with apple trees worth 2s. (10p) six pigs at £3 10s. (£3.50), five bushels of potatoes at 8s. 3d. (41p), and a small tub costing 1s. 6d. (7.5p).

The provision of credit was risky and possibly could not have been sustained in a fully cash economy. When William Marshall, a carpenter and shopkeeper of Lodsworth, died in 1816, his shop debts amounted to £70 17s. 7½d. (£70.88) owed by eleven individuals. All but £5 was lost as the estate required cash settlements that could not be met. Probate inventories frequently show similar cases of desperate debts which once translated into cash, cannot be honoured.[56]

An impression is gained that at least until mid-century, there was a sector of the economy in which the cash nexus was only partially operative. Small farmers and tradespeople were in this way partially shielded from market fluctuations, and also provided a shield for the poor who were able to obtain some essential requiremens by barter and credit. The benefits were two-way. Tradespeople and small farmers might depend on the poor for labour at crucial times, or for the supply of raw materials for their various enterprises.

The vigorous existence of this phenomenon makes it possible to suggest that the production and reproduction of labour power for capitalist agriculture, was partly borne by the family sector. Barter and credit may have enabled capitalist farmers to pay wages that were lower than subsistence level, indeed were it not for the well documented provision of long-term credit, usually partly settled with harvest earnings, it is inconceivable that the abysmal level of weekly wages could have been sustained.

Nor should we assume that any economic importance that these groups might have had was necessarily only a local one. A clue may also be found to the identity of the migrant harvest worker. E.J.T. Collins has detailed a number of migrant routes in nineteenth-century England, including that from the Weald to the coastal plain of Sussex. He categorises routes by several criteria, observing that the 'quantitatively most important movement was that between the small-farm subsistence and large-farm capitalist sectors of British agriculture', by which he means the so-called 'Celtic fringe'.[57] In fact, all the routes mentioned seem to be from areas of small-scale farming to areas in which such farms were few. Labourers in the receiving areas thought migration was depressing their wages. In the Aldingbourne area of the Sussex coastal plain in 1831 the workforce attempted to 'set up a resolution that no outparishioners at all should be employed however this may protract the Harvest, and that instead of 8s. (40p) an Acre for which the Farmers can get the wheat reaping done, they will have 14s. (70p).'[58] If workers in areas with significant numbers of small farms and holdings were able to subsist partly outside of the market, then they would have been able to work for lower wages than their counterparts in the receiving areas.

This possible wider significance may also be demonstrated by the well-known system of agisting[59] by which sheep were sent from Romney Marsh or the South Downs, into the Weald for the winter. We have already seen how John Payne sent his own stock onto the land of more opulent neighbours each winter, yet at precisely the same time, he was accepting sheep from distant downland farms for the winter. In 1826 he 'fetched 20 2-toothed wheather Sheep from Master Tuppers at Bignor to keep until Ladyday at 4s. (20p) p. h.', and in the same year, '10 lambs were sent by Mr Foard of Glattin to keep until Ladyday at 5s. (25p) per head'.[60] The account books of capitalist downland farmers frequently show payments for agisting to Wealden dwellers. Whenever it has been possible to identify the Wealden farmer, he is always a small family land-user. Why then did downland farmers entrust their sheep to smallholders when, if Payne is at all typical, the larger farmers in the locality kept the smallholders' own stock? We can perhaps speculate. Payne was a family farmer who therefore did not need to gain a surplus from a hired labour force, so that his charges might have been lower than those a capitalist farmer would have had to charge. The sending of his own stock was of mutual importance since in an economy where cash was not universal, it was necessary to provide goods and services in order to obtain others.

Whatever the validity of this speculation, it is clear that by sending stock into the family sector, the downland or marsh farmer was spared the investment needed to provide facilities, foodstuffs and labour for winter keeping, thereby enhancing rates of capital accumulation. Possibly a similar phenomenon lies behind Cobbett's observation that the small Wealden farmer bred the cattle fattened by the capitalist marshland stock-keeper.[61]

Thus the small farmers and tradespeople may be seen to have considerable economic significance in the nineteeth century. The capital accumulation arising out of, and necessary for, agricultural improvement may have been at least partly dependent upon these groups as well as the workforce who, of course, effectively financed it directly. But the significance of these people is not simply an economic one.

IV

Class relations are power relations. It was the labourers who felt the full brunt of that power. At work they were subject to their employer's power; at home to their landlord's; in their dealings with the parish, to the vestry's and the clergy's; and overarching all was the power of the gentry, resident or on the magistrates bench, or both. The very intricacy of class relations though, meant that power was mediated; laws, rules, and instructions were interpreted by persons and groups whose interests were not uniform and were often opposed. What has been called 'the collective conspiracy of the village rich',[62] is a tempting but over-simplified notion, since the rich were themselves not always united, and were opposed not only by the labourers, but often by those who actually administered the rulings of the rich. In short, the rich did not get things all their own way, neither in detail nor in principle.

Historians' attraction for a model of rural society in which only capital and labour are of significance – in effect, a polarised social formation – has had unfortunate consequences for the study of rural conflict. Since in a capitalist society, capital has ultimate power, in a polarised social formation, it has total power, while the other group, labour has none. Conflict is therefore restricted to a category called 'protest', usually covertly carried on in the rickyard or the pheasant wood, or very occasionally overtly in instances of doomed collective action like Swing.[63] The concept of a polarised social formation leads us relentlessly into conspiracy or social control theory; to a society in which 'power is exercised by an affluent arbitrary minority'.[64]

Class relations are seldom that straightforward. A model that incorporates the real complexity of rural society is long overdue. We need to see the social formation as including a variety of potentially possible alliances between various classes and class fractions. We can then accommodate the undoubted fact that power is almost always mediated. Rural conflict, shifts in attitude to gender divisions and shifts in gender roles, the changing characteristics of the family in different social groups, and so on, cannot be separated from their context in class society, and a complex class society at that.

Conflict, then as now, occurred in every arena of life, and was not simply expressed by arson, poaching, or other types of 'social crime' or 'social protest'. We need to examine conflict within the labour process in greater detail than has yet been done for the countryside,[65] and to investigate ways in which the repressive intentions of those in authority may have been mediated. Roger Wells has argued that in the open Sussex parish of Burwash, repression was every bit as harsh as in any closed parish.[66] Research elsewhere in Sussex suggests that intentions expressed in vestry minutes are a poor guide to what was actually put into practice.[67] In many Sussex parishes, officials were often small farmers and trades-people, and this was even more true of the lower and more arduous administrative posts within the parochial administration. In this type of parish, it can be seen that the intentions and wishes of gentry and capitalist farmers were often thwarted.

J.V. Mosley has demonstrated with much evidence from the south-east that the aims of the Poor Law commissioners and their supporters were frequently frustrated by local evasion of the law.[68] The New Poor Law was a constant source of friction in Lodsworth. Hasler Hollist, the resident magistrate, a large landowner, member of the county bench, chairman of the Board of Guardians of the newly formed Midhurst Union, active member of local agricultural societies, and later to become a member of the county police committee, was a powerful and influential figure, with a wide range of connections with leading local and national political figures. He was anxious to implement the spirit and the letter of the new law but was soon disillusioned, noting in February 1837, that the Guardians 'are not going on right at present'.[69] As Mosley points out, evasion of the Act's requirements was widespread in Sussex, and especially so at the level of the parish. This was where Hollist's biggest problem lay. His principal tenant, John Naldrett Farhall, who may at this time be safely considered his surrogate, told the Petworth Agricultural Association that:

> to relieve any but the aged and infirm from the poor rate is . . . nothing more than to encourage our labourers in idleness, and we all know that

idleness is the forerunner of vice, and consequently produces want and misery.[70]

This exhortation was not complied with in Lodsworth, where both he and Hollist lived. In accordance with vestry decisions, reached as always by the multiple votes of the wealthy inhabitants, warrants were frequently issued at Petty Sessions for non-payment of poor rates, but they were much less frequently served. One example will suffice. In 1843 the Lodsworth overseer asked the magistrate at Petty Sessions, if he could return distress warrants against two poor persons, having had them for a year and been unable, despite frequent attempts, to serve them.[71] One wonders whether it was really so difficult, in a small parish, to serve warrants, or whether the officials, who were usually small farmers and tradespeople, were less than enthusiastic.

In defiance of vestry decisions, officials refused to pay the legally required contribution towards the cost of relieving their own poor, and towards the common expense of running the Union. In addition the favourite Sussex ruse of manipulation of the highway rate, to finance the employment of paupers on the roads instead of putting them in the workhouse, seems to have occurred at Lodsworth just as elsewhere.[72] Except in 1841–2, responsibility for the roads was firmly in the hands of tradespeople and there is little doubt that expenditure rose following the formation of the Poor Law Union. Certainly most roads in the parish were constantly repaired with the significant exception of those leading to Hollist's own home, despite his threats and eventual resort to legal action.[73]

Hollist's writ did not run unchallenged among the small farmers and tradespeople of Lodsworth, in spite of his residence in the centre of the village and his many powerful connections. In common with gentry and establishment figures everywhere, he intervened in every area of social life. The pub, which he owned, was no exception. The 'Hollist Arms' became the scene of a protracted struggle between Hollist and the village at large in the 1840s and 1850s. Pubs were often dark places in the eyes of authority. The centre of alternative values, even of alternative authority, they were viewed with suspicion. In the closed downland village of Glynde, later in the century, it is argued that the pub:

was divided up so that the workers sat in one corner with the casuals, and those on the fringes of social life in the tap room, while the farmers sat at the opposite end of the bar from the workers.[74]

In Wealden and similar villages, status was quite likely to be turned on its head, or at least be based on quite different principles, unknown, and therefore worrying:

(The) fireplace was surrounded by high-backed settles coming out in a kind of semi-circle, so that each drinker might see the blaze. During the daytime these settles were common property, but as soon as the shades of evening began to gather they became sacred and might only be pressed by certain privileged cronies. No doubt the privilege was obtained according to certain fixed laws, as all recognised it, but no outsider was ever able to fathom the mystery. . . . Thomas Hodges, a mere labourer, with a summer wage of eleven shillings a week, and a winter stipend from the parish, was entitled to a corner, while Jabez Bunch, a farmer and a man reputed warm, had to content himself with a windsor chair outside the charmed circle. William Day too, although he came from a neighbouring parish, had a place on the settle, yet James Brooker, whose fathers had been carriers and dwelt under the shadow of their own vines and fig-trees anytime for the last two hundred years, was cast out. . . . (A) place was reserved for the landlord. . . . Yet were none of the privileged order present, no villager ever dreamed of sitting on the settles. . . . It was here, within this charmed circle, that all the important business of the parish was conducted. . . .[75]

It was here, in the pub, that the village justice of the skimmington was organised along with other activities unwelcome to the local gentry and their allies.[76] It was, then, a place that needed watching, where authority's rules were not observed. Hollist performed this function over many years. The details of the struggle have been described elsewhere.[77] Briefly, the landlord Richard Gill, who was no respector of his squire, permitted 'the sort of licences and dissipations which is the ruin of a country village'.[78] Hollist repeatedly and more and more apoplectically sought Gill's removal, but only succeeded after several years when a pub fight ended in a fatality. A boycott seems to have ensued immediately. Three landlords came and went, unable to make a living. The brewers asked to be released from their lease, which Hollist refused, but he admitted their claim that 'all customers' had gone to 'the other public houses'. By the end of the 1850s, Hollist was beaten and Richard Gill returned as landlord, a position that his son and grandson were to hold after him, and no doubt the customers returned as well.[79]

Perhaps the most sustained challenge to Hollist was over the enclosure of Gosdens Heath, a bounded common to the west of Lodsworth. This enclosure in 1836, was intended to give exclusive possession to Hollist, Mullens Dennett, and W.S. Poyntz, and coincided with the enfranchisement of Hollist's and Dennett's copy-hold properties within the manor of Lodsworth. Enfranchisement removed the few remaining areas of common interest with the rest of the village, rights of common on the manorial waste. The enclosure was immediately resisted.[80] Banks and ditches were repeatedly thrown down; the parish officials, all small farmers and tradespeople, refused to accept responsibility for the upkeep of a new road across the heath, despite several judgements at Petty Sessions that they should do so. Hollist was eventually forced to accept liability for the road out of his own pocket, an arrangement that was not reversed until 1894.[81] In 1850, 383 newly-planted trees had their tops cut off, and '85 laurels (were) torn up by the roots' and permanent watchers had to be stationed on the heath. These facts were recalled with pleasure in the local press nearly fifty years later, when the dispute was still a major cause of schism in the village, and when the contemporary tradespeople were preparing to take the current owner of the Hollist estate to court with the aid of the Commons Preservation Society, a case which, regrettably, they lost.[82]

In every dispute so far studied, opposition to the gentry and capitalist farmers was led by the small farmers and tradespeople of Lodsworth. The labourers, no doubt advisedly, were less open in their resistance and therefore are less visible to the historian.[83] Power in Lodsworth lay theoretically, and ultimately practically, in very few hands. Yet in every real dispute that power was opposed at every turn. The main *visible* opposition came from groups that were neither wage labourers nor capitalist, and who had different material interests. The obvious result of their opposition was that the *intended* repressiveness of the gentry and their allies, was seldom translated into practice in any straightforward way. The effect of this opposition on the *processes* of rural change awaits research.

These kinds of incidents are of course, of mainly local significance, though local events are not without importance to developments on the wider canvas of national political and social change. The common element each time is the involvement of the local gentry, as agents of central government in the case of the New Poor Law, or simply as opponents to customary forms of behaviour or to customary use rights. They were to be found in opposition to custom all over the country, and the kinds of struggle outlined above were likewise a national phenomenon.[84] Whether the groups that this article is concerned with were as prominent in conflicts elsewhere as they were in Lodsworth can only be decided after the appropriate research, but it is possible to infer in a whole range of developments and occurrences, that the small farmers and tradespeople played significant roles in a more generalised way. Two examples may indicate some possibilities.

We have seen how the spirit and the letter of the New Poor Law was to some extent frustrated in Lodsworth by the local tradespeople and small farmers. It is also quite possible that these groups played a significant role in opposing certain aspects of the old Poor Law, thereby easing the passage of the new legislation, or at least strengthening the arguments of the commissioners. The campaign against the various forms of Labour Rate is the clearest example. The very idea of a labour rate makes little sense in a society in which all producers are capitalist, since to force each to take on more labour than required is the very antithesis of capitalism. In this respect, it would be interesting to compare the class structures of parishes with labour rates, and those with none.

The authors of the Poor Law Report, when they considered labour rates, realised that 'the practice seems to be not a sharing in fair proportion of the burthen amongst all, but a shifting of the burthen from one class to some other'.[85] The most frequent form of rate required rate-payers to employ labourers in proportion to their assessment, and was so devised, according to the Commissioners, that:

> either the whole surplus labour is cast upon trades, and the whole of the agriculturalists share the advantages; or the larger agriculturalists, or those whose proportion of arable land is large, cast the weight upon the small occupier, the occupier of grass land, the occupier, who alone or with his sons can do all the labour his farm requires, and the tradespeople and householders.[86]

Despite some differences in the way the rate was assessed, the common factor is – an attempt by employers of labour to place the burden of paying for unemployment upon some or all non-employers, by forcing them to take on hands they did not require.

It is perhaps not entirely fortuitous that the driving force behind the Labour Rate Bill,[87] which sought to make the rate compulsory in parishes where a sufficient number of ratepayers approved, should have been a large landowner, Sir Charles Burrell, in the Weald of western Sussex, where there were many family producers upon whom capitalist farmers could place the burden of the unemployed.

The voluminous correspondence to the Poor Law Commissioners on this subject was published as Appendix D of the Poor Law Report. It contains a wealth of virtually untapped information on small farmers and tradespeople, who with few exceptions were implacably opposed to the system, and who provided most of the evidence used by the Commissioners to argue against it. It is clear that these groups were of great importance in that they, along with the workforce, carried the can for the inability or unwillingness of capitalist farming to provide employment.

Captain Swing provides our second example of the potential significance of these groups. Once again, more research is needed. In seeking to explain the distribution of disturbances in 1830–1, Hobsbawm and Rudé suggested that the 'riotous' village:

would tend to be above average in size, to contain a higher ratio of labourers to employing farmers than the average, and a distinctly higher number of local artisans; perhaps also of such members of rural society as were economically, socially and ideologically independent of squire, parson and large farmer: small family cultivators, shopkeepers and the like.[88]

On the evidence of the south-east, this is quite right and it is a pity that more has not been made of it. In this region, collective action at the time of Swing occurs where there is a *mix* of large-scale capitalist farming and small-scale family enterprise. It does not occur where either form is absent. Michael Winstanley has argued that machine breaking in Kent was most common where small farmers were numerous,[89] and this is true of Surrey, Sussex, and probably Hampshire. Even in the few areas where it appears not to be true, such as the Pagham area of western Sussex, study of the local sources reveals that the crowds originated in areas – in this case around Walberton and Barnham – where there *were* small farmers. It is worth repeating that it is not simply the presence of these groups that is important, but their admixture with large-scale capitalist farms. The existence of this mix is usually ignored by historians. It has been suggested that in Hampshire, Swing was confined to areas of purely large-scale farming. This can only be sustained by statistical manipulation of a high order, and in fact the areas referred to again exhibit precisely this mix of capitalist and family producers.[90]

What this means is impossible to decide as yet. The presence in Swing crowds of small farmers and, especially tradespeople, is well attested to,[91] and as we have seen, it is probably unwise to make too sharp a distinction between them. Similarly, it is hazardous to rely on the prison and judicial records for the occupations of those persons arrested for involvement in Swing who, we are told 'were predominantly "peasants" or country labourers'.[92] Research at the local level can alone qualify the data derived from judicial records. An embryonic beginning has been made for Sussex and it is possible to suggest – tentatively – that many 'labourers' were in fact artisans or small farmers, or at least children of such people. There seems sufficient evidence to justify a call for further investigation of Swing as a movement that was not simply 'the last labourers' revolt' but was rather a movement of labourers and family producers.

Having demonstrated that small farmers and tradespeople were both numerous and significant in the English countryside during the nineteenth century, it remains necessary to try to locate them theoretically within the context of the capitalist social formation.

V

That England was a capitalist country in the nineteenth century is not of course, in dispute. But it does not mean that every producer was a capitalist using hired labour. The capitalist mode of production is characterised by the commoditisation of labour power in the form of wage-labour, and by the expropriation of the surplus product in the form of surplus value.[93] It follows that producers who do not hire labour or who do so without deriving surplus value from it, are not capitalist, and therefore work a different mode of production. Confusion over the use of this term is commonplace. Gary Littlejohn rightly points to Marx's use of the term to indicate firstly, a 'system of production' referring to the organisation of the labour process, and secondly, in a wider sense, an 'economy structured by the articulated combination of the relations and forces of production, ideology and . . . politics'.[94] Marx consistently pointed out that modes of production in the wider sense usually contained more than one mode of production narrowly defined. For the purposes of this discussion I follow Shanin[95] and adhere to the 'narrow' definition of the term, using the concept of 'social formation' instead for the wider sense. It should be remembered that any given 'social formation' may contain within it several 'modes of production'. The character of the social formation will be determined by the dominant mode of production. In nineteenth-century England, the social formation was capitalist, since capitalism was far and away the dominant mode of production, but it was not the only one, though historians of the English countryside have preferred to ignore this, adhering instead to what amounts to a model of a polarised social formation in which capital and labour are the only classes meriting consideration. This article has sought to demonstrate the existence and importance of groups that were not capitalist since they produced by means of family labour, with hired labour where used, being only a supplement to that of the family. They worked, in other words, a different mode of production to the capitalist farmer.

How then, should they be conceptualised? In one sense it might be considered unimportant, since it is their significance as a group that needs study and that has been argued here. On the other hand, their significance is *precisely* due to the fact that they worked a distinct non-capitalist mode of production and therefore have different material interests from both capital and labour. The label used so far in this article – 'small farmers and tradespeople' – is inadequate since it does not indicate this distinction.

The reliance upon family labour immediately brings to mind the concept of 'peasant'. The first quotation at the head of this article expresses the orthodoxy concerning peasants in nineteenth-century England. Recently Dennis Mills has argued for the widespread existence of peasants during this period, but his basis for definition is wholly inadequate.[96] Within a far wider debate the whole problem of definition of 'peasant' and 'peasantry' is currently being reappraised.[97] None of the contributors to the debate have managed to establish a consensual definition, and there have been calls to dispense with the concept entirely, at least for capitalist social formations and to replace it with concepts such as, for example, 'simple commodity producer',[98] or else its retention as 'merely heuristic delineation of types of roles, structures, or situations to which, and only to which, the term is to apply, these classes of events to be distinguished from others of a similar order by criteria which are of theoretical (not political) interest'.[99]

A large part of the problem seems to be that scholars have devoted their efforts to finding an essentialist definition of 'peasant' and 'peasantry'. Failing to do so they sometimes opt for concepts which may in their turn be essentialist. Accordingly, most of the 'essential' characteristics should be dropped. The groups covered in these wide-ranging discussions have probably only one thing in common – they produce predominantly by means of family labour. This is surely sufficient to categorise a rural production unit as 'peasant'. S.H. Franklin has used this criterion in defining peasant enterprises as having the family as the institutional basis of the enterprise and providing labour (and, under the *chef d'entreprise* or head), control and direction. Distribution is by barter and/or the market, with kind and/or money providing the media of distribution.[100] Such a description fits the people described in this article rather well, and justifies their categorisation as 'peasants'.

Of course this is insufficient, since class is not a category, but a relationship. It has been well said that 'the hard part is to move from static categories to processes'.[101] Peasants are individuals. To move from the individual to the class, we need to talk about the 'peasantry'. As a concept, 'peasantry' tells us nothing about how work is controlled, surpluses appropriated or systems reproduced. 'Peasantry' is not, it has been convincingly argued, a mode of production.[102] Not, that is, in any generic sense. But *specific* peasantries do work *specific* modes of production in *specific* social formations. Specificity is the keyword, and the vital first step in undertaking the 'hard part'. It has been suggested that any understanding of social roles 'involves fairly exhaustive holistic descriptions of societies as such . . . (and) a sophisticated typology of whole-societal forms. . . .'[103] Put another way, we require 'a theorisation of the relationship between the unit of production and social formation'.[104] We cannot discuss 'peasants' and 'peasantries', or for that matter 'capitalists' and 'capitalism', abstracted from the historical context of specific social formations. 'Peasants' can be defined by their reliance upon family labour, but 'peasantries' can only be defined within the context of the social formation of which they are a part.

This article has discussed some prominent groups in the English countryside of the nineteenth century. It seems adequate, as a first step, to consider them as peasants. We have begun, but no more, to indicate their relationships with other groups in the social formation, and it is these relationships that are so important for moving beyond categorisation to the study of process. The sources give the impression, but so far no more, that production for subsistence is widespread during the first half of the century, but that simple commodity production becomes dominant later on. As yet no comment can be made upon the process within which this shift occurs. The significance of these groups upon the entire processes of rural change are similarly more or less unexplored. Whether the people in these groups are subsistence producers or simple commodity producers[105] should not affect their classification as peasants, though it is clear that there would be a difference in their relationships with other classes and in their material interests. In fact, it is unlikely that two categories are mutually exclusive, any more than tradespeople and small farmers are.

Capitalist producers do not all have identical material interests. Industrialists and farmers, landlords and tenants, have different interests in some respects, and make up different fractions of the capitalist class. Similarly peasant producers with land will have different interests, to a degree, from those without land, just as subsistence producers will have, again to a degree, differing concerns from simple commodity producers. They will though, still be peasants, but will comprise different peasant fractions rather than fundamentally different groups or classes.

The thrust of this article has been to demonstrate that the social formation of the English countryside was a complex one, rather than the simple polarisation favoured by historians generally, with capitalists (large or small), on the one hand, and labour on the other being the only classes of significance. By arguing for the existence of a group or groups that are neither capitalist nor labour, it is suggested that there was a mediation of economic and social – class – relations that may have important implications for our understanding of the countryside. In his work on north-east Scotland, Ian Carter made a plea for analyses 'studying the alliances and conflicts between the separate material interests of landlords, capitalist farmers, peasant fractions, and landless labourers'.[106] Perhaps this article will stimulate similar studies of rural England in the nineteenth century.

Notes

I must thank several people for their help with various drafts of this article. My supervisor, Alun Howkins, has also given valued guidance throughout my research to date. Ena Ainsworth and Ken Lunn made valuable comments. In particular, Anna Davin made very detailed and constructive comments that led to a complete restructuring with extremely beneficial results. I must also thank Sue and Cecil Barnes of Lodsworth, and Reg Thompson of Kirdford, for the loan of valuable documents.

1   E.J. Hobsbawm and George Rudé, *Captain Swing*, Harmondsworth 1973, p. 3; Sheila Kaye-Smith, *Sussex Gorse: The Story of a Fight*, 1924, pp. 105–6.

2   E.J. Hobsbawm, *Industry and Empire*, Harmondsworth 1969, p. 98. Similar views abound in the work of many historians, especially those of radical or socialist persuasion. See for examples: J.L. and Barbara Hammond, *The Village Labourer* throughout; A.J. Peacock, *Bread or Blood*, chaps 1–4; E.P. Thompson, *The Making of the English Working Class*, chap 7; Hobsbawm and Rudé, *Captain Swing*, chap 1; Roger A.E. Wells, 'The Development of the English Rural Proletariat and Social Protest 1700–1850', *Journal of Peasant Studies* (hereafter *JPS*), vol. 6, 1979, pp. 116–17.

3   For the survival of small-scale agriculture during the nineteenth century, see David Grigg, *The Dynamics of Agricultural Change*, 1982, pp. 206–10; J.V. Beckett, 'The Debate over Farm Sizes in Eighteenth and Nineteenth Century England', *Agricultural History* vol. 57, 1983, Lodsworth 1780–1860' unpub. MA Thesis, Univ. of Sussex, 1982 pp. 15–25 and throughout; J.D. Chambers and G.E. Mingay, *The Agricultural Revolution, 1750–1880*, 1966, throughout; B.A. Holderness, 'The Victorian Farmer' in (ed.) G.E. Mingay, *The Victorian Countryside*, 1981, pp. 227–44. Such arguments usually get short shrift. Chambers and Mingay have been criticised by E.P. Thompson ('Land of our Fathers', *Times Literary Supplement*, 16 Feb. 1967) and John Saville ('Primitive Accumulation and Early Industrialisation in Britain', *Socialist Register*, 1969, pp. 247–71). Both point to the small proportion of acreage and workforce exploited by the small farmer. Thompson is concerned that many small farmers were not 'bona-fide' (whatever that means); while other historians have been equally concerned that they often had dual or multiple occupations, which apparently justifies their exclusion from any discussion of rural society: J.R. Wordie, 'Social Change on the Leveson-Gower Estates, 1714–1832' *Economic History Review*, 2nd ser. XXVII, 1974, pp. 601–2; Wells, 'The Development of the English Rural Proletariat', p. 117; Hobsbawm and Rudé, *Captain Swing*, p. 4. Another tactic is to ignore such arguments altogether. Holderness's article in *The Victorian Countryside* demonstrates the varied types of 'farmer' in the nineteenth century, pointing out that small farms, subsistence farms, and part-time farmers were common enough in the countryside, yet his article does not even warrant a mention in the most recent extended review of this book (Alan Everitt 'Past and Present in the Victorian Countryside', *Agricultural History Review*, vol. 31, 1983, pp. 156–69). Such omissions are not of course sinister, but merely indicate how deeply rooted is the conviction that these groups are of, at most, peripheral interest.

4   In *The Agricultural Revolution*, Chambers and Mingay are anxious to refute the Hammonds' thesis that enclosure was the death-knell of the small farmer, but as they are mainly concerned to investigate the 'agricultural revolution' and 'improvements' in

farming practice, they are forced to dismiss the small farmers as poor and ignorant, since they seldom flocked to implement the suggestions of the improvers. Grigg and Beckett (see note 3 above) draw no conclusions from their observations upon the survival of small farms, which seem to be for them, only an interesting but insignificant diversion.

5 James Obelkevich, *Religion and Rural Society: South Lindsey 1825–1875* (Oxford 1976), pp. 17 and 49. Similar decisions are made by Hobsbawm and Rudé in chap 1 of *Captain Swing*.

6 Hobsbawm and Rudé, *Captain Swing*, p. 4.

7 Agricultural statistics for 1885 BPP 1886 (c. 4847) LXX. The national figures are as follows:

Holding Size	Great Britain	England
¼ to 19.9 acres	308,044	233,583
20 to 100 acres	148,864	106,039
over 100 acres	98,937	75,328
Total	555,855	414,950

It might be argued that the returns relate to holdings only, and give no insight into multiple holding by farmers which could seriously reduce the true number of agricultural occupiers, or that many holdings were really 'leisure' holdings. One can only say that contemporaries considered this to be so only in 'a small proportion' of cases. In 1908 it was reckoned that perhaps 4 or 5,000 holdings out of over a million were so held. Agricultural statistics BPP 1912–13 (c. 6227) XX p. 545. The same commentator states that only 6% of British holdings were *not* 'farmed for business' p. 545n.

8 Léonce de Lavergne, *The Rural Economy of England Scotland and Ireland*, 1855, p. 108.

9 F. Beavington, 'The Development of Market Gardening in Bedfordshire', *Agricultural History Review*, vol. 23, 1975, pp. 23– 31; G.E. Fussell, *The Dairy Farmer, 1500–1900*, 1968, p. 303.

10 Peter McPhee, 'A Reconsideration of the "Peasantry" of Nineteenth-century France' *Peasant Studies*, vol. 9 no. 1, Fall 1981, p. 7.

11 Hobsbawm and Rudé, *Captain Swing*, p. 3. Roger Wells elevates the virtual absence of these groups to the status of 'an elementary fact of English agricultural history': Wells, 'The Development of the English Rural Proletariat', p. 115.

12 1831 Census, BPP 1833 XXXVI and XXXVII. On this last point, it was noted at the beginning of the century that farms in the extreme west of the coastal plain were sometimes 'unusually small'; Revd Arthur Young, *General View of the Agriculture of the County of Sussex*, 1813, p. 24.

13 Select Committee Report on Agricultural Distress, BPP 1837 (c. 464) V, p. 180; J.A. Eggar, Remembrances of Life and Customs in Gilbert White's, Cobbett's and Charles Kingsley's Country (no date), p. 6.

14 Poor Law Report, BPP 1834 (c.44) XXXVIII app. D, pp. 73D, 129D, and 164D.

15 Report on Employment of Children, Young Persons and Women in Agriculture, BPP 1867–8 (c. 4068–1) XVII p. 83; Select Committee Report on Small Holdings BPP 1889 (313) XII p. 335; Royal Commission on Agriculture, BPP 1895 (7623) XVI p. 15. For a useful discussion of the Wealden poultry industry, see Brian Short 'The Art and Craft of Chicken Cramming: Poultry in the Weald of Sussex 1850–1950' Agricultural History Review, vol. 30, 1982, pp. 17–30.

16 Grigg, Dynamics of Agricultural Change, p. 208.

17 For a discussion of the difficulties with the census schedules, see P.M. Tillot, 'Sources of inaccuracy in the 1851 and 1861 censuses' in (ed.) E.A. Wrigley, Nineteenth Century Society, Cambridge 1972.

18 Herman Levy, Large and Small Holdings: A Study of English Agricultural Economics, 1966, p. 99; Ian Carter, Farm Life in North-east Scotland: The Poor Man's Country 1840–1914, Edinburgh, 1979, p. 28.

19 Census of 1851, BPP 1852–3 (1691–1) LXXXVIII pt. I–1; Agricultural Statistics, BPP 1880 (2727) LXXVI; see also note 7 above.

20 B.A. Holderness, 'Rural Tradesmen 1660–1850: A Regional Study in Lindsey', Lincolnshire History and Archaeology vol. 7, 1972, p. 77; for some of the very few studies of rural tradespeople see J.A. Chartres, 'Country Tradesmen' and J.A. Chartres and G. Turnbull, 'County Craftsmen' both in (ed.) Mingay, The Victorian Countryside; Barbara Kerr, Bound to the Soil: Social History of Dorset 1750– 1918, 1968; Pamela Horn, The Rural World 1780–1850: Social Change in the English Countryside, 1980.

21 BPP 1852–3 (1691–I) LXXXVIII Pt. I.

22 BPP 1834 (c. 44) XXXVIII pp. 163D and 173D.

23 Compiled variously from the census schedules for 1841 and 1851, Kelly's Directory 1852, Tithe award for Lodsworth 1841, and West Sussex Records Office (hereafter WSRO) Cowdray Mss. 281 and 282.

24 Raphael Samuel, 'Village Labour', in (ed.) R. Samuel, Village Life and Labour, 1975, p.6.

25 Henry Evershed, 'Farm Labourers and Cow Plots', The Fortnightly Review vol. 14, 1873, pp. 79–81. Samuel refers to 'a whole class of cow-keepers' still surviving east of Oxford in the 1860s. Samuel, 'Village Labour', p. 6.

26 Samuel, 'Village Labour', p. 6.

27 Richard Heath, The English Peasant: Studies Historical, Local and Biographical, London, 1893, p. 143. Chap 7 of this book gives fascinating glimpses of life in these areas of common in the 1860s and 1870s. For equally interesting glimpses, scattered through an otherwise romantic novel, see A.C. Bickley, Midst Surrey Hills: A Rural Story, 1890; see also Gertrude Jekyll, Old West Surrey, 1904.

28 Sussex Daily News, 3 April 1886.

29 East Sussex Records Office RF/2C, interviews of W.A. Raper with old foresters.

30 E.L. Jones, 'Environmental Buffers of a Marginal Peasantry in Southern England' Peasant Studies Newsletter vol. 3 no. 4, Oct. 1974, pp. 13–16.

31 Anon. 'Our Kentish Parish', Blackwoods Magazine vol. 124, 1878, pp. 75–6.

32 See pp. 226–7.

33 Hollist to Puttock, 5 July 1848, Hollist Letter Books. I am indebted to Cecil and Sue Barnes for the loan of these letter books. Complete photocopies are in my possession. Kerr has pointed out the existence of widespread sub-letting in Dorset during the eighteenth and nineteenth centuries. *Bound to the Soil*, pp. 39–40.

34 Michael Turner, 'The 1801 Crop Returns for England' (unpub. typescript, London Inst. of Hist. Research, 1978); WSRO Add. Ms. 22650, Account Book of Phillip Rapson.

35 WSRO Add. Ms. 22650; John Payne's Memo Book. I am indebted to Reg Thompson for the loan of this latter item.

36 Thompson, *Making of the English Working Class*, p. 118; Wells, 'The Development of the English Rural Proletariat' p. 117; Hobsbawm, *Industry and Empire*, p. 98.

37 For a discussion of this problem, see R. Samuel, 'Village Labour' and '"Quarry Roughts": Life and Labour in Headington Quarry, 1860–1920. An Essay in Oral History' both in *Village Life and Labour*, 1975.

38 Hobsbawm, *Industry and Empire*, p. 98.

39 Martine Segalen, *Love and Power in the Peasant Family: Rural France in the Nineteenth Century*, Oxford 1983, p. 2. For some recent studies of the rural family in France see John W. Shaffer, *Family and Farm: Agrarian Change and Household Organisation in the Loire Valley 1500–1900*, Albany, New York 1982; James R. Lehning, *The Peasants of Marlhes: Economic Development and Family Organization in Nineteenth-century France*, 1980.

40 See for example, Pamela Horn, *The Victorian Country Child*, 1974; Marion Lochhead, *The Victorian Household*, 1964.

41 Samuel, 'Village Labour', p. 3.

42 See p. 213 above.

43 Kaye-Smith, *Sussex Gorse*, p. 87.

44 Flora Thompson, *Lark Rise to Candleford*, 1948, p. 73.

45 John Eldridge, 'Mayfield 70 to 130 Years Ago' in Fred Lester, *Looking Back Mayfield*, no date, p. 15. See also Thompson, *Lark Rise*, p. 73.

46 Evershed, 'Farm Labourers', p. 82.

47 John Coker Egerton, *Sussex Folk and Sussex Ways*, 1924, p. 39.

48 Report of the Royal Commission on Agriculture BPP 1895 (c. 7623) XVI, p. 15.

49 I follow John Shaffer in defining household structure as not simply 'how many and which relatives co-reside in a given household – but rather the entire network of property rights accorded family members, the division and allocation of family labour, and the uses to which family income is employed'. *Family and Farm*, p. 17.

50 E.P. Thompson, 'The Grid of Inheritance: a Comment' in (ed.) Jack Goody, Joan Thirsk, E.P. Thompson, *Family and Inheritance: Rural Society in Western Europe 1200–1800*, 1976, p. 129.

51 William Marshall, *The Rural Economy of the Southern Counties: comprising Kent, Surrey and Sussex*, 1798, p. 132; James Caird, *English Agriculture in 1850–51*, 1852, pp. 126–7; de Lavergne, *Rural Economy*, pp. 202–3; George Lemaitre, *Le Weald des Comtés de Kent, Surrey, Sussex, Hampshire: Études de Geographie Economique et Humaine*, Paris 1931, p. 358.

52 William Stevenson, *General View of the Agriculture of the County of Surrey*, 1813, p. 88. I am grateful to Ian Dyck for this point.

53 Thea Vigne and Alun Howkins, 'The Small Shopkeeper in Industrial and Market Towns', in (ed.) Geoffrey Crossick, *The Lower Middle Class in Britain 1870–1914*, 1977, p. 201.

54 John Payne's Memo Book.

55 WSRO Add. Ms. 22650.

56 See for example WSRO (uncatalogued) Acc. 4842 Box 5/5.

57 E.J.T. Collins, 'Migrant Labour in British Agriculture in the Nineteenth Century' *Economic History Review*, 2nd ser. vol. 18, 1976, pp. 43–5. The use of the phrase 'celtic fringe', ought to be dropped forthwith. It embodies all the centripetal tendencies of English historians and in practice consigns Wales, Scotland, Ireland and the south-west peninsula of England to a merely peripheral status. The arguments in this article would apply with even greater force to the relationship between these areas and the capitalist agriculture of England.

58 William Tyler to Egremont 27 July 1831, WSRO Petworth House Archive (uncat.); I am grateful to Alison McCann for drawing my attention to this source. Surrey Wealden workers were also visitors to the coastal plain for the harvest. In 1842 it was noted that:

> The number of labouring men from Surrey, journeying through here (Midhurst) towards the south, in search of harvest work and turnip hoeing, although at all times great, has this year been without precedent.

> *Sussex Agricultural Express*, 30 July 1842. See also George Sturt, *The Bettesworth Book*, Firle 1978, pp. 59–66.

59 John Farncombe, 'On the Farming of Sussex' *Journal of the Royal Agricultural Society of England* (*JRASE*) vol. 11, 1850, pp. 81–3; Siday Hawes, 'Notes on the Wealden Clay of Sussex and on its Cultivation' *JRASE* vol. 19, 1858, p. 195; William Wood, *A Sussex Farmer*, 1938, p. 69.

60 John Payne's Memo Book.

61 William Cobbett, *Rural Rides* (1830), Harmondsworth 1967, p. 190.

62 Hobsbawm and Rudé, *Captain Swing*, p. 32.

63 Wells, 'The Development of the English Rural Proletariat'; Roger A.E. Wells, 'Social Conflict and Protest in the English Countryside in the early Century: A Rejoinder' *JPS* vol. 8, 1981; Andrew Charlesworth, 'The Development of the English Rural Proletariat and Social Protest: A comment' *JPS* vol. 8, 1980; J.E. Archer, 'The Wells-Charlesworth Debate: A Personal Comment on Arson in Norfolk and Suffolk' *JPS* vol. 9, 1982.

64 Wells, 'Social Conflict and Protest', p. 519.

65 Alun Howkins, 'Structural Conflict and the Farmworker: Norfolk 1900–1920' *JPS* vol. 4, 1977; Reed, 'Social and Economic Relations', pp. 42–51.

66 Wells, 'Social Conflict and Protest' throughout.

67 Reed, 'Social and Economic Relations' pp. 64–81.

68 John V. Mosley, 'Poor Law Administration in England and Wales 1834–1850: with special reference to the problem of able-bodied pauperism' unpub. PhD Thesis, Univ. of London, 1975, throughout.

69 Hollist to Brown 10 Feb. 1837, Hollist Letter Books.

70 *Sussex Agricultural Express*, 30 May 1840.

71 *Sussex Agricultural Express*, 18 March 1843.

72 Mosley, 'Poor Law Administration', pp. 213–43.

73 Reed, 'Social and Economic Relations', pp. 74–6.

74 N.J. Griffiths, 'Firle: Selected Themes from the Social History of a Closed Sussex Village, 1850–1939', unpub. MA Thesis. Univ. of Sussex, 1976, p. 87.

75 Bickley, *Midst Surrey Hills* vol. III, pp. 75–6.

76 *Midst Surrey Hills* chaps 7 and 8; A.C. Bickley, 'Some Notes on a Custom at Woking, Surrey' *Home Counties Magazine* vol. 4, 1902, pp. 25–9; E.P. Thompson, '"Rough Music" et Charivari: quelques reflexions complémentaires' in (ed.) Jacques Le Goff et Jean-Claude Schmit, *Le Charivari: Actes de la table ronde organisée à Paris (25–27 Avril 1977) par l'École des Hautes Études en Science Sociale et le Centre National de la Recherche Scientifique,* Paris 1981, p. 281.

77 Reed, 'Social and Economic Relations', pp. 79–80.

78 Hollist to Gatehouse 4 August 1852, Hollist Letter Books.

79 Hollist to Gatehouse 30 August 1855, Hollist Letter Books.

80 For a fuller account, see Reed, 'Social and Economic Relations', pp. 69–72.

81 WSRO Par 128/12/3, entry 27 March 1894.

82 WSRO (uncat.) Acc. 4842 Box 5/5.

83 Some examples of resistance by labourers in Lodsworth can be found in Reed, 'Social and Economic Relations' throughout.

84 For recently published examples of work in this field, see Alun Howkins, 'The Taming of Whitsun: the Changing Face of a Nineteenth-Century Rural Holiday'; Vic Gammon, '"Babylonian Performances": the Rise and Suppression of Popular Church Music 1660–1870'; both in (ed.) Eileen and Stephen Yeo, *Popular Culture and Class Conflict 1500–1914: Explorations in the History of Labour and Leisure,* Hassocks 1981. R.W. Bushaway, *By Rite: Custom, Ceremony and Community in England 1700–1885,* 1982.

85 S.G. and E.O.A. Checkland, *The Poor Law Report of 1834,* Harmondsworth 1973, p. 296.

86 Ibid., pp. 295 and 296–7.

87 2&3 Will. IV, c. 96 (1832).

88 Hobsbawm and Rudé, *Captain Swing,* p. 158.

89 Michael Winstanley, *Life in Kent at the Turn of the Century,* Folkestone 1978, p. 57.

90 Ronald Windle, 'Hampshire Agrarian Society 1815–1846', unpub. PhD Thesis, (CNAA), Portsmouth Polytechnic, 1973. Windle notes that most incidents occurred where farms tended to be very large (p. 224). His way of arriving at this conclusion is bizarre to say the least. He constantly excludes holdings smaller than 20 acres. In the parishes of Dummer and North Waltham, which he characterises as areas of medium and large farms, (using Clapham's classification by which medium farms are from 100 to 300 acres and large from 300 to 500 acres), the tithe maps show 145 holdings smaller than 20 acres, nine between 20 and 100 acres, and twelve over 100 acres. By ignoring those below 20 acres, he arrives at the total of twenty-one holdings. Since twelve of these are over 100 acres, he feels justified in considering the area as one of medium and large farms. This ignores not only the 145 holdings below 20 acres (many of which would admittedly be cottage gardens), but also those between 20 and 100 acres. In fact the area is a marvellous example of a finely graduated range of holding sizes.

91 Hobsbawm and Rudé, *Captain Swing,* pp. 206–8.

92 Ibid., p. 204. 'Peasant' in this context is of course, synonomous with 'country labourer'.

93 Gary Littlejohn, 'Peasant Economy and Society' in (ed.) Barry Hindess, *Sociological Theories of the Economy,* 1977, p. 144.

94 For some recent discussions of the problems of definition see Littlejohn, 'Peasant Economy'; E. Paul Durrenberger, 'Chayanov and Marx' *Peasant Studies* vol. 9 no. 2,

Winter 1982; J. Ennew, P. Hirst and K. Tribe, 'Peasantry as an Economic Category' *JPS* vol. 4, 1977;' Teodor Shanin, 'Defining Peasants: Conceptualizations and De-conceptualizations Old and New in a Marxist Debate' *Peasant Studies* vol. 8 no. 4, Fall 1979, pp. 48–55.

95   Shanin, 'Defining Peasants', p. 51.

96   Dennis R. Mills, *Lord and Peasant in Nineteenth Century Britain*, London 1980, pp. 43–5. Mills follows Alan Macfarlane (*Origins of English Individualism*, Oxford 1978, esp. pp. 17–33) in listing a number of arbitrary characteristics by which a peasantry is defined. He does not claim that his nineteenth-century 'peasantry' fits many of these characteristics, and ultimately they are revealed merely as small-scale entrepreneurs who are distingushed from other entrepreneurs simply by the scale of their enterprises.

97   For examples of this debate see Shanin, 'Defining Peasants'; Ennew, Hirst, and Tribe, 'Peasantry as an Economic Category'; Harriet Friedmann, 'Household Production and the National Economy: Concepts for the Analysis of Agrarian Formations' *JPS* vol. 7, 1980; Henry Bernstein, 'African Peasantries: a Theoretical Framework' *JPS* vol. 6, 1979; Littlejohn, 'Peasant Economy'; Anthony Leeds, 'Mythos and Pathos: Some Unpleasantries on Peasantries' in (ed.) R. Halperin and J. Dow, *Peasant Livelihood: Studies in Economic Anthropology and Cultural Ecology*, New York, 1977; S.H. Franklin, 'Systems of Production: Systems of Appropriation' *Pacific Viewpoint* vol. 6, 1965.

98   Friedmann, 'Household Production'; see also Peter McPhee, 'A Reconsideration of the "Peasantry" of Nineteenth-century France' *Peasant Studies* vol. 9 no. 1, Fall 1981.

99   Leeds, 'Mythos and Pathos', p. 231.

100   Franklin, 'Systems of Production', p. 149.

101   Frederick Cooper, 'Peasants, Capitalists, and Historians: A Review Article' *Journal of Southern African Studies*, vol. 7, no. 2, 1981, p. 286.

102   For discussions of the peasantry as a mode of production, see Ennew, Hirst, and Tribe, 'Peasantry as an Economic Category': Mark Harrison, 'The Peasant Mode of Production in the work of A.V. Chayanov' *JPS* vol. 4, 1977; Bernstein, 'African Peasantries'; Friedmann, 'Household Production'; Cooper, 'Peasants, Capitalists, and Historians'; Shanin, 'Defining Peasants'.

103   Leeds, 'Mythos and Pathos', p. 232.

104   Friedmann, 'Household Production', p. 158.

105   For simple commodity production, see Harriet Friedmann, 'Simple Commodity Production and Wage Labour in the American Plains' *JPS* vol. 6, 1978; Friedmann, 'Household Production'; McPhee, 'Reconsideration of the "Peasantry"'; and of course Marx. Discussions of simple commodity production are scattered through the three volumes of *Capital*, the *Grundrisse*, and *Theories of Surplus Value*. Like subsistence production, simple commodity production has 'a subsistence logic and usually has as its aim the exchange of use-values (commodity – money – commodity) rather than the profit aim of capitalist farming (money – commodity – money plus surplus value)'. McPhee, 'Reconsideration of the Peasantry', p. 9.

106   Carter, *Farm Life*, p. 183.

11

Net Fishermen and the Salmon Laws: Conflict in Late Victorian Devon

J.H. Porter
University of Exeter

The value of the British salmon industry in 1863 was assessed at £18,000; by 1880, thanks to successful conservation it was estimated at £100,000 a year. Accompanying the growth of the industry and stricter laws of conservation was an increase in poaching. The increase in the incidence of the crime was both a function of the growth of the salmon resources and the increasing specificity and rigour of the legislation and powers of enforcement. As soon as the first salmon act had been passed in 1861 a meeting was held chaired by Sir Stafford Northcote and attended by the Earl of Devon, Col. Acland and the Mayor of Exeter. Their enthusiasm for the new law was evident. First, we must examine the succession of salmon laws in late Victorian England and see why they so appealed to riparian owners and the rod and line men and why consequently they were to be a contentious matter for the more plebeian net men in common and tidal estuary waters.[1]

Offences committed under the first Salmon Act of 1861 were to be tried before two justices and had provisions relating to pollution and weirs but here the concern is only for those provisions which directly affected the net fishermen. The principal provisions prohibited the use of a light, spear, gaff or line to catch salmon, or possessing these items in suspicious circumstances which betrayed an intent to use them. The mesh of their nets was not to be less than two inches from knot to knot. Further, no 'fixed engine' was to be set and that included nets secured by anchors. Unseasonable or unclean salmon were not to be taken, nor were young salmon, and fishing in the close season from 1 September–1 February was prohibited. Furthermore, no fish was to be caught or killed other than by rod and line between 12 noon on Saturday and 6am on Monday. For each breach of these clauses a fine of up to £5 could be imposed with up to £2 for each fish taken and instruments or nets could be forfeit.[2]

The Quarter Sessions justices were to appoint conservators and could authorise a water bailiff, constable or conservator to enter and search premises and seize engines or salmon. The 1861 Act was amended in a

minor way in 1863 to prevent the export of unclean or unseasonable salmon.[3]

Conservators had their powers expanded in 1865 to secure more effective enforcement.[4] The justices at Quarter Sessions were empowered to apply to the Home Office for the establishment of a Fishery District for salmon rivers. Members appointed by the Home Office, all justices for the county who were owners or occupiers of land of not less than £100 a year ratable value adjoining a salmon river and having fishing rights, and all those who paid a duty of £50 or over under the Act, were to be ex-officio members of the Board of Conservators. The Board should determine a closed time to be approved by the Home Office and appoint bailiffs and constables who were to be paid by the Board. On their evidence it should initiate prosecutions. Any conservator or bailiff could examine or seize any engine or fish, search boats, nets or baskets and were deemed to be a constable while so acting. Penalties on conviction were also increased so that on a third offence imprisonment of up to six months could be imposed. Although a justice could not try an offence committed on his own land, his being a conservator or subscriber to any society for the protection of salmon did not disqualify him from hearing the case.

The Salmon Fisheries Act of 1873 introduced further restrictions upon the professional fishermen.[5] First, any fisherman who shot or worked a seine or draft net across the whole width of a salmon river, or even more than three-quarters of it within 100 yards of a net being similarly used was liable to a £5 fine. Fishermen who caught eels were not to use baskets, nets, traps or other engines between 1 January and 24 June in any salmon river. If they did a fine of up to £2 a day for each engine could be imposed.

The representational coverage of the Boards of Conservators was marginally widened. In addition to the appointed members the ex-officio categories were extended. Owners or occupiers of a fishery assessed at £30 a year poor rate as well as owners of lands with a frontage of one mile and lands of £100 a year who had both a right and a licence to fish were included. Additionally, representatives of the net men who fished in public or common waters were to have one representative for every £50 in aggregate licence fees paid and one for every additional £50 or part of it. Voting was to be on the basis of licence fees paid and for the personating of voters there was to be a fine of up to £20 or three months' hard labour.

While the Board might be made marginally more democratic the autocratic powers of the water bailiffs were considerably extended. Their powers of search and seizure were confirmed and they could now enter any lands on a written order from the Chairman of the Board and such an order had a life of two months. Breaches of any of the Boards' bye-laws carried the same penalty, up to £5, as any breaches of the principal clauses of the legislation. Further, the licence duties were increased.

As far as ground game was concerned the use of police as rate financed gamekeepers for private preserves was a controversial matter and even if the Boards paid for the hire of county constables similar attitudes applied. Moreover, just as gamekeepers had a doubtful reputation for morality so too did some water bailiffs.[6] While the need for salmon conservation in the long run was desirable, for there is no doubt that fishermen took young salmon peel as well as overfishing the mature salmon, the structure of the Boards of Conservators as well as the nature of the legislation meant that power was vested in the gentry rod and line men and their fellows and allies the country justices, and not with the more necessitous estuary fishermen whose livelihood was dependent on their netting.[7] In parallel with this shift of power was the more general attack on perceived or actual common law right in rivers and estuaries as landlords and lords of manors exercised their legal rights in the face of pressure from falling agricultural prices and the increasing capitalisation of agriculture.[8]

Some of the most violent incidents over salmon took place on the river Wye in Breckon at Radnor but Welsh protest had an extra element, a nationalist resistance to English officialdom. While such an element was not present in Devon the increasing vigour of the legislation emanating from London and its local enforcement by the gentry provided for a distinct feeling on the part of the net men that they were a minority suffering considerable discrimination.[9]

Salmon poaching in Devon must also be placed in the context of the overall number of poaching prosecutions which came before the Devon county and borough sessions 1860–99. During that period there were 6,298 prosecutions against poachers of ground and winged game and fish and fishery offences, of which 873, or 14 per cent, were for offences against the salmon acts, though not all of those were by net fishermen but involved individual poachers on the higher reaches of the salmon rivers. Where offenders received prison sentences they more commonly were for six to eight weeks which suggests they were frequent offenders. The majority paid fines from under £1 to as much as £10 for a frequent offender.[10]

As might be expected the Devon county bench comprised the aristocracy, gentry and principal rectors and retired naval and military gentlemen. The characteristics of the benches may be illustrated by three which operated in the principal salmon districts where prosecutions against fishermen occurred. Cases brought by the Exe Board of Conservators came primarily before the Wonford division sitting at the Castle in Exeter. Here sat the Devonshire aristocracy and gentry such as the Aclands, Addington, Bamfylde, Chichester, Courtenay, Devon, Haldon, Iddesleigh and Poltimore. The Teignbridge bench had an aristocratic and

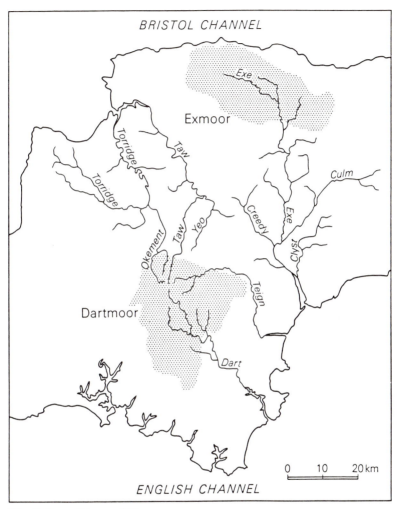

The Salmon Rivers of Devon
(Map produced by Department of Geography, University of Exeter)

military tone; Lord Clifford of Ugbrooke, Earl Morley, Admiral Cornish Bowden and Generals Lucas and Reynell Taylor. In north Devon the Braunton division included numerous members of the Chichester family and Sir William Williams of Heanton and Sir Henry Bouchier Toke Wrey of Tawstock Court.[11]

The three principal fishery districts with which this chapter is concerned are associated with the rivers Teign, Exe and in the north Devon the Taw/Torridge district (see map p. 243).

The districts of the Teign and the Exe saw less conflict than in the Taw/Torridge area, nevertheless there are examples. Pleading ignorance of the law did not save Edmund Cox when he killed a salmon in July 1881. The Teignmouth bench fined him 20s. (100p) inclusive of costs. Shortly afterwards Thomas and William Boynes, father and son escaped penalty by convincing the bench that the bailiff who charged them had been 200 yards away and that they had only a conger. The next year four more fishermen were caught by the bailiff and a constable with three salmon peel in an unlicensed net and each paid 19s. (95p) and had their net forfeited. A further five were fined for fishing during closed time. A similar offence was again committed by William Boynes and another of his relatives in 1886 when three fishermen were fined 8s. 6d. (42.5p) for fishing in the close season.[12]

The fishermen's frustration at what they regarded as illegitimate harassment was seen in court in 1889. George Venton, John Smith and Frank Youldon were charged with using a net in salmon pools out of season. They had only caught rough fish and the crowd in the court noisily supported the defence of their livelihood and claimed that, in addition, the boundary of the Teign conservators' district was based on a shifting bar which they could not locate. The magistrates latched on to the latter and dismissed the case.[13] The Conservators next pursued net fishermen both on this matter and net mesh size. This was a double trap; if the net mesh was over two inches they would catch no rough fish, if it was less they would be using an illegal net in closed time. In 1890 seven were caught on the Teign in this way.[14] During the years 1893–8 the target changed, twenty-one fishermen were charged with having fixed nets across the Teign. While some escaped because they could prove their nets had become accidentally fouled one frequent offender faced escalating fines. In 1893 John Frost was fined 5s. (25p) and costs, next year he avoided conviction but in 1896 and 1897 he paid £2 10s. (£2.50). Finally in 1898 he was fined with costs £3 3s. 2d. (£3.16).[15]

The chairman of the Teignmouth bench in 1896 had expressed his dissatisfaction for 'illegal fishing had become such a common practice among the fishermen of both Teignmouth and Newton (Abbott) [and] should be stopped'. The fishermen had other views, as George Newton and Henry Smith said in their defence in 1898; they were 'dismayed at the fine and times were hard and they had caught hardly any fish'.[16]

On the Exe it was principally the fishermen of Topsham who faced the wrath of the Conservators in the 1880s. In 1882 six of them were jointly charged after the bailiff swore they had caught a salmon in their nets and refused to be searched. The bailiff said he knew how it was done as he had done the same thing in the past. Despite the hilarity this caused in court and attacks on the uncorroborated evidence of an old poacher, the Wonford bench fined each fisherman 10s. 6d. (52.5p).[17] James Luxton and three other fishermen were in 1886 charged with illegal salmon fishing. They brought witnesses to prove they were in public waters but the court determined it was the private right of the Earl of Devon and fines were imposed. Later in the year two more were fined for the same offence. It seems clear that this was a private right being freshly re-imposed against customary practices. Three years later four men were fined for fishing with nets in a mill leat on the river Clyst though the miller had given them permission and swore he had never seen salmon there in his thirty-seven years. The men were each fined 15s. (75p). For fishing outside daylight hours and catching ten salmon four young net men were fined £2 and costs in May 1891.[18]

The Conservators continued to attempt to enforce their rules on the fishermen right up to the end of the century when this survey ends. On 18 December 1898 Robert Wreford, William Voysey, Daniel Pym, Thomas Cobley and Frederick Wannell, all from well-known Topsham fishing families, were caught fishing out of daylight hours and the permitted net area. The bailiff admitted in court that for the first time in twelve years there were a lot of sprats in the river and the men had taken advantage of them in what had been a hard season. The Wonford bench recognised this as a mitigation for the fine was only 3s. (15p) inclusive with a week to pay, which was very unusual in such cases.[19]

One of the most frequent witnesses for the Exe Board prosecutors was Topsham water bailiff Henry Luxton, but he had been convicted of taking a salmon in February 1883. He had got into a boat, rowed into the river, smacked a salmon on the head and taken it home. In court he said the fish was wounded, that he took it home to save others from temptation and that the witnesses were malicious men who had been themselves convicted. He was fined 44s. 6d. inclusive.[20]

Whilst the Conservators of the Exe and Teign were not in physical conflict with the fishermen, in north Devon events turned out differently with more physical attacks on bailiffs and police. In north Devon the Conservators were more active almost from the inception of the legislation. In April 1865 John Clarke and Henry Passmore were charged before the Braunton bench with taking two salmon. Passmore failed to appear, Clarke was fined £5 and costs and their net confiscated. The following November the Barnstaple county bench fined Thomas Hammett £5 or three months' imprisonment for taking two salmon in the close season. His companion was charged £2 or two months. Two years later in August 1868 the South Molton justices chaired by Revd Joshua Bawden fined two Chittlehampton fishermen £5 and costs for taking three Taw salmon with a net.[21] All these fines were at the top of the range.

The Barnstaple borough police court saw an affray in 1868. The Conservators' watchers found a salmon in the possession of four fishermen on 13 October. When the case came to court two did not appear and Frank Curtis and Richard Ross swore the evidence false. The bench disbelieved them, fined each £2 and costs and forfeited their nets. Curtis and his wife then attacked the witnesses, abused the justices and fought with the police. For that they were given an extra two months' imprisonment.[22] The next year saw a lull, but in August 1870 three fishermen were charged with taking salmon peel from the private waters of Sir F. Williams of Ashford. They claimed they were public waters; the bench rejected this but only imposed a one shilling (5p) nominal fine. The following year Williams secured a similar conviction.[23]

The hazards facing fishermen were clearly illustrated in 1874 when a strict interpretation of legislation and Board rules was in evidence. William Mitchell and three of his employees were charged with using a net with mesh one quarter of an inch too small. Mitchell paid £6 plus costs and the net, worth £14, was confiscated. The same year three fishermen were charged with catching salmon peel at Fremington. They pleaded that none had ever been caught there or expected. This was accepted and a nominal fine imposed. Less fortunate was Thomas Dark in 1879 when the Mayor of Bideford imposed a £10 fine for taking a salmon without a licence.[24]

The pace of prosecution quickened over 1880–1; particularly active was water bailiff Bastard. In December 1880 William Borrow and William Macmanus of Appledore were fined a total of £9 for killing a Taw salmon on a Sunday. Bastard got them again in 1881 for fishing on a Sunday in Sir William William's private waters and having netted two salmon.[25] The water bailiff's energy caused the Appledore fishermen to protest to the Home Office in 1881, twenty-three signed, saying it was wrong that they should be prevented from fishing merely because their nets *might* catch salmon. The Conservators' view was revealed in a case in June at Barnstaple where an Appledore fisherman was fined for using a small mesh net and taking salmon fry which he threw back. The Conservators in this case said they believed he had not known the law and therefore only asked for a nominal fine. The fisherman appealed to the high court but the conviction was confirmed. Two other fishermen faced test cases at Bideford where, after the high court judgement, a nominal fine was imposed with a warning of substantial fines thereafter.[26]

More prosecutions over net mesh size following in 1886–7 raised tempers further. In November James and Henry Passmore, J. Ridd and J. Parminter refused to allow the water bailiff to search their boat, tried to run him down and threatened to knock his brains out. The Barnstaple justices deplored their behaviour but as the bailiff had not produced his warrant they escaped. In October James, William and Joseph Cox had been charged with using a one-inch mesh net at Appledore. Their defence successfully claimed that they were in shallow water catching mullet and bass and in forty years' fishing there they had never seen a salmon.[27] The same plea was put by George Evans and his three sons in January 1887. Their defence was that they only caught bass and mullet and if the use of the nets were stopped a large number of families in Appledore and Barnstaple would be out of work. The issue was still unresolved later in 1887 before the Braunton sessions when the defence claimed there must be intent not mere capability to catch salmon and that the real question was whether nets should be kept out of the water altogether in the close season. In this and another case in 1888 where a draft net was used in public waters in the close season the justices decided to duck the issue and dismiss the charges with leave to appeal.[28] Their dismissal was popular with the fishermen in court but probably doubtful in law and though the result of the appeal is not recorded it is likely that the cases were referred back for conviction. In March 1888 three Evans brothers were fined for refusing to let a watcher search their boat and each paid £1 while Thomas Vanstone paid £3 and costs.[29]

The sitting of the Braunton division at Barnstaple in January 1889 was completely disrupted by fishery cases when two groups of fishermen came for trial on the same day: Robert Kivell, Robert Goss, Thomas Ridd, Thomas Sampson and Richard Cole were charged with using a spear in the Taw. Also awaiting trial were Thomas Light, Albert Nott, Albert Toms, William Pow and Reginald Nott accused of taking a salmon at Heanton in the close season. The last three were also charged with assaulting the bailiff. At the end of the day all the cases had not been heard and a two-day adjournment announced. Uproar resulted; there were cries that their children would starve, men stood on the seats and a general fight started between bailiffs Cowler and Howard and the fishermen. Before the borough police could arrive the bailiffs and a witness had been 'severely handled' and attempts made to throw them down the court's steps. The women screamed at the witnesses and urged the men on to attack the county police in court before the borough police arrived. It took ten borough police to clear the court and water bailiff PC Howard had been so severely kicked he could not stand. The fishermen still waited outside the court house and when the defence solicitor asked them to disperse and what they had to gain, the response was 'Nothing, but send us out the policemen'. More borough police and the superintendent had to be called and not till 7.30pm could the bailiffs and county police be escorted to the borough boundary and the railway station.[30] When the sessions next resumed twenty police controlled the court and all the defendants were convicted, mostly fined £2 or £1 10s. (£1.50). The cases took six hours and the bailiffs were loudly jeered as they left the court.[31]

The National School room at Appledore saw a protest meeting of fishermen over the Conservators' decision to allow no net mesh of less than four inches instead of the three-inch net mesh used, which would cost £600 to replace. The Conservators were relentless however. In July they decided to prosecute anyone with nets within two yards of each other; in October two were prosecuted for using an unlicensed draft net and in November two with obstructing a bailiff. All were convicted. In December two Barnstaple and three Appledore fishermen were prosecuted. In another case of three more Appledore men, two policemen had chased them and, when stuck in the mud, were pelted with stones.[32] During 1891 eight fishermen were convicted of taking salmon during the close season, two for using too small a mesh; fines ranged from 7s. (35p) to £5. The following year a further seven were convicted of close season violations, many of them being men previously convicted such as the Barrow, Passmore and Nott families.[33] Thomas Barrow received a month's imprisonment for attacking bailiff Vowles in 1893. As soon as he was released he was again fined for obstructing bailiff Cowler and with three others was also fined for a small net mesh.[34]

Even this activity was deemed insufficient by the newly-formed Taw Fishery Protection Association at its first annual meeting in December 1893. The meeting, chaired by Capt. Hon. A.G. Fortescue attacked the Taw Board for being insufficiently vigilant and reckoned four tons of salmon found its way to London in the close season.[35] Perhaps in response to this eleven fishermen of Appledore and Instow were fined for close season offences in November 1894, one Charles Fishleigh, paid a further £1 for trying to force down the throat of bailiff Shackston a young salmon. Another, Isaac Short, protested that his conviction was unjust when rod men were still permitted to fish.[36]

On 25 September 1895 water bailiff Pidler was reported to be 'in a very critical state'. At 6.20am he and bailiff Shackston had gone to search a boat in the Taw. In the boat was the coxswain of the Appledore lifeboat, John Williams Berry. He refused to let Pidler board and beat him about the head with an oar. When Shackston shouted Pidler was nearly killed Berry replied 'he would finish the . . .'. At assize Berry was sentenced to four months hard labour, mitigated by his previous good reputation.[37] In November two more fishermen were fined for unseasonable salmon fishing and two more in 1896.[38]

Another test case took place before the Torrington Bench in 1896 as to whether waters at Weare Giffard were public tidal waters or the private waters of Viscount Ebrington. Fishermen's employer William Mitchell said he had fished there for forty years and no previous attempt had been made to exclude fishermen. Chairman of the Bench JC Moore Stevens found against the three fishermen charged and fined each a nominal 2s. 6d. (12.5p).[39] By the end of 1899 at least another ten fishermen had been prosecuted for salmon offences and seven of them convicted.[40]

It is clear from this account that the Conservators and justices in north Devon were much more rigorous in their pursuit of net fishermen than were those of the Exe and Teign districts. The fines and alternatives of prison sentence were much greater than those handed out by the Wonford or Teignbridge divisions. Further, the assiduousness of Cowler, Pidler, Bastard and Shackston contributed towards the violent incidents. Cowler himself was convicted of assault in 1895 after he had stamped on a fisherman's hand to force him to give up his net.[41] The fact that Berry could resort to such violence as to disable Pidler and still gain a petition in his favour from the people of Northam suggests the strength of feeling. It does in many ways seem that the actions of the Conservators in pursuing prosecutions for net mesh size even in areas where no salmon had been seen or suspected put the fishermen's livelihood in more jeopardy than their nets did to the salmon. If this be so the gentlemanly rod men were unduly partial, being less concerned with conserving the salmon than in ensuring it for their taking.

Notes

1 R.M. McLeod, 'Government and Resource Conservation: the Salmon Acts Administration 1860–86', *Journal of British Studies*, vii, (1968), pp. 114–50.
2 24 & 25 Vict C109.
3 26 Vict C10.
4 28 & 29 Vict C121.
5 36 & 37 Vict C71.
6 P.B. Munsche, 'The Gamekeeper in English Rural Society 1660–1830', *Journal of British Studies*, XX, (1981), pp. 82–105; Carolyn Steedman, *Policing the Victorian Community*, (1984), pp. 30–1.
7 McLeod, *Journal of British Studies*, vii, (1968), pp. 114–50.
8 J.H. Porter, 'Poaching and social conflict in late Victorian Devon', in *Rural Social*

Change in Conflicts since 1500, (ed.) Andrew Charlesworth, (Hull, 1983), pp. 96–107; Peter Bartrip, 'Food for the body and food for the mind: the regulation of freshwater fisheries in the 1870s', *Victorian Studies*, xxviii, (1985), pp. 285–304; J.H. Porter, 'Teign Oyster Beds', *Devon and Cornwall Notes and Queries*, xxv, 5, (1984), pp. 174–80.

9 David Jones, 'The second Rebecca riots: a study of poaching on the Upper Wye', *Llafur*, ii, (1972), pp. 32–56; Melvin Firestone, *Anthropological Studies in Great Britain and Ireland*, (Arizona, 1982), pp. 73–76.

10 Source: data file compiled from the petty session reports in the *Devon Weekly Times* (*D.W.T.*).

11 Devon Record Office (DRO) Q.S. 30/1.

12 *D.W.T.*, 15 July, 23 Sept. 1881, 18 May 1887, 22 Oct. 1886.

13 *D.W.T.*, 25 Oct., 28 Nov. 1889, 28 Feb. 1890.

14 *D.W.T.*, 23 May 1890.

15 *D.W.T.*, 22 Sept. 1893, 26 Jan., 9 Feb. 1894, 31 May 1895, 15 May, 17 July 1896, 11 May 1897, 20, 27 May 1898.

16 *D.W.T.*, 27 May 1898.

17 *D.W.T.*, 14 July 1882.

18 *D.W.T.*, 12 March, 7 May 1886, 27 Sept. 1889, 12 June 1891.

19 *D.W.T.*, 3 Feb. 1879.

20 *D.W.T.*, 22 March 1883.

21 *D.W.T.*, 21 April 1865, 23 Nov. 1866, 21 Aug. 1868.

22 *D.W.T.*, 6 Nov. 1868.

23 *D.W.T.*, 19 Aug. 1870, 10 Nov. 1871.

24 *D.W.T.*, 11 Sept. 1874, 20 June 1879.

25 *D.W.T.*, 10 Dec. 1880, 18 Feb. 1881.

26 *D.W.T.*, 20 May, 24 June, 16 Nov., 23 Sept., 21 Oct. 1881.

27 *D.W.T.*, 1 Oct., 31 Dec. 1886.

28 *D.W.T.*, 4 Feb. 1887, 13 Jan., 4 May 1888.

29 *D.W.T.*, 2, 30 March 1888.

30 *D.W.T.*, 25 Jan. 1889.

31 *D.W.T.*, 8 Feb., 8 Mar., 12 April 1889.

32 *D.W.T.*, 12 April, 19 July, 11 Oct., 14, 29 Nov., 13 Dec. 1889.

33 *D.W.T.*, 3 April, 7 Aug., 16, 23 Oct. 1891, 22 July, 16 Sept., 23 Dec. 1892.

34 *D.W.T.*, 23 June, 4 Aug. 1893.

35 *D.W.T.*, 29 Dec. 1893, 9 Mar. 1894.

36 *D.W.T.*, 9, 16 Nov. 1894.

37 *D.W.T.*, 4, 25 Oct., 15 Nov. 1895.

38 *D.W.T.*, 22 Nov. 1895, 8 May 1896.

39 *D.W.T.*, 8 May, 17 June 1896.

40 *D.W.T.*, 7 Aug. 1896, 2 Dec. 1898, 27 Jan. 1899, 12 Jan. 1900.

41 *D.W.T.*, 22 Nov. 1895.

Index